D1487367

Rise of Environmental Consciousness

Voices in Pursuit of a Sustainable Planet

First Edition

Edited by

Beth S. Caniglia
Regis University

Thomas Jerome Burns,
Rachel M. Gurney, and Erik L. Bond
Oklahoma State University—Stillwater
University of Oklahoma

Bassim Hamadeh, CEO and Publisher
Michael Simpson, Vice President of Acquisitions
Jamie Giganti, Senior Managing Editor
Miguel Macias, Graphic Designer
Angela Schultz, Acquisitions Editor
Michelle Piehl, Project Editor
Alexa Lucido, Licensing Coordinator
Allie Kiekhofer and Rachel Singer, Interior Designers

First published in the United States of America in 2016 by Cognella, Inc.

Trademark Notice: Product or corporate names may be trademarks or registered trademarks, and are used only for identification and explanation without intent to infringe.

Cover image copyright © Depositphotos/njnightsky.
    copyright © Depositphotos/file404.
    copyright © Depositphotos/Maks_Narodenko.
    copyright © Depositphotos/kokoroyuki.
    Copyright © Depositphotos/hristianin.

Printed in the United States of America

ISBN: 978-1-63189-180-9 (pbk) / 978-1-63189-181-6 (br)

www.cognella.com   800-200-3908

Contents

PART 1

Native Voices

The Indigenous View of Environmentalism: Tribe, Nature, and Kinship

Introduction by Erik Bond
University of Oklahoma

Thishis section of the text focuses on stories told by peoples indigenous to North America. We cover many tribes, including the Creek, Micmac, Iroquois, Paiute, Penobscot, Klamath, Algonquin, Ojibwe, Cheyenne, Cherokee, Inupiaq, Lenape, Squamish, Sioux, and Mohawk. Although we use these stories to explore indigenous perspectives on nature, it is important to remember that they are not stories about "*The Environment.*" The word "environment" originates from "environ," which means to surround, enclose, or encircle (*Etymology* n.d.). The term has become what Burns (1999) calls a "Summary Symbol." A summary symbol is "a word or short phrase that implies an accompanying package of thoughts, values, emotions, or beliefs" (Burns 1999). Burns says that summary symbols are developed in a social context but used by individuals in thought and communication. We see the natural world framed in this "environmental" context often: in the media, in education, in general conversation. The Environment is a thing that is *other*—either a surrounding arena in which humans conduct their business of living or a resource that *humans* have enclosed and now manage for their purposes. In short, "The Environment" is contemporary Western culture's summary symbol for all aspects of the world that are "natural," which generally connotes anything that was not processed for human use. However, the Environment summary symbol is not universal and is most notably absent within traditional indigenous cultures. If we are to understand both the Western and the Indigenous American symbols for the natural world, we must investigate the social and physical factors that characterize their cultural stories.

Summary symbols are powerful because (1) they simplify complex mental concepts, (2) they appear less value-charged than examining a multifaceted issue in detail, and (3) they are thus more easily assimilated into a person's worldview (Burns 1999). The Environment summary symbol is the focal point of a modern cultural story about the world, and it serves the same explanatory purpose as does any other mythology. The Environment story uses separate lexicons for describing human affairs versus those of non-human life, thus perpetuating a cultural perspective of human-nature separation wherein one party always encloses the other. Agrawal (2005) coined the term "Environmentality" to refer to an individual person's acceptance of the environment as an object to be managed. The Environment story is a story about the way things are from one perspective, just as the Greek or Roman or Norse myths were in their heyday. By contrast, we see stories and summary symbols in Native American lore that do not delineate the human and natural worlds—at least not in the same way as do many Western cultural stories.

Native American tales treat the natural world as almost seamless: humans, animals, plants, and the earth itself are all characters and, in many ways, are depicted as living similar lives and having similar thoughts. In "How Coyote Stole Fire," we see the Klamath depicting animals as humanity's allies. The text refers to them as "the People," and they display the same kinds of rational thought, action, and verbal exchanges as do humans. In "The Snake with Big Feet," we meet several animals who live just like humans, utilizing tools, living in built homes, and creating clothing. While it is true that there are distinct categories to some characters in these stories, the similarities vastly outweigh the differences. Although it might be easy to dismiss these anthropomorphized depictions as the fanciful concoctions of more "primitive" cultures, doing so would overlook important sociocultural implications hidden just under the surface. The language used to depict the natural world in these stories presents signposts pointing to a worldview distinct from the Western standard of human-nature separation. The summary symbol in many Native American stories is not "humans" or "nature" but "the world." The commonalities (as members of these cultures see them) between human and non-human creatures are significant for understanding and learning from these indigenous tales because they are windows into ecologically sensitive cultures. The fact that they explained the world as a unified web of systemic interactions, far from displaying primitivism, suggests a remarkable level of cultural and semantic complexity.

To unpack some of the differences between Western and Native American stories about human-nature relationships, we can study the ways in which the storytellers make their livings—their *modes of subsistence*. Cultural stories (alternatively labeled "history" or "myth" depending on the cultural hegemony of the moment) often serve the purpose of explaining the way people should or must live in present social and physical conditions. Burns and LeMoyne (2003) offer a theoretical framework that helps describe this function of cultural story symbolism: "[t]he degree of centrality of a summary symbol is a function of its relationship with *other* ideas needed for the individual to negotiate his/her life world." In short, a summary symbol's importance in the mind depends on its usefulness for navigating life in a particular social and physical setting. For example, when a class of American elementary school students is taught about the formation of the United States, the students are likely to hear about the oppressive British government and the Founding Fathers' courageous quest for freedom. Although this story may serve as a history lesson, it also helps to explain the way that American society works today: the freedoms we enjoy, the rules we follow, and what makes America unique and special. It should almost go without saying that there are multiple sides to this story, any of which may be as valid as any other. In this case, the "truth" taught to the grade-schoolers consists of a story relevant to the lives they are presently living and the goals of their elders.

In the same vein, the stories told in Western society about The Environment elaborate truths about the ways that people in these societies navigate their lives. Some of the most popular motifs for presenting environmental concerns today include "conservation" of natural resources, "protection" of wildlife, and "stewardship" of nature. All of these motifs come bound up with certain unspoken presuppositions, chief among them being the superiority and separation of the *human* subject from the *natural* object. While it is true that the Native American folklore in this chapter depicts humans taking responsibility for ethical treatment of animal and plant life, the indigenous stories depict that responsibility as a kinship obligation or a mandate from a higher authority. This dynamic is distinct from the Western version of human dominion.

The Western semantic separation between the human and the natural parallels the physical separation between humans in the developed world and the materials that they depend on in daily life. For example, it is estimated that the average American diet contains 70% processed foods and that the average American meal travels approximately 1,500 miles to get to the consumer's plate (CUESA). These kinds of spatial and temporal gaps between person and resource are far greater than those found in small agricultural communities just a century ago, to say nothing of comparisons with indigenous hunters, gatherers, and horticulturalists across most of human history. Research shows that people will use the smallest subset of meaningful schema that is pragmatic to their daily lives (Burns and LeMoyne 2003, Weber and Crocker 1983, Deaux et al. 1985). We should thus find it unsurprising that Westernized peoples would tend to assign a different set of meanings to the resources they use than would those living in close connection to those same resources in their natural state. The semantic-meaning changes are obvious in the language now used: "chicken" stops representing a living bird and begins to represent a mass of meat on a plate; "cereals" come from boxes rather than being planted, tended, harvested, and ground into edible states. It is only reasonable to expect that such fundamental subsistence changes would come with attendant psychological and sociocultural changes in human perceptions of the natural world.

One major difference between indigenous and modernized perspectives of natural resources is that the *natural* state of those resources becomes obscured to the Westernized population by social and political infrastructure. This is not to suggest that a natural state is objectively superior to a processed state; however, the natural state contains important information that is lost in the processed state: that an animal is a living, feeling creature, or that a type of tree is disappearing from an ecosystem, or that a river is rapidly filling with toxic chemicals. Burns and LeMoyne (2001) suggest that the historically superior success rates of local environmental movements (as compared with national or international efforts) can be attributed to the acuteness of local issues garnering priority status with a particular citizenry. Burns's and LeMoyne's observation describes a broader and more basic premise: issues with practical and immediate consequences receive more social energy than do those with theoretical, philosophical, or physically/temporally remote consequences. We can see this correlation in the most popular "green" practices in the United States and other developed nations.

"Going Green" and "Green Living" are popular catchphrases that promote more environmentally friendly lifestyle choices in the United States. Adults and children in America are encouraged toward practices such as turning off and unplugging appliances when not using them, recycling used materials, and using reusable (as opposed to disposable) food and drink containers whenever possible. Such behaviors display good intention, but they are inextricably constrained within certain practical and semantic frameworks. For example, they presume a lifestyle that makes use of non-essential appliances, off-site recycling services, and pre-prepared consumables. According to the theory posited by Burns and LeMoyne (2003), new information taken in by people in such a lifestyle will be organized and prioritized based on their existing social context. In many developed and developing countries, for example, energy-consumptive appliances and disposable conveniences are heavily integrated into advantaged lifestyles and higher class statuses. People living in such lifestyles may be more likely to accept changes that minimize the negative effects of convenience and consumption rather than changes that dispose of those practices altogether. The mindset of minimizing the damaging aspect of a practice—as opposed to shifting to a less- or non-damaging practice altogether—will naturally be less effective at ameliorating problems.

For a contrast to the Westernized perspective, we can look to the cultural constructs of certain indigenous populations regarding human relationships to the natural world and resources. We will do so by analyzing the oral traditions transcribed in this section of the book. Although only a few of these selections focus explicitly on environmental issues, they all serve to explain important facets of the human-nature relationship. A common theme runs throughout the human/non-human relationships depicted here, as well as in much of the collective body of Native American folklore. Salmón (2000) terms this theme "kincentric ecology." Salmón (2000) describes kincentric ecology as the view (common among indigenous peoples) that humans and nature are "part of an extended ecological family that shares ancestry and origins." Because humans are seen as one integrated component in a complex system of ecological interactions, human-nature relationships take on protective, edifying characteristics similar to those in a healthy, human family. According to some authors of indigenous descent, this familial worldview becomes deeply ingrained from childhood due to the ubiquitous presence of folk stories told by tribal elders (Silko 1996). In fact, these constructs are so embedded in the languages of these cultures that distinguishing labels such as "kincentric ecology" might seem nonsensical—as redundant to them as would be phrases such as "manmade technology" or "social culture" to us.

The stories in this section of the book offer diverse examples of kincentric ecology, where the whole ecological network is the summary symbol. The "Micmac Creation Story" describes one culture's fable about the beginnings of the world. The Micmacs were a semi-nomadic culture of hunter/fishers and foragers, and their creation mythology reflects this lifestyle. The tale describes how each part of existence—the sun, the earth, and all life—was created to exist in relationship to all others. When Glooscap, the first human, is created directly from the earth, he is forced to stay still and observe the world for a long time. He is finally granted autonomy, thanks the earth for giving him life, and then explores the farthest reaches of the land. When it comes time for Glooscap and his grandmother, Nogami, to eat, he calls for a fish and asks it to surrender its life for them. The fish, Abistanooj, agrees, but after it has been killed, Glooscap feels sad and recognizes that all animals are his brothers and sisters. Nogami tells Glooscap that the animals will always provide humans with the resources they need to live. Glooscap and Nogami go on to live life relying on and respecting one another for their unique and complementary skills. In this one creation legend, we see the origins of a kincentric ecological worldview: humans come from the world, are dependent upon one another, are kin to all other creatures, and are responsible to respect and appreciate the creatures that must die for humans' survival.

The premise that the human and non-human worlds shape one another is ubiquitous in Native American lore. The Iroquois Nation was a confederacy of Native American tribes: the Mohawks, the Oneidas, the Senecas, the Cayugas, the Onondagas, and (later) the Tuscaroras. The Nation had its own creation story that tied each tribe to its regional origins and major natural resources. Moreover, the mythology links those physical/geographical characteristics to cultural attributes of the tribes themselves: "To the patient Oneidas, I give the nuts and the fruit of many trees. To the industrious Senecas, I give beans. To the friendly Cayugas, I give the roots of plants to be eaten. To the wise and eloquent Onondagas, I give grapes and squashes to eat and tobacco to smoke at the camp fires" ("The Five Nations"). As Burns and LeMoyne (2003) explain, position in a stratification system influences meaningful organization of information among people. Although the Iroquois Nation may not have exhibited a strict hierarchical stratification system, we see in its origin story that organization within the larger confederacy influences cultural explanations of the human-nature relationship while simultaneously explaining how the world provides for each in unique but plentiful ways. Highlighting each tribe's assets in the creation legend embeds in the collective culture an appreciation of their unique contributions to the confederacy, as well as recognition of their ties to the world's resources.

A number of our selections demonstrate the common theme of animals and other creatures seeking to aid humans with their "birth" into the world. In this context, humans are often treated as a younger sibling in the family of all life, requiring guidance and protection to survive. In "How Coyote Stole Fire," we see that the other animals pity humans for their frailty and inability to survive the winter months. The animals seek to help the humans by acquiring fire for them. There are three important things to note about this goal: first, the text refers to animals as "the People"; second, animals have no need of fire for themselves; and third, the "Fire Beings" who selfishly guard fire are not themselves animals. In other words, the tale is a prime example of depicting humans and animals as members of a single family. Over the course of the tale, the animals put themselves at great personal risk to secure fire for humans. Each of the animals winds up with a scar for his participation in the venture: Coyote's, Squirrel's, and Frog's tails, and Chipmunk's stripes. These visual cues are an elegant lesson-reinforcement mechanism: whenever a child who has heard this tale sees one of these animals, he or she is reminded that that animal bears scars for helping the child's people survive.

The kinship between humans and animals runs both ways. "The Snake with Big Feet" describes an anthropomorphized snake who is rejected by the other snakes for his differences. He journeys to find friends and is helped along the way by other animals that are distinctly human-like, including a deer who lives in a hut and teaches Snake how to make deerskin moccasins and a porcupine who teaches him how to use porcupine quills to decorate his moccasins. After encountering and killing many hostile humans, Snake finally finds a tribe of people that take him in to live and hunt and fight alongside them. The only thing he cannot do is marry the chief's daughter (with whom he is smitten) because, for all his anthropomorphic traits, he is still a snake. When the tribe's medicine man succeeds in transforming him into a human, the story makes clear that he and his descendants retain snake blood. In this story, animals are depicted not only living like humans, but also using animal products the way that humans do, showing that they do not disapprove of having their bodies used as resources. We also see that characteristics can flow fluidly from animal to human, that animals are welcomed into human society, and that humans can even share blood kinship to certain animals.

Several selections in this section discuss the obligations that humans have to non-human life and nature in general. This premise follows logically from the previously discussed ideas that humans are kin (often younger siblings) to all other life. In fact, we might think of this part of kincentric ecology as taking the character of familial obligation. In "Buffalo and Eagle Wing," we see how a young man is gifted with great speed of foot by a powerful buffalo on the condition that he promises to keep his people from hunting the buffaloes. When his aspirations of tribal leadership lead him to kill many buffaloes, all of nature, from mountains to plant life, agrees to change itself to prevent humans from running quickly again. A similar lesson occurs in "The Legend of

Wountie," where a greedy fisherman overfishes the stream and has his entire catch turned to sticks and branches and his nets ruined. The river's guardian spirit explains that this is the fisherman's punishment for having "broken the faith with the river and with nature, by taking more than he needed for himself and his family." The tale of "Yellowstone Valley and the Great Floor" recounts the culturally ubiquitous legend of a worldwide flood but, in this case, pins the disaster on humans who do not respect their obligations to the world.

In "An Unwritten Law of the Sea," Herbert Anungazuk explains how humans' faith obligation with nature manifests in everyday activities. He tells of how the hunting and gathering lifestyle, which depends on the bounty of nature and the sacrifice of animals, requires people to respect the creatures they must prey upon to survive. Anungazuk offers an example tale from the Inupiaq tradition, wherein hunters out in a boat encounter a heard of *Aqlu* (orca whales). Inupiaq tradition warns that disturbing an *Aqlu* is punishable by death, and in return for peaceful passage, the hunters in the story promise to give the *Aqlu* a piece of each thing they kill that day. However, the legend also says that when in need, the Inupiaq may also call on the *Aqlu* to provide a portion of meat from their own prey. Anungazuk explains that survival skills and moral lessons are handed down from tribal elders as a package and that, being the sole repositories of such knowledge for future generations, their words are greatly respected by all. This point hints at important ways that the kincentric-ecology worldview shapes not just human activity, but organization within human societies.

It has been well-documented (e.g., Berman 2000, Harris 1990) that a society's cultural and social organization is influenced by its subsistence practices, but case studies of societies that practice kincentric ecology offer rich insights into these interrelationships. In "Keepers of the Water," Lois Beardslee describes how relationships to the natural environment help reinforce a cooperative group structure. In Ojibwe culture, "The Keepers of the Water" are the women of the tribe. Beardslee explains that this title refers to the daily activities (cooking, cleaning, etc.) that require carrying water from a natural source to the home site, as well as to important duties like managing waste water and avoiding water-source contamination. Women also hold this responsibility in ceremonial and educational activities, and they are responsible for passing relevant knowledge to subsequent generations.

Whereas in the Western world a division of labor often creates interclass conflict, Beardslee tells us that the Ojibwe division of labor is a unifying force, reminding all members of the tribe that each has a valuable contribution to make to the tribe's survival based on his or her individual abilities. This cultural solidarity reinforces a kincentric ecological perspective: because the world generously provides resources and resource-use practices shape the social structure, the natural world indirectly shapes the tribe's social organization. This phenomenon is fundamentally different from the common Western subsistence pattern where both workers (people) and resources (money) are standardized. We previously explored an example where important semantic information about a resource is lost the more it is processed out of its natural state (e.g., a live chicken versus a cooked chicken breast). A similar pattern occurs in the Western employment model. As the means of survival becomes more distanced from raw resources and more dependent on complex infrastructure, both person and activity lose significance. The uniqueness of both worker and job fade away, their values becoming associated with the only remaining measure: the size of their compensation (i.e., paycheck). The Ojibwe example in "Keepers of the Water" shows us how cultural solidarity both reinforces and is reinforced by interaction and identification with the natural world. This pattern logically makes cultures practicing kincentric ecology highly resilient so long as their traditional modes of connecting with the world remain intact. Such societies do not need "Green" practices, since their cultures are fundamentally held together by a meaningful relationship with nature.

This collection of Native American lore is replete with environmental lessons. However, these stories do not treat "The Environment." Instead, they discuss humans' familial obligations to the collective body of all life. Although popular fiction has often characterized these cultures as inherently noble and altruistic, for the people who originally told these stories, they were instructions in survival. Little or nothing separated Native peoples from the resources on which they depended, and they had little or no buffer from consequences resulting from abuse of those resources. All societies have moral standards for how people ought to treat one another. Kincentric ecological societies extend their interpersonal morals to include the natural world, which serves the logical purpose of preserving each society's time-tested modes of survival. Contemporary Western culture's well-meaning "Green" efforts are grounded in a survival practice that is inherently removed from the physical reality they seek to protect. This survival practice consists of acquiring resources from a "safe" distance via industrial and political infrastructure. The resultant loss of meaningful reality is evident in the rhetoric of Environmentality: the human subject manages the natural object, maximizing usefulness first, minimizing damage second. Whether a stable human-world relationship can be created from such a distance remains to be seen.

References

1. Agrawal, Arun. *Environmentality: Technologies of Government and the Making of Subjects*. Durham, NC: Duke University Press, 2005.

2. Berman, Morris. *Wandering God*. New York: State University of New York Press, 2000.

3. Burns, Thomas J. "Rhetoric as a Framework for Analyzing Cultural Constraint and Change." *Current Perspectives in Social Theory* 19, no. 1 (1999): 165–185.

4. Burns, Thomas J., and Terri LeMoyne. "How Environmental Movements Can Be More Effective: Prioritizing Environmental Themes in Political Discourse." *Human Ecology Review* 8, no. 1 (2001): 26–38.

5. Burns, Thomas J., and Terri LeMoyne, "Epistemology, Culture, and Rhetoric: Some Social Implications of Human Cognition." *Critical Theory: Diverse Objects, Diverse Subjects* 22, no. 1 (2003): 71–97.

6. CUESA. "How Far Does Your Food Travel to Get to Your Plate?" *Cuesa*. http://www.cuesa.org/learn/how-far-does-your-food-travel-get-your-plate.

7. Deaux, K., W. Winton, M. Crowley, and L. L. Lewis. "Level of Categorization and Content of Gender Stereotypes." *Social Cognition* 3, no. 1 (1985): 145–167.

8. Harris, Marvin. *Our Kind: Who We Are, Where We Came From, Where We Are Going*. New York: HarperCollins, 1990.

9. Online Etymology Dictionary. "Environ." *Etymonline*. http://www.etymonline.com/index.php?term=environ&allowed_in_frame=0.

10. Salmón, Enrique. "Kincentric Ecology: Indigenous Perceptions of the Human-Nature Relationship." *Ecological Applications* 10, no. 5 (2000): 1327–1332.

11. Silko, Leslie M. *Yellow women and a beauty of the spirit*. New York: Simon and Shuster, 1996.

12. Weber, R., and J. Crocker. "Cognitive Processes in the Revision of Stereotypic Beliefs." *Journal of Personality and Social Psychology* 45, no. 1 (1983): 961–977.

Creek
How the Clans Came to Be

In the beginning, the Muscogee people were born out of the earth itself. They crawled up out of the ground through a hole like ants. In those days, they lived in a far western land beside tan mountains that reached the sky. They called the mountains the backbone of the earth. Then a thick fog descended upon the earth, sent by the Master of Breath, Esakitaummesee.

The Muscogee people could not see. They wandered around blindly, calling out to one another in fear. They drifted apart and became lost. The whole people were separated into small groups, and these groups stayed close to one another in fear of being entirely alone. Finally, the Master had mercy on them. From the eastern edge of the world, where the sun rises, he began to blow away the fog. He blew and blew until the fog was completely gone.

The people were joyful and sang a hymn of thanksgiving to the Master of Breath. And in each of the groups, the people turned to one another and swore eternal brotherhood. They said that from then on these groups would be like large families. The members of each group would be as close to each other as brother and sister, father and son. The group that was farthest east and first to see the sun, praised the wind that had blown the fog away.

They called themselves the Wind Family, or Wind Clan. As the fog moved away from the other groups, they, too, gave themselves names. Each group chose the name of the first animal it saw. So they became the Bear, Deer, Alligator, Raccoon, and Bird Clans. However, the Wind Clan was always considered the first clan and the aristocracy of all the clans. The Master-of-Breath spoke to them: "You are the beginning of each one of your families and clans. Live up to your name. Never eat of your own clan, for it is your brother.

You must never marry into your own clan. This will destroy your clan if you do. When an Indian brave marries, he must always move with his wife to her clan. There he must live and raise his family. The children will become members of their mother's clan. Follow these ways and the Muskhogeans will always be a powerful force. When you forget, your clans will die as people."

Micmac
Creation Story

ONE: GISOOLG

Gisoolg is the Great Spirit, the Creator who all things. Gisoolg is the Mik'Maq word that means both "you have been created" and "the one credited for your existence." Gisoolg is genderless, neither He nor She, and gender is of no concern to Gisoolg. We do not try to explain how Gisoolg came to be; we only acknowledge that everything we see comes from Gisoolg: past, present, and future.

TWO: NISGAM

Nisgam is the name of the sun, the second thing and Gisoolg's first creation. Nisgam bestows life on all the earth through its gifts of light and warmth. Nisgam helped Gisoolg to create all the people of the earth. All of Nisgam's children revere its power, and Nisgam reveres Gisoolg, the Great Spirit.

THREE: OOTSITGAMOO

Ootsitgamoo is the earth, the land upon which grow all the people and animals and plants to which Nisgam gives life. Oetsgitpogooin means "the person or individual who stands upon this surface" or "the one who is given life upon this surface of land." The Mik'Maq people can travel all the land of Ootsitgamoo, which Gisoolg created and placed within Nisgam's embrace. Nisgam cares for Ootsitgamoo and lights its path as it travels through night and day.

FOUR: GLOOSCAP

Ootsitgamoo was created by Nisgam and Gisoolg, and plants and animals grew upon its surface when Gisoolg decided to create again. Lightning struck the surface of Ootsitgamoo, forming the shape of a human from the earth. From this earth, Glooscap was created to be the first human.

Another bolt of lightning granted life to Glooscap's form, but he was still only a shape in the earth. His head pointed toward Oetjgoabaniag, the east, from whence the sun and the summer weather emerge. His feet pointed toward Oetgatsenoog, the west, where the sun sets and from whence the winter winds blow. His right hand pointed toward Oatnoog, the north, and his left hand toward Opgoetasnoog, the south. He watched the world turn from his back. He watched Nisgam's journey across the sky day after day. He watched all the things grow and live and die.

One day, he asked Nisgam to grant him freedom and, with a third bolt of lightning, Glooscap was free to wander the Mik'Maq world. He turned round seven times, taking in the world, then turned his face to the sky and thanked Gisoolg for his life and freedom. He turned his face to the ground and thanked Ootsitgamoo for giving him his flesh. He turned inward and thanked Nisgam for his soul and spirit. Finally, he turned to each of the four directions—east, west, north, and south—and gave thanks to them. In this way, Glooscap gave thanks seven times.

Glooscap set out to explore the world he'd watched for so long. He walked toward the sunset until he came to the ocean. He walked toward the south until the land was so narrow that he could see an ocean on either side of him. He walked into the northern regions to see the ice and snow. Finally, he settled in the east, where he had been given life. He sat and watched everything once more: the animals, the plants, the sky, and the land. Under Gisoolg's guidance, he learned about the world by watching it work. After much time had passed and he had learned many things, he turned once more to Gisoolg and Nisgam and asked why he had been created. They told him that he would soon meet someone who would answer that question for him.

FIVE: NOGAMI

One day after Glooscap had been living some time in his home in the east, he stumbled upon an old woman while he was out hunting. Glooscap was surprised, thinking he was the only person who had been created, and so he asked the old woman how she had come into the Mik'Maq lands. The woman said that her name was Nogami and that she was grandmother to Glooscap. She told him that she had also been created by Nisgam, and the sun's fire burned inside her as well. With Gisoolg's guidance, Nisgam had warmed a dew-covered stone in a misty morning valley. Gisoolg had transformed that stone into the shape of an old woman, and that shape was given life by Nisgam's warmth so that Glooscap might have a grandmother.

Nogami told Glooscap that she had been created already old and wise so that she would be a source of strength and wisdom for Glooscap, so long as he treated her with respect and honor. Glooscap was overjoyed, and he called upon the fish of the stream to come ashore so that he and his grandmother might have something to eat. From the stream emerged Abistanooj, a marten who was willing to surrender his life so that Glooscap and Nogami might live. Nogami thanked Abistanooj and quickly snapped his neck, placing him on the ground for preparation. But Glooscap was stricken with regret and fear that he had hurt his relationship with the animals, so he asked Gisoolg to return Abistanooj's life.

Glooscap was touched by Abistanooj's sacrifice, and he thereafter saw all the animals as his brothers and sisters. Nogami taught Glooscap that the animals would always be glad to give the people food and clothing, tools and shelter. Abistanooj returned to the river, pledging brotherhood with Glooscap. Gisoolg provided another marten for Glooscap and his grandmother to eat. Nogami taught her grandson the ways of preparing food: gathering wood, building a fire, spreading the coals, cleaning and cooking the fish. This first fire grew into the Great Spirit Fire still known to this day, and it served Glooscap and his grandmother well. Glooscap revered his grandmother and learned many things from her about survival and compassion. Nogami came to respect her grandson for his strength, and their interdependence brought many years of life and prosperity to them both.

Iroquois
The Five Nations

When the world was young, it was covered by the deep waters. There were no people, no animals of the land, only fish in the oceans and birds in the air, and in the depths where no sunlight reaches, great monsters roamed freely. When the First Woman came, she fell from the greatest heights of the sky, tumbling endlessly through the clouds. The great birds that soared through the air met with the great birds that glided over the water's surface to decide what to do.

"We must stop her from falling beneath the waves. How can we do this if she cannot fly through the air or glide over the water's surface?" they asked.

They devised a plan to spread their wings together in midair so that she would land gently on their soft feathers. Each bird spread its great wings to interlock with another, and so the woman reached the earth in safety.

Upon her arrival, the monsters of the deep held a council of their own. "We must protect this beautiful woman from these deep waters. She cannot roam freely through them as we do," they said. But the monsters did not have the ability to protect her as they wished. Only one among their number—Giant Turtle—could help her. Giant Turtle, of course, was happy to help, and he offered his back for her to rest upon. He then began to grow; he grew and grew until he became the first island in the great oceans.

What the birds and the monsters did not know was that the Celestial Woman was pregnant. She carried twin boys, whom she eventually gave birth to on the back of the Giant Turtle. Her children were the Spirits of Good and Evil. One made all those things of the earth that bring life and benefit to humans and animals: corn and wheat and fruit and the trees that offer shade. The other created all those things that drain life from the humans and animals: weeds and insects and the swarms that kill the crops.

The Celestial Woman cared for her twins as they grew, and as they grew, so did Giant Turtle, causing the land to spread over ever more of the oceans. From time to time, Giant Turtle would stretch mightily, and the ground beneath their feet would tremble and shudder. The Sky-Holder, whom we call Ta-rhu-hia-wah-ku, watched all of this for a long time. After some years, it came upon the Sky-Holder to create people to live and walk on the growing land. Taking inspiration from the Spirit of Good, he created these people to be beautiful, strong, and brave. From the heart of the land he created six pairs of these new people.

The first pair settled near the great river Mohawk, and they carry its name still today. The second pair made their home in a land of giant stones near Oneida Lake, and they are called the Oneidas.

The third pair took the name Onondagas, and they now live on the high hills. The fourth pair were the first Cayugas, and the fifth pair were the parents of all Senecas, and both pairs lived in what is today the state of New York. The sixth pair went up the Roanoke River into what we now call North Carolina, and they were the first Tuscaroras. When these people had all made their settlements, the Sky-Holder built a home with them so that he could teach them the wise knowledge and the arts and crafts that their descendants would always need to make a living for themselves. Each of the six tribes today teaches that theirs is the favored tribe because the Sky-Holder made his home with them. The Onondagas say, "We have the council fire, and so we are the chosen people." Over many years, the families grew and spread over New York, into modern-day Pennsylvania, the Midwest, and southern Canada. Those that lived in the region where bear was the principal game became called The Bear Clan. Those who lived where there were many beavers became called The Beaver Clan. Other clans were named after the deer, the wolf, the snipe, and the tortoise, to name a few. Each of them, however, was a family of the Iroquois.

Paiute
The Snake with the Big Feet

BY GLENN WALKER

Long ago, in that far-off happy time when the world was new, and there were no white people at all, only Indians and animals, there was a snake who was different from other snakes. He had feet-big feet. And the other snakes, because he was different, hated him, and made life wretched for him. Finally, they drove him away from the country where the snakes lived, saying, "A good long way from here live other ugly creatures with feet like yours. Go and live with them!" And the poor, unhappy Snake had to go away.

For days and days, he travelled. The weather grew cold and food became hard to find. At last, exhausted, his feet cut and frostbitten, he lay down on the bank of a river to die.

The Deer, E-se-ko-to-ye, looked out of a willow thicket, and saw the Snake lying on the river bank. Pitying him, the deer took the Snake into his own lodge and gave him food and medicine for his bleeding feet.

The Deer told the Snake that there were indeed creatures with feet like his who would befriend him, but that some among these would be enemies whom it would be necessary to kill before he could reach safety.

He showed the Snake how to make a shelter for protection from the cold and taught him how to make moccasins of deerskin to protect his feet. And at dawn the Snake continued his journey.

The sun was far down the western sky, and it was bitter cold when the Snake made camp the next night. As he gathered boughs for a shelter, Kais-kap the porcupine appeared. Shivering, the Porcupine asked him, "Will you give me shelter in your lodge for the night?"

The Snake said, "It's very little that I have, but you are welcome to share it."

"I am grateful," said Kais-kap, "and perhaps I can do something for you. Those are beautiful moccasins, brother, but they do not match your skin. Take some of my quills, and make a pattern on them, for good luck." So they worked a pattern on the moccasins with the porcupine quills, and the Snake went on his way again.

As the Deer had told him, he met enemies. Three times he was challenged by hostile Indians, and three times he killed his adversary.

At last he met an Indian who greeted him in a friendly manner. The Snake had no gifts for this kindly chief, so he gave him the moccasins. And that, so the old Ones say, was how our people first learned to make moccasins of deerskin, and to ornament them with porcupine quills in patterns, like those on the back of a snake. And from that day on the Snake lived in the lodge of the chief, counting his coup of scalps with the warriors by the Council fire and, for a long time, was happy.

But the chief had a daughter who was beautiful and kind, and the Snake came to love her very much indeed. He wished that he were human, so that he might marry the maiden, and have his own lodge. He knew there was no hope of this unless the High Gods, the Above Spirits took pity on him, and would perform a miracle on his behalf.

So he fasted and prayed for many, many days. But all his fasting and praying had no result, and at last the Snake came very ill.

Now, in the tribe, there was a very highly skilled Medicine Man. Mo'ki-ya was an old man, so old that he had seen and known, and understood, everything that came within the compass of his people's lives, and many things that concerned the Spirits. Many times, his lodge was seen to sway with the Ghost Wind, and the voices of those long gone on to the Sand Hills spoke to him.

Mo'ki-ya came to where the Snake lay in the chief's lodge, and sending all the others away, asked the Snake what his trouble was.

"It is beyond even your magic," said the Snake, but he told Mo'ki-ya about his love for the maiden, and his desire to become a man so that he could marry her.

Mo'ki-ya sat quietly thinking for a while. Then he said, "I shall go on a journey, brother. Perhaps my magic can help, perhaps not. We shall see when I return." And he gathered his medicine bundles and disappeared.

It was a long and fearsome journey that Mo'ki-ya made. He went to the shores of a great lake. He climbed a high mountain, and he took the matter to Nato'se, the Sun himself.

And Nato'se listened, for this man stood high in the regard of the spirits, and his medicine was good. He did not ask, and never had asked, for anything for himself, and to transform the Snake into a brave of the tribe was not a difficult task for the High Gods. The third day after the arrival of Mo'ki-ya at the Sun's abode, Nato'se said to him, "Return to your own lodge Mo'ki-ya, and build a fire of small sticks. Put many handfuls of sweet-grass on the fire, and when the smoke rises thickly, lay the body of the Snake in the middle of it."

And Mo'ki-ya came back to his own land.

The fire was built in the centre of the Medicine lodge, as the Sun had directed, and when the sweetgrass smouldered among the embers, sending the smoke rolling in great billows through the tepee, Mo'ki-ya gently lifted the Snake, now very nearly dead, and placed him in the fire so that he was hidden by the smoke.

The Medicine-drum whispered softly in the dusk of the lodge: the chant of the old men grew a little louder, and then the smoke obscuring the fire parted like a curtain, and a young man stepped out.

Great were the rejoicings in the camp that night. The Snake, now a handsome young brave, was welcomed into the tribe with the ceremonies befitting the reception of one shown to be high in the favour of the spirits. The chief gladly gave him his daughter, happy to have a son law of such distinction.

Many brave sons and beautiful daughters blessed the lodge of the Snake and at last, so the Old ones say, his family became a new tribe-the Pe-sik-na-ta-pe, or Snake Indians.

Penobscot
The Legend of the Bear Family

BY GLENN WALKER

The story concerning the Bear family was revealed through a descendant of the original hero of the following tale. He owned a very old powder horn bearing an incised representation of his mother, who was a Bear, seated in the bow of a canoe travelling to the hunting grounds with her husband.

Many, many generations ago, a Penobscot, his wife, and their little son started out from their village to go to Canada. They were from Penobscot Bay, bound for a great council and dance to be held at the Iroquois village of Caughnawaga. They went upriver to the point where they had to make a 20-mile portage to reach another river that would take them to the St. Lawrence.

The man started ahead with the canoe on his back, leaving his wife to pack part of the luggage to their first overnight campsite. The little boy ran alongside of her. While she was busy arranging her pack, her son ran on ahead to catch up with his father.

The man had gone so far ahead, the boy became lost. The mother assumed the boy was with his father. When she arrived at the campground, they discovered that their son was with neither of them. They began a search immediately, but they could not find him.

The parents returned home to tell their story to their tribe. All of the men turned out for a wide search party, which lasted for several months without success. In March of the next year, the Penobscots found some sharpened sticks near the river. They concluded that the boy must be alive and had been spearing fish. Footprints of bears were seen, and they thought perhaps the boy had been adopted by a bear family.

In the village, there was a lazy man who did not enter into the search, but lay around idly. Everyone asked him, "Why don't you help hunt for the boy? You seem to be good for nothing."

"Very well, I will," he replied. He went right to the bear's den and knocked with his bow on the rocks at the entrance. Inside, a great noise arose where the father, mother, baby bear, and adopted boy lived. The father-bear went to the entrance, holding out a birch-bark vessel. The lazy man shot at it and killed the bear.

The mother-bear says, "Now I will go." She took another vessel, held it out at the entrance, and also was killed. The baby bear did the same and was killed. All of the bears were laid out dead in the cave. Then the lazy man entered and saw the little boy terribly afraid and huddled in a dark corner, crying for his relatives and trying to hide.

The lazy hunter gently carried him home to the village and gave him to his parents. Everyone gave the lazy man presents: two blankets, a canoe, ammunition, and other good things. He became rich overnight.

The boy's parents, however, noticed that their son seemed to be turning into a bear. Bristles were showing on his upper back and shoulders, and his manners had changed. Finally they helped him to become a real person again, and he grew up to be a Penobscot Indian like his father. He married and had children. Forever after he and all of his descendants were called Bears.

They drew pictures of bears on pieces of birch-bark with charcoal and left them at camps wherever they went. All of their descendants seemed to do this and declared, "I am one of the Bear family."

Klamath
How Coyote Stole Fire

Mankind is a younger brother among the People. Though he came into the world long ago, the land was already old. Man missed the early days of mighty upheaval and change, enjoying in his youth long days of peace. He breathed in the warm, moist winds of spring on which the thunder rode. He watched the summer sunshine darken his children to a lush, ruddy copper. He harvested the thick stalks of corn that stretched tall in the morning mists of autumn. In these days of plenty, mankind enjoyed a richness and peace seldom paralleled throughout history.

We today know that all such days come to an end: the autumn months pass, the sun's light thins and the shadows grow longer, dusk chills both bones and spirit. In his youth, however, man had to learn this doom by harsh experience. As winter approached and the rest of the land fell into slumber, young mankind fell into the grip of fear. He feared for the young ones, who had not the means nor the strength to sustain themselves. He feared for the elders, the carriers of ancient wisdom, who doubted they would see another spring. He feared for the sick and infirmed and for all those who would succumb to frost and darkness, never again to thaw.

Unlike young mankind, the elders among the People had grown to be more at home with the inevitable changes of the land. Sister Squirrel hid food away all year long so that she would have plenty at hand when the trees were bare. Brother Salmon hid beneath the ice of the lake, protected by the very harshness that threatened him. Brother Bear grew fat and slept, deep underground, until the first hints of spring. Likewise, Coyote gave no thought to the creeping veil of winter. No thought, that is, until one crisp, spring day when he was tracking a rabbit on the outskirts of a human village. A soft, mournful tune floated to him on the breeze, and he followed it. He found the tribe's women, gathered arm-in-arm, singing for the young, the old, and the sick who had fallen asleep in winter's embrace. Their moans sat heavy in Coyote's empty belly; their wails raised the hairs on his neck.

He listened to the men lament. "The Sun warms us and lights our way all the days of the year," said one. "He warms our huts and our hearts and the stones on the riverbank; he brings us life. Why, then, does he abandon us to frigid darkness? If only he would leave a piece of himself for us, we could guard it all winter long."

Coyote felt pity for his younger brothers and sisters. Why had Father Sky and Mother Earth not gifted them with the same protections as the rest of their children? He knew he must help his siblings if he could. He thought of the great mountaintop where the Fire Eaters lived—man-like creatures that jealously guarded the source of their power and sustenance. Till now, no other members of the People had had need to challenge them, and there was nothing to be gained. However, Coyote knew that mankind had need of this gift, and he would do what he could.

Coyote made the journey to the top of the mountain, and he crept to the edges of the Fire Eaters' camp. As he came near, the three creatures sitting around the fire leapt to their feet and hissed angrily. Their eyes burned like coals, and their clawed fingers clenched and unclenched like the talons of great birds of prey.

"Who's there! Show yoursssself!" hissed one.

"A thief, no doubt! Come to steal what's ours!" shrieked another.

The third creature, quieter and cleverer than the others, simply watched, its eyes darting back and forth among the trees. It spotted Coyote, who quickly made out to be nosing around the underbrush as if he was searching for rodent burrows.

"It is only a simple, grey coyote!" it cried, pointing. The other two looked where it pointed and saw the same: a simple, grey coyote scouring for a modest meal. They sat back down and paid him no more attention.

Coyote, disappearing softly into the tree line, watched the creatures all day and all night. He saw how they kept their fire: feeding it pine cones and branches, poking it with twigs, blowing new life into it if it grew dim. He saw how they guarded it, chasing down and stamping out sparks and embers that tried to escape. And he saw how, after dusk fell, they took turns sitting by the fire all night long—two asleep, one awake.

Finally, the dewy light of dawn crept over the furthest hills, turning the land pink and orange. The creature watching the fire stretched side-to-side, shivered, and lurched sleepily to its feet, scampering into the hut. "I am tired!" it called to its fellows. "Come watch the fire so I may sleep!" But its replacement was no more eager to sit alone in the cold, damp morning hours than it had been. Inevitably, the replacement would take a precious few minutes to dig out from beneath its bed of furs and skins, tottering into the misty morning with a head full of fog and dreams.

Coyote saw in this flaw an opportunity, and he ran down the mountain and gathered some of his friends among the People: sister Squirrel, brother Frog, sister Deer, brother Wood. He told them of poor, furless man, slave to the fear and death of winter. He told them of his watch at the Fire Eaters' camp and of how they kept a piece of the sun that they guarded jealously throughout all the seasons. All the People shared in Coyote's pity for mankind and agreed they must help in his efforts to steal fire.

Coyote returned to the mountaintop and nestled into a deep pile of brush to wait. He waited and watched all through the day until dusk fell and two of the watchers retreated to the hut to sleep. He watched all night as they took turns relieving each other of guard duty, rubbing their eyes and yawning as they passed in the darkness. Finally, the air began to warm, and the ground grew damp with dew as a new day approached. The creature on guard stretched and yawned and cleared its throat, croaking as it walked toward the hut, "Get up, you lazy thing! Come and watch the fire while I rest!"

The second creature woke slowly, as Coyote had expected. It climbed, slow and sleepy, from its mountain of furs, grumbling, "Yes. Yes, I am coming. Do not shout so."

Coyote seized his moment, leaping from the brush on nimble paws. He snatched up a roiling ingot of the fire and lunged with all his might down the mountainside.

A chorus of screeches split the peaceful dawn air, and the Fire Eaters roared after him. For all his gift of speed, the creatures still caught up to poor Coyote in just moments. One creature shot out a grasping claw, clutching at his tail. Though it caught only the tip, the merest touch was enough to turn the hairs white as ash, and that symbol of Coyote's selflessness marks all coyotes to this day. Coyote squealed in fright, flinging the fire away. But the other People were ready and waiting in case they were needed, and Squirrel leapt into action. She caught the tumbling fire and fled through the treetops.

The Fire Eaters scrambled up into the trees, catching Squirrel with terrible speed. The fastest of them breathed flame at her, scorching her back and curling her tail, and this too marks all Squirrels still. Squirrel threw the fire down through the branches to sister Deer, who caught it and darted deftly between the trees. Still, the Fire Eaters charged her, unstoppable in their pursuit. One creature drew so close that it was breathing down her neck. It sputtered red-hot with fury, showering her back with glowing cinders, leaving white spots that commemorate her bravery on the hides of all her descendants. With a grimace, she threw the fire to Frog, who ran for his life. One creature was upon him too quickly, grasping his tail as he leapt. But Frog was not caught so easily and bounded away, leaving his tail behind. That frogs have had no tails ever since is a testament to his strength of will.

Still, the creatures tore after him, and Frog was growing weary. He flung the fire to Wood, and Wood—having nowhere to go—swallowed it. The Fire Eaters turned their fury onto Wood, but Wood was unfazed. They had no idea how to get their fire back from Wood. They promised it wonderful gifts. They sang beautiful, fearsome songs to it. They screeched and screamed at it in the morning light. They tore at it with their knives, struck it with stones, twisted it in their gnarled claws, but Wood did not surrender fire. The Fire Eaters were at a loss, knowing defeat for the first time. They retreated, grumbling and shuffling all the way, to their mountaintop camp far from all the People.

But Coyote alone, clever as he was, knew how to get fire out of Wood. He took Wood to the village of men and shared his wisdom. He showed them that they could rub two dry sticks together to produce heat. He taught them to make glowing embers by spinning a sharpened stick in a hole made in another piece of wood. And mankind was grateful to his older siblings, for he now had a piece of the sun that he could keep safe in his huts to stave off the icy darkness of winter. The songs in the spring were no longer songs of mourning, but of hope, and always of gratitude.

Algonquin
How Glooskap Found the Summer

When the world was a younger place, the Wawaniki—the Children of Light—lived far to the east, near the rising sun. Their chief was known as Glooskap, and he was a kind chief who always sought to protect his people

Midway through the time of Glooskap's leadership, the warm days began to shorten and the land grew colder. Snow blanketed the land more frequently and for longer periods; the crops became weak and many disappeared altogether; the people fell into despair—they could not even build campfires strong enough to stave off the bitter chill.

Glooskap's heart broke for his people, and he knew he must do something quickly to lighten their suffering. He set out on the long journey to the Great North, where the ice rules the land. Here, he found the old giant, Winter, alone in his wigwam—just as Winter liked it. Glooskap knew at once that Winter was responsible for the killing frost that had beset his people.

The old giant welcomed Glooskap inside with a disingenuous smile, offering him drink and a pipe. The two sat and smoked and talked of things. Winter spun tales of the ancient days when snow and ice covered all things, talking of its purity and austere beauty. As he spoke, his words wove a charm of chill and sleep around Glooskap, and the chief fell into deep slumber. He slept for months under the spell of Winter, much like a bear does. But Glooskap was mighty, and he eventually shook off Winter's spell and emerged with renewed vigor.

The Loon, a great bird who was Glooskap's friend and ally, had been searching for Glooskap since his disappearance. Now he found Glooskap and brought him important news. He told Glooskap of a land far to the south, the opposite of Winter's in every way: always warm, lush, and green. This land was ever-bountiful for the people who dwelled there thanks to their kind mistress, Summer. Glooskap knew immediately that Summer would have the power to free his people from Winter's embrace, and so he set out to find her.

Glooskap journeyed to the coast, where he sang the old song that calls the whales. From beneath the waves emerged an old friend: a great whale who often served as Glooskap's ferry when he traveled out to sea. When he asked for her assistance, she reminded him of her rule for travelers: that he must keep his eyes closed and allow her to navigate the waters. "If you do not," she told him, "I will surely run aground, and you and I shall both be doomed."

Glooskap agreed, and the two traveled together over the waves for many days. As they went, the harsh chill gradually faded from the air, replaced by warmer winds and a breeze that grew ever sweeter. The odors that wafted from the shore ran rich with notes of fruit and spice and colorful flowers that grew from great vines and bushes.

One day, when the pair was soaked in the warm air of the far-southern shores, the water beneath them grew suddenly very shallow. Beneath them, tiny sea creatures sang warnings, trying to save them from running aground. Glooskap heard the creatures and opened his eyes to see that they spoke the truth. His urgency was so great that he neglected to tell his friend the whale, who promptly beached herself. Glooskap leapt from her head onto dry land, eager to continue his trek. "Why did you not warn me?" she cried. However, Glooskap did not abandon his friend. Instead, he used his mighty bow as a lever against the whale's enormous flank. He heaved with all his might, freeing her from the bank and launching her out into deeper water, and so they parted ways.

Glooskap journeyed inland, finding the air warmer and the soil richer with every step. At last, he came upon a clearing in the middle of which danced a troop of beautiful, brown-skinned girls. At the center of them all was the woman Glooskap instantly recognized as Summer: rich and ruddy skin, dark locks of curly hair, and a crown of violet flowers, with more blossoms overflowing from her arms. Glooskap knew she would be able to charm Winter out of the frozen death grip he held on the land, and so he leapt at her and would not let go until she heard his tale. Together, the pair retraced the long journey back to the north and the wigwam of old, stubborn Winter.

Winter was unfazed, feeling sure he would be able to lull Glooskap to sleep once more. This time, however, Summer worked her magic while Glooskap and Winter talked. The old giant soon broke into a sweat and realized his power was broken. Even his icy home began to melt. Summer danced, waking animals from their slumber, bringing life to the grass and trees, filling the rivers and lakes with snow melt.

Old Winter wallowed in his defeat, but Summer struck a bargain. She said, "All the country to the far north is still yours, as it has always been and ever shall be. As for the lands of the Children of Light, we will share them. For half of each year, you may return and enjoy reigning over them, but more gently than before. I will return from the south for the other half of the year so that they may warm themselves and replenish their stores." Old Winter accepted this without resistance, and so the bargain between Summer and Winter remains intact to this day. Each year, Winter comes back and lulls the land to sleep with frost, and each year, Summer chases him away with her gifts of warmth and joy.

Keepers of the Water

BY LOIS BEARDSLEE

According to tradition, we Ojibwe women consider ourselves "keepers of the water." It is a title we bestow upon ourselves, an honor. It was once a pragmatic term, we are certain, a reference to the fact that we once hauled it for cooking and cleaning in the family camps. There is honor in the division of labor between the sexes and between people of different ages and abilities. It means that we each have value. Our culture cannot survive without each and every one of us.

As keepers of the water in the home, we made sure that our nearby water supply was not defiled with waste and runoff. We instructed the children carefully in the disposal of wash water and other wastes so that they could do their daily chores with minimal supervision. No one can live without water and yet it becomes spoiled so easily, with the tiniest contamination.

In ceremonial and teaching contexts, it is the women only who handle the water. This is to remind all of us of the important roles that women play in our everyday lives, families, and society, as well as in our history.

Some elders say that our Mother Earth was populated with the *Anishnabeg*, or human beings, by the first woman, Kiishigokwe. She is the bringer of all life, not just human life. Her name means Cloud Woman. She exists in the air, in great sweeping cloud banks, and in mists. On warm days, she takes up the moisture from the lakes surrounding our homes and stores it in the breezes. She releases it to the plants and the lake basins in the form of life-giving precipitation. The water is continually recycled and reused, always changing forms, not unlike Kiishigokwe. She takes on many personifications and has the power of multiplicity—she can be in many places at one time. We do not distinguish between her earthly personification (present within all Ojibwe women) and her historic, or supernatural identity. Her role is a beneficial and loving one. She is, in her manner of generosity and behavior, a role model for all *Anishnabe* women. Like Kiishigokwe, we make essential contributions to the life cycle. We are the keepers of the water.

Cheyenne
Yellowstone Valley and the Great Flood

BY GLENN WALKER

"I have heard it told on the Cheyenne Reservation in Montana and the Seminole camps in the Florida Everglades, I have heard it from the Eskimos north of the Arctic Circle and the Indians south of the equator. The legend of the flood is the most universal of all legends. It is told in Asia, Africa, and Europe, in North America and the South Pacific." Professor Hap Gilliland of Eastern Montana College was the first to record this legend of the great flood.

This is one of the fifteen legends of the flood that he himself recorded in various parts of the world:

He was an old Indian. His face was weather beaten, but his eyes were still bright. I never knew what tribe he was from, though I could guess. Yet others from the tribe whom I talked to later had never heard his story.

We had been talking of the visions of the young men. He sat for a long time, looking out across the Yellowstone Valley through the pouring rain, before he spoke. "They are beginning to come back," he said.

"Who is coming back?" I asked.

"The animals," he said. "It has happened before."

"Tell me about it."

He thought for a long while before he lifted his hands and his eyes. "The Great Spirit smiled on this land when he made it. There were mountains and plains, forests and grasslands. There were animals of many kinds—and men."

The old man's hands moved smoothly, telling the story more clearly than his voice.

The Great Spirit told the people, "These animals are your brothers. Share the land with them. They will give you food and clothing. Live with them and protect them.

"Protect especially the buffalo, for the buffalo will give you food and shelter. The hide of the buffalo will keep you from the cold, from the heat, and from the rain. As long as you have the buffalo, you will never need to suffer."

For many winters the people lived at peace with the animals and with the land. When they killed a buffalo, they thanked the Great Spirit, and they used every part of the buffalo. It took care of every need.

Then other people came. They did not think of the animals as brothers. They killed, even when they did not need food. They burned and cut the forests, and the animals died. They shot the buffalo and called it sport. They killed the fish in the streams.

When the Great Spirit looked down, he was sad. He let the smoke of the fires lie in the valleys. The people coughed and choked. But still they burned and they killed.

So the Great Spirit sent rains to put out the fires and to destroy the people.

The rains feil, and the waters rose. The people moved from the flooded valleys to the higher land.

Spotted Bear, the medicine man, gathered together his people. He said to them, "The Great Spirit has told us that as long as we have the buffalo we will be safe from heat and cold and rain. But there are no longer any buffalo. Unless we can find buffalo and live at peace with nature, we will all die."

Still the rains fell, and the waters rose. The people moved from the flooded plains to the hills.

The young men went out and hunted for the buffalo. As they went they put out the fires. They made friends with the animals once more. They cleaned out the streams.

Still the rains fell, and the waters rose. The people moved from the flooded hills to the mountains.

Two young men came to Spotted Bear. "We have found the buffalo," they said. "There was a cow, a calf, and a great white bull. The cow and the calf climbed up to the safety of the mountains. They should be back when the rain stops. But the bank gave way, and the bull was swept away by the floodwaters. We followed and got him to shore, but he had drowned. We have brought you his hide."

They unfolded a huge white buffalo skin.

Spotted Bear took the white buffalo hide. "Many people have been drowned," he said. "Our food has been carried away. But our young people are no longer destroying the world that was created for them. They have found the white buffalo. It will save those who are left."

Still the rains fell, and the waters rose. The people moved from the flooded mountains to the highest peaks.

Spotted Bear spread the white buffalo skin on the ground. He and the other medicine men scraped it and stretched it, and scraped it and stretched it.

Still the rains fell. Like all rawhide, the buffalo skin stretched when it was wet. Spotted Bear stretched it out over the village. All the people who were left crowded under it.

As the rains fell, the medicine men stretched the buffalo skin across the mountains. Each day they stretched it farther.

Then Spotted Bear tied one corner to the top of the Big Horn Mountains. That side, he fastened to the Pryors. The next corner he tied to the Bear Tooth Mountains. Crossing the Yellowstone Valley, he tied one corner to the Crazy Mountains, and the other to Signal Butte in the Bull Mountains.

The whole Yellowstone Valley was covered by the white buffalo skin. Though the rains still fell above, it did not fall in the Yellowstone Valley.

The waters sank away. Animals from the outside moved into the valley, under the white buffalo skin. The people shared the valley with them.

Still the rains fell above the buffalo skin. The skin stretched and began to sag.

Spotted Bear stood on the Bridger Mountains and raised the west end of the buffalo skin to catch the West Wind. The West Wind rushed in and was caught under the buffalo skin. The wind lifted the skin until it formed a great dome over the valley.

The Great Spirit saw that the people were living at peace with the earth. The rains stopped, and the sun shone. As the sun shone on the white buffalo skin, it gleamed with colours of red and yellow and blue.

As the sun shone on the rawhide, it began to shrink. The ends of the dome shrank away until all that was left was one great arch across the valley.

The old man's voice faded away; but his hands said "Look," and his arms moved toward the valley.

The rain had stopped and a rainbow arched across the Yellowstone Valley. A buffalo calf and its mother grazed beneath it.

Cherokee
Buffalo and Eagle Wing

BY ELLA E. CLARK

A long time ago there were no stones on the earth. The mountains, hills, and valleys were not rough, and it was easy to walk on the ground swiftly. There were no small trees at that time either. All the bushes and trees were tall and straight and were at equal distances. So a man could travel through a forest without having to make a path.

At that time, a large buffalo roamed over the land. From the water, he had obtained his spirit power—the power to change anything into some other form. He would have that power as long as he only drank from a certain pool.

In his wanderings, Buffalo often travelled across a high mountain. He liked this mountain so much that one day he asked it, "Would you like to be changed into something else?"

"Yes," replied the mountain. "I would like to be changed into something nobody would want to climb over."

"All right," said Buffalo. "I will change you into something hard that I will call 'stone.' You will be so hard that no one will want to break you and so smooth that no one will want to climb you."

So Buffalo changed the mountain into a large stone. "And I give you the power to change yourself into anything else as long as you do not break yourself."

Only buffaloes lived in this part of the land. No people lived here. On the other side of the mountain lived men who were cruel and killed animals. The buffaloes knew about them and stayed as far away from them as possible. But one day Buffalo thought he would like to see these men. He hoped to make friends with them and persuade them not to kill buffaloes.

So he went over the mountain and travelled along a stream until he came to a lodge. There lived an old woman and her grandson. The little boy liked Buffalo, and Buffalo liked the little boy and his grandmother. He said to them, "I have the power to change you into any form you wish. What would you like most to be?"

"I want always to be with my grandson. I want to be changed into anything that will make it possible for me to be with him, wherever he goes."

"I will take you to the home of the buffaloes," said their guest. "I will ask them to teach the boy to become a swift runner. I will ask the water to change the grandmother into something, so that you two can always be together."

So Buffalo, the grandmother, and the little boy went over the mountain to the land of the buffaloes.

"We will teach you to run swiftly," they told the boy, "if you will promise to keep your people from hunting and killing buffaloes."

"I promise," said the boy.

The buffaloes taught him to run so fast that not one of them could keep up with him. The old grandmother could follow him wherever he went, for she had been changed into Wind.

The boy stayed with the buffaloes until he became a man. Then they let him go back to his people, reminding him of his promise. Because he was such a swift runner, he became a leader of the hunters. They called him Eagle Wing.

One day the chief called Eagle Wing to him and said to him, "My son, I want you to take the hunters to the buffalo country. We have never been able to kill buffaloes because they run so very fast. But you too can run fast. If you will kill some buffaloes and bring home the meat and the skins, I will adopt you as my son. And when I die, you will become chief of the tribe."

Eagle Wing wanted so much to become chief that he pushed from his mind his promise to the buffaloes. He started out with the hunters, but he climbed the mountain so fast that they were soon left far behind. On the other side of the mountain, he saw a herd of buffaloes. They started to run in fright, but Eagle Wing followed them and killed most of them.

Buffalo, the great one who got his power from the water, was away from home at the time of the hunt. On his way back he grew so thirsty that he drank from some water on the other side of the mountain not from his special pool. When he reached home and saw what the hunter had done, he became very angry. He tried to turn the men into grass, but he could not. Because he had drunk from another pool, he had lost his power to transform.

Buffalo went to the big stone that had once been a mountain.

"What can you do to punish the hunter for what he has done?" he asked Stone.

"I will ask the trees to tangle themselves so that it will be difficult for men to travel through them," answered Stone. "I will break myself into many pieces and scatter myself all over the land. Then the swift runner and his followers cannot run over me without hurting their feet."

"That will punish them," agreed Buffalo.

So Stone broke itself into many pieces and scattered itself all over the land. Whenever the swift runner, Eagle Wing, and his followers tried to run over the mountain, stones cut their feet. Bushes scratched and bruised their bodies.

That is how Eagle Wing was punished for not keeping his promise to Buffalo.

An Unwritten Law of the Sea

BY HERBERT O. ANUNGAZUK

In his work for the National Park Service, Herbert Anungazuk has provided invaluable assistance to anthropologists and other researchers working in and around the Bering Land Bridge National Preserve, an area which is a remnant of the ancient land connection between North America and Asia. Anungazuk's native village of Wales sits on the westernmost point of the North American continent at Cape Prince of Wales, on the shores of Bering Strait across from the Diomede Islands and East Cape, Siberia in Asia. A fluent speaker of the Inupiaq language, Anungazuk's writings and talks often present his Inupiaq culture. The essay that appears here, "An Unwritten Law of the Sea," delves deeply into essential aspects of life and worldview that distinguish the Inupiat, particularly from non-Native peoples. The text begins with the relationship between all people and the earth, which sustains and nourishes them. Clearly, this relationship differs from one group to another, and Anungazuk points out how special the relationship is in the case of hunters and gatherers like the Inupiat, who depend on animals and must treat their prey with respect in order to achieve success in hunting. He tells us how traditions essential to physical and cultural survival are passed on by Inupiaq elders, and how this fundamental role makes elders the primary storytellers and pillars of the society. Unfortunately, Inupiaq beliefs and ceremonies have not been well understood by Western people, who often disparage them, failing to recognize concepts that have long since disappeared from agriculture-based and urban societies. Anungazuk tells us that these traditions are not lost or discarded but have gone underground, because culture does not go away easily, particularly where the underpinnings of an entire people are concerned. In the essay, some words and names are spelled in the standard Inupiaq orthography, some in the author's own system, and others in the author's spelling, followed by standard orthography in brackets, e.g., *aqlu [aaglu]*.

—LDK

We have an alliance with the earth. Each one of us does, and some of us as a people have continued to grasp this alliance and have anchored it into our hearts, our minds, and our souls. We have an alliance with the mammals, birds, and fish because through them we have gained a lasting balance as their flesh provides the nutrients which have, since dawn immemorial, continued to nourish our bodies. From this alliance our being probes into the world of our prey and learns their ways so we can increase our chances for a successful harvest. The implements used by our ancestors that continue to be found in ancient house pits commemorate the mammals, birds, and fish that provide for our survival. The jawbones of the mighty whale, skulls of the polar bear, and skin boats or kayaks adorn the graves of noble hunters. In my society, even in death a hunter lies according to his stature while he was among the living: his grave and those of his family lie high upon the mountain. His status as an *umialik* grants him the privilege of lying in state above many others on the mountain, and in time, the remains become naturally absorbed by the earth.

The lifeways of a people cover an entire spectrum, a spectrum so wide and profound that it continues to astound the Western mind as non-Inupiat learn more about us. Indigenous people are certainly a profound people but we too are astounded as we learn more about what was related to us by our elders. The flame of wonder about our culture and heritage may have been lit long, long ago by the story of an elder, but the flame may not mature with each one of us until decades later. You must share what you have heard, what you have learned. Sharing is how the people have endured up to this very day. You must never become obsessive because it is our way to share. It is known that if you do not share your harvest with others, you will meet with ill fortune in your effort to continue as a provider for your family and the community. No hunter would ever want to fall victim to that prophecy. Sharing knowledge with others has been the way of the people, because through knowledge we survive.

Our land is not only known as Wales, Alaska. It is a place of a multitude of names. Place names are a part of the voice of the land. Place names take us into our own geographical world, since the names relate directly to the land. The names show our union, our total existence, and our uniform standing with our universe. The names ring out: Ugalaturuaq, the place of many Arctic hares; Mapsaturuaq, an area of extreme danger where the land is prone to avalanches in the winter; Izraqit, a rocky slope resembling diced foods prepared for the table. The language of the Kingikmiut [Kinikmiut] has been reverberating over the land through countless ages. Although the language may have been temporarily silenced from the land when the people left ages ago for unknown reasons, the language returned with us when we found that our new land could not support our need for sea mammal oil. One voice may be just a whisper, but to speak the language shows an act of respect for the land because from the land came the language. When Kingigin [Kinigin] was first settled is no longer in the memory of the oldest elders. Whether occupation of our land occurred as stated in a context not of the people, one can only assume when the greatest event of my people's history took place, that of the settlement of our community, Kingigin. We are certain that we have long been on the land despite the fact that we moved away from Kingigin on one occasion. From that point forward, the people came to call themselves Kingikmiut, because we are "people of Kingigin."

The ways and methods of teaching by the elders are similar in indigenous societies. One elder will not know everything about the culture, but he will know many different elements. Our way of life revolves in a continual circle that, in turn, revolves around the spectrum of reality. Even the mere task of gathering wood is a part of the intricate realities of survival because from wood come many things. Special types of wood are used to make the shaft of a harpoon, or the frame of an *umiaq*, or in making a drum. Most of our elders are authorities in several categories of knowledge specific to the culture, be it knowledge of species of wildlife, geography within its natural realm, or diplomacy between people. These things are learned and are among the many elements that fulfill the completeness of a culture or society. The creatures of the land and sea are teachers also, but you need to catch them while they are teaching. If the elders are uncertain about any information that is asked of them, they are very quick to relay your question to someone else. No one is ever denied an answer.

The elders are very forthright in offering help because it is their duty to pass on to the new generations what they learned from the elders before them. Both man and woman are entrusted to teach and they teach in the same way as the persons who taught them. There is only one way, but there can be alternatives in very rare instances. We have never stated to one another to stay away from the old ones, but we have been thrust into a new age. The new generations with a wish to learn are drawn to the elder. Other societies are now seeing the importance of the elder, because the elder, for generation after ancient generation, has always been in the forefront of our quest to survive. The elders are and always have been the pillar of our society. To hear the words of wisdom of the elder, their vision and encouragement is a loud voice even though it is expressed in quiet tones.

It is rare for a hunter to call an animal an animal. To us they are our prey, and each and every one of them has a name. In our belief, each one of them has a spirit regardless of how other societies have arranged them in classes. Some of the creatures of the sea have been gifted with multiple names because of their importance to us as a source of survival. A whale is a whale until you identify the species. A walrus is a walrus until it too identifies itself in terms of where the Iñupiat have placed this mammal within their society. For example, a bull walrus is a *nugaaġruk,* which quite literally, in a fond way, can mean your younger sibling. Multiple definitions of words do occur. An *izavgalik* is a mother with calf, while she can be identified as an *aġnazaluq. Aġnazaluq,* or *aġnaq,* meaning female or woman, can be applied to any species: man, mammal, bird, or fish. The walrus, like the whale, is a mammal of many uses. The skin is used to cover the *umiaq* that ply the waters in search of the mammals that provide our livelihood. The inner membrane of the stomach covers the drum whose sound reverberates over the land in ceremony, ritual, and song. The bones can be made into a variety of tools that are useful in the everyday lives of the Iñupiat. Where do the whale, walrus, and seal spend their winters? There can be so many of them that you wonder why others who travel the same waters and who have the potential of winter encounters say so little about them. The Iñupiat know when the mammals, birds, and fish return, yet they can only assume where the animals go in winter.

When others come to the elders, they say, "I know where the animals are, I know when the animals will come to me." We know, for we have been anticipating the return of the sea mammal since the dawn of time. This thought continues in the hearts and minds of the new generations of hunters, because the glories of a successful harvest rest in every hunter. In this new age, the young continue to learn and to fulfill their duties as hunters, but the winds of change have taken over.

Hunters are maritime people. We are Imaaġmiut, people of the sea; we are Taġiuġmiut, people of the salt water. We are Tapqaamiut, coastal people, because the sea is our doorstep to survival. The sea sustains us, yet the sea can claim us if we do not heed its warning, since the sea has a character all her own. We have a strong relationship with the sea that goes beyond what other societies can understand. We live in a world where we need to know what we are doing. In our world, every second of every day, a whale, a walrus, a seal comes up from the depths and takes a breath of the very air that fills our lungs. Although we do not share the same watery existence, we share the same environment with the life that is found on the land and in the sea. Our sea is the most productive part of the earth and that is why many of the villages in Alaska are situated on or near the coast. The sea supports an entire people. Very few of the life-forms of the sea are not eaten. Although most forms are edible, you cannot be sustained nutritionally for indefinite periods because your body needs a variety of nutrients to survive. Our fate is set if we have only one form of food to sustain our bodies. Meat, leaves, berries, and undersea life forms create a balance as they have since the first dawn. The seasons decide what will be placed upon the table.

The stories of our ancient past are very complex. Stories are immeasurable wealth to any people. Some stories require intense hours, days, weeks, and even months before the story is deemed complete by the one relating the story. In reality, the storyteller is saying, "Let me read you a story from my mind," and the stories elevate your interest if you can see what is being told in your mind. You can see places as they are being related to you in the story. You can actually see the faces and hear the voice of a person you are learning about, or the voice of the walrus as stories are being related about them. Storytelling is a special skill that cannot exist without someone going through a complex process of learning our ways. Some societies place words into special categories that restrict their use in normal speech. Some of these words are for prayer and are sacred; these words have long been used by indigenous people from the depths of their hearts. The deadly sins that occur in other societies are also recognized by indigenous beliefs. Customs and rituals were seen as sinful in the eyes of others, and the young were warned to stay away from the old, not realizing that the elder is the teacher of the people. Indigenous beliefs were treated in a very disrespectful manner at the time of the first encounters with other societies from the east.

As mentioned, the hunter has a profound alliance with the mammals of the sea, an alliance that involves the spiritual beliefs of many, many hunters. This belief is that the people cannot survive without a hunter/prey bond that was begun by our ancestors ages ago. This belief conforms with those of many hunting cultures in the northern hemisphere. One belief among many, that respect must be paid to the spirit of the mammals, birds, or fish, is no longer observed, but many hunters continue to respect animals in spirit. From the first moments of contact with people from the East, our societies and cultures clashed because what was put in place of others' proven ways was not a perfect match with our concepts. Fortunately, in many ways, parts of the culture important to ceremony and observances of special events were just put underground and not discarded, because culture is necessary to read the story of a people. Efforts were made to obliterate the culture, and this trend continues in many different forms today. Culture is a crucial part of a people's being. Our culture is not uniform with that of other societies because we have our own ways. Its compelling power is revealed by a person telling a story, and this story is absorbed by the listener, to be told again to eager ears.

The traditions of the people define our relationship with the land, the sea, and the creatures that reside therein. Each village is a society, a nation, distinct on its own, and each and every group has a story of their own that defines and describes this relationship. Let me relate a story told by my grandfather Sigiaqluq on his first encounter with the *aqlu [aaġlu]* as a child. To us, the killer whale or orca is *aqlu*. The name does not signify that the mammal is a wanton killer, but the *aqlu* is a supreme predator. The *aqlu* is a hunter and he has gained an extremely high status in the lore of the northern hunter, yet is not a mythical being, although to some who do not understand our ways, the *aqlu* may have the nature of a myth. In the ancient stories of the Iñupiat the *aqlu* is at its own level in the hierarchy of predator and prey, and the majestic mammal resides at the top of its own universe. His position is absolute. Elderly hunters, refined in the art form of hunting on the northern ice and seas, will say to their crews, "Someone is already hunting here," when the *aqlu* is encountered during hunts. The hunters leave in search of other hunting grounds immediately.

Every young boy is an aspiring hunter, and my grandfather was certainly no exception; before a boy is taken onto the ice, his father conditions him to the life of a hunter by taking him to the *qargi* at a very young age. This is the time of awareness. The child is now conscious and begins his life as a human being. Prior to that time, the society entrusts him to a woman, and she takes complete responsibility for his livelihood. My grandfather was very young when my great-grandfather Kiapiq began to take him along on walrus hunts as the icy winter weather was being replaced by the warmth of spring. The weather can still be extremely cold, but even so, a boy child must be conditioned. A hunter is not born to hunt; he has to be made.

Stories begin in the life of a hunter at a very tender age, and as an aspiring hunter begins his training in the month when the weather begins to warm, it is usually the encounters with walrus that are his first awareness. The most menial of jobs is handed the aspiring hunter, and it will be years before someone considers him able to lead a crew. He will have filled every position on a crew before he can become an *umialik,* or someone who is truly capable of providing for others besides himself. He is made to know that he has a responsibility that must be continually fulfilled. The life of any hunter fulfills the life of only one individual, but in all cases, many lives can be influenced by the actions of a single individual. Some hunters attain an elite rank in the society of hunters at an early period, but some may never attain a high status until late in life. Some, despite a lifetime of hunting, never attain a high rank. A hunter never retires. Although he may no longer accompany the crew, he serves the community of hunters by teaching them what he learned from the elders who taught him the ways of the ice. The life of a hunter is a unique story, best told in the *qargi* during specific times of day when the night begins to wane and the young become restless.

Our ancient relationship with the sea is a relationship that you will not see among other groups of people. The relationship extends to all creatures that the sea and ice harbor, and it is this relationship that has made us into a class of hunters unmatched among other societies. Yet even as we are unmatched, we are not invincible. We are mortal, and in the ways of mortal beings, we have learned to adjust as best as we can within our environment. In fulfilling the responsibilities of a hunter, my grandfather gained the status of an *umialik,* but this honor was not accomplished in a short period. He went through a lifetime of training, observing men who taught him what they had learned in a lifetime of learning. In my society, every man and woman is a teacher, and their credential in life is their knowledge of survival in what is considered one of the most inhospitable of regions on earth. My grandfather had two *umiaqs* and one kayak when death overtook him before his time during an influenza epidemic in the winter of 1944. My grandmother, Tuġutaq, of Cape Espenberg origin, followed in death three days later. My grandfather told a story to my mother and the rest of the family while she was a young girl, and I heard her relate the story to us when we were very young. I never knew my grandparents. I only know them through a photograph that I cherish.

I will attempt to tell a story in the way that my grandfather may have told the story of an encounter with the beings of the sea during his lifetime. He would have begun, "Do you know the *aqlu?*" and saying that, he would have gained the immediate attention of everyone, young and old. The entire *qargi* would have gathered around to hear him speak in his soft voice as he began to tell the story. He would continue by explaining that there was no more night, but the time was late as the walrus season was near its end. A spring storm had kept the hunters off the ice for many days, but the days were again prime to pursue their efforts to fatten winter stores. The horizon glowed white in the distance revealing an expanse of ice, but the ice dances high above the sea, as a mirage. The boat moved as fast as the gentle northeast wind toward the islands in the middle of the sea, and the crew knew that the ice could not be reached in a short time. The ice insures a successful hunt, and the boat plied effortlessly over the water. With a gentle wind, the sea was light, but the men were grateful for the wind since it kept them from their paddles.

Since my grandfather was in training, he occupied the stern of the boat. His position in the crew placed him under the guidance of the hunter who steered the craft, and in complete view of those who manned other positions. The *umialik* was a seasoned hunter, as were the other crew members. His father, Kiapiq, was young but already envisioned himself as an *umialik,* and his position was in the bow of the boat, a position you cannot attain without being assigned to it by a person in authority. His actions insured a kill, and he did not take his responsibility for granted, nor did he take any unjust action.

The boat crept closer to the ice under full sail from the gentle wind. The rays of an early morning sun put my grandfather into a near stupor, but he struggled to remain awake as he knew everyone was watching him. He had been told that he must be observant, since an observant hunter is a successful hunter. The crew, including my grandfather, whiled the time away by tending to their equipment or scanning the sea for any prey they might encounter, but their minds were on reaching the ice and the promise of success. There is an intense quiet in an *umiaq* carried by the wind, and only the swish of the water parted by the bow of the boat can be heard. All was quiet, but suddenly the men were startled by the loud sound of a large mammal expending its breath just out of sight of the bow. Some of the men stood and some craned their necks to see what had surfaced before them. On seeing that it was an *aqlu,* many of the men were afraid because bothering an *aqlu* in any form violated a strict rule that must never be broken. To do so was a fault punishable by death, and the *aqlu* does not rest until it deals with the wrongdoer. Many of the men sat down, resigned to what might happen when suddenly the sea around them exploded with scores of *aqlut [aaġlut]* in perfect formation alongside them. Immediately the men began to ask themselves, "What is happening to us?" "What have we done?" "Who among us has broken the rule of the *aqlu?*" My grandfather had heard many, many times that you must not bother the *aqlu* in any way, and he could see and sense the tension and uneasiness among the crew members.

The *umialik* and Kiapiq assessed their situation. The pair and every member of the crew realized that many *aqlut* had surrounded the boat in two V formations, diving and surfacing in unison. The closest consisted of adolescent *aqlut* with an older one leading them. The farthest consisted of large *aqlut* with a larger one leading the formation. Leading both formations was an extremely large *aqlu* whose *inuk* was taller than Kiapiq, and Kiapiq was a tall man. The Inupiat call the dorsal fin of the *aqlu* the *inuk* or "person," for this is where the *inua* or spirit of the *aqlu* resides. The *umialik* wondered what could be done as he realized they might now be in peril, being in the open sea far from the islands of the strait and also the mainland.

Among the crew was an aspiring *angatkuq [anatkuq],* a shaman who was an unseasoned, but determined man. He came forward to the bow of the boat, grasped both gunwales, and prepared for what he felt he must do. Some of the men felt there was no alternative but to meet their fate.

The *umialik* and Kiapiq welcomed his coming forward because they did not know what could be done in a time like this. The *angatkuq* began by stating, "We are hunters, like you. We are hunting, as you are. We have families. We have families to feed, as you do. Please let us continue what we are doing and I will give you the tongues of our harvest today as a share of our success" The *aqlut* kept pace with the *umiaq*, swimming on the surface and occasionally diving, but never completely disappearing into the water. Surely a voice could not be heard over the commotion made by the water, but the *aqlut* dove in perfect unison after hearing the plea of the *angatkuq*. The boat was in the middle of the sea, and the crew searched the horizon around them, but the *aqlut* did not surface so they could be seen. The crew continued on despite their encounters, and in time the ice field was reached. Throughout the day, the men harvested seal and walrus, and each time a successful harvest occurred, the *angatkuq* removed the tongues and dropped them into the water after saying he had repaid a part of his debt to the *aqlut* during the hunt. After the hunt was over, the debt was no more. You can ask the *aqlut* for a share of their harvest when you see them hunting, and a share of their harvest will be given to you. We are told that even if the current is not likely to cast anything ashore, your share, as if cut by a sharp knife, will drift in. This is an unwritten law of the sea that many aspiring hunters learn early in life in the Bering Strait region. I am sure many other young hunters of other nations learn this commandment very early in life. In the *aqlu* resides a powerful spirit. This majestic mammal has the power to transform into a man or a wolf, but that is a story best told elsewhere and in other times reserved for learning.

In seeking to understand the ways of the people, you must probe into the ways of survival of the northern hunter. This is where you hear the song of subsistence, for subsistence is the song of survival. The chorus of this song contains many unique elements, and each of these elements tells a special story. We give thanks to the Creator before each meal, and our thanks are also a silent prayer before the hunt. Prayers are stated for favorable winds and safe seas so that we can replenish winter stores for another season of survival. The quest to survive stands in a class all its own. The way of life of the northern hunter is a life of sincerity with oneself and of personal union with one's family and people.

In closing let me read a previous note that was shared as an abstract in a paper entitled "The Indigenous Identity in Framework, Collaboration, and Compromise with the Alaska Native Informant." The abstract begins, "From a simple flake of stone or ivory arise many questions. Where, when, how, or why is a specific product obtained, if the resource is not available within an immediate region?" Who is responsible is usually known except in rare cases, and the scope and depth of the question can astound even the descendants, as they become knowledgeable of their ancient past. Survival is a universal quest, as the will to survive was decided eons ago by the Ancient Hunter. Indigenous man identifies himself with the Ancient Hunter very easily because it is his story that is related to him by his elders. Some Arctic research began over a century ago, but with decades of lapses in between, and only in the last three decades, also with lapses, has research been renewed by a new generation of researchers. Even if this is very welcoming, it is possibly occurring only in what may be the twilight period for many groups of people; fortunately for all, there has always been a sunrise that follows. There is no time to waste, but the lack of funding cripples the efforts of many people. Some of the elders may have been consulted for only short periods, but always, the information they contribute adds much to the story. Remember Ruth Milligrock of Little Diomede who stated that "Our land is getting old; like an old woman she is changing" So little of the story of our periods of time with eras such as *issaq* or *aipaani* are documented. *Issaq* and *aipaani* are time periods of unwritten history thousands of years old that are only supported by oral tradition, and so little of the elders' knowledge of this period has been presented. Ernest Oxereok of Wales, just months before his passing, stated that from the earth came our health, as he related information about the abundant plants that grow upon our land, as traditional uses of these plants continue today. Patrick Ongtowasruk, also of Wales, is young in comparison to other elders that we have talked with. He stated that when the crust of the earth was thin there were many spirits roaming the earth. The elders of the 1930 to 1935 era may be considered "young" by some researchers, but this is the generation that lived a life being entirely Inupiaq, before the society and its culture became wholly immersed into Western ways. They can surely share the wisdom, pride, and honor that are the ways of the Inupiat. We have only to ask if they would like to share their lifetime of learning with us. Quyaana.

Lenape
The Hunter and the Owl

Once a Delaware man and his wife went on a long hunt quite a way from the village. They had been out several days without having any luck when one night as they were sitting around their camp fire an owl hooted from a tree nearby and after hooting laughed. This was considered a good omen, but to make sure of this the hunter took a chunk of fire and retired a little way from the camp under the tree where the owl was perched, and laid the chunk of fire on the ground, and sitting by it began to sprinkle tobacco on the live coal and talk to the owl. He said: "Mo-hoo-mus (or Grandfather), I have heard you whoop and laugh. I know by this that you see good luck coming to me after these few days of discouragement. I know that you are very fond of the fat of the deer and that you can exercise influence over the game if you will. I want you to bring much game in my way, not only deer, but fur-bearing animals, so that I may return home with a bountiful supply of furs as well as much dried meat, and I will promise you that from the largest deer that I kill, I will give you the fat and heart, of which you are very fond. I will hang them in a tree so that you can get them." The owl laughed again and the hunter knew that he would get much game after that.

The next morning he arose early, just before day, and started out with his bow and arrow, leaving his wife to take care of the camp. He had not gone far before he killed a very large buck. In his haste to take the deer back to camp so that he could go out and kill another before it got too late, he forgot his promise to the owl and did not take out the fat and heart and hang it in the tree as he said he would do, but flung the deer across his shoulder and started for camp. The deer was very heavy and he could not carry it all the way to camp without stopping to rest. He had only gone a few steps when he heard the owl hoot. This time it did not laugh as it had the night before.

The owl flew low down, right in front of the man, and said to him: "Is this the way you keep your promise to me? For this falsehood I will curse you. When you lay down this deer, you will fall dead." The hunter was quick to reply: "Grandfather, it is true I did not hang the fat up for you where I killed the deer, but I did not intend to keep it from you as you accuse me. I too have power and I say to you that when you alight, you too will fall dead. We will see who is the stronger and who first will die." The owl made a circle or two and began to get very tired, for owls can only fly a short distance. When it came back again, it said: "My good hunter, I will recall my curse and help you all I can, if you will recall yours, and we will be friends after this." The hunter was glad enough to agree, as he was getting very tired too. So the hunter lay the deer down and took out the fat and the heart and hung them up. When he picked up the deer again it was much lighter and he carried it to his camp with perfect ease. His wife was very glad to see him bringing in game. She soon dressed the deer and cut up strips of the best meat and hung them up to dry, and the hunter went out again and soon returned with other game.

In a few days they had all the furs and dried meat they could both carry to their home, and the hunter learned a lesson on this trip that he never afterwards forgot—that whenever a promise is made, it should always be fulfilled.

Squamish
The Legend of Wountie

BY BAMARIVER

This legend is from the Squamish Nation, Coast Salish, on the west coast of Canada. The Cheakamus River is north of the town of Squamish and flows into Howe Sound.

A long time ago, even before the time of the flood, the Cheakamus River provided food for the Squamish people. Each year, at the end of summer, when the salmon came home to spawn, the people would cast their cedar root nets into the water and get enough fish for the winter to come.

One day, a man came to fish for food for his family for the winter. He looked into the river and found that many fish were coming home this year. He said thanks to the spirit of the fish, for giving themselves as food for his family, and cast his net into the river and waited. In time, he drew his nets in, and they were full of fish, enough for his family for the whole year. He packed these away into cedar bark baskets, and prepared to go home.

But he looked into the river, and saw all those fish, and decided to cast his net again. And he did so, and it again filled with fish, which he threw onto the shore. A third time, he cast his net into the water and waited.

This time, when he pulled his net in, it was torn beyond repair by sticks, stumps and branches, which filled the net. To his dismay, the fish on the shore and the fish in the cedar bark baskets were also sticks and branches. He had no fish; his nets were ruined.

It was then he looked up at the mountain and saw Wountie, the spirit protecting the Cheakamus, who told him that he had broken the faith with the river and with nature by taking more than he needed for himself and his family. And this was the consequence.

And to this day, high on the mountain overlooking the Cheakamus and Paradise Valley, is the image of Wountie, protecting the Cheakamus.

The fisherman? Well, his family went hungry and starved, a lesson for all the people in his family.

Sioux
The Forgotten Ear of Corn

An Arikara woman was once gathering corn from the field to store away for winter use. She passed from stalk to stalk, tearing off the ears and dropping them into her folded robe. When all was gathered she started to go, when she heard a faint voice, like a child's, weeping and calling:

"Oh, do not leave me! Do not go away without me."

The woman was astonished. "What child can that be?" she asked herself. "What babe can be lost in the cornfield?"

She set down her robe in which she had tied up her corn, and went back to search; but she found nothing.

As she started away she heard the voice again:

"Oh, do not leave me. Do not go away without me."

She searched for a long time. At last in one corner of the field, hidden under the leaves of the stalks, she found one little ear of corn. This it was that had been crying, and this is why all Indian women have since garnered their corn crop very carefully, so that the succulent food product should not even to the last small nubbin be neglected or wasted, and thus displease the Great Mystery.

Mohawk
Prophecy of the Seventh Generation

The prophecy of the Seventh Generation is common to many American Indian nations. Young native people, especially young Mohawk people, should pay attention to and consider.

According to the prophecy, after seven generations of living in close contact with the Europeans, the Onkwehonwe would see the day when the elm trees would die. The prophecy said that animals would be born strange and deformed, their limbs twisted out of shape. Huge stone monsters would tear open the face of the earth. The rivers would burn aflame. The air would burn the eyes of man. According to the prophecy of the Seventh Generation, the Onkwehonwe would see the day when birds would fall from the sky, the fish would die in the water, and man would grow ashamed of the way that he had treated his mother and provider, the Earth.

Finally, according to this prophecy, after seven generations of living in close contact with the Europeans, the Onkwehonwe would rise up and demand that their rights and stewardship over the Earth be respected and restored.

According to the wisdom of this prophecy, men and women would one day turn to the Onkwehonwe, and particularly to the eastern door of the Confederacy, for both guidance and direction. It is up to the present generation of youth of the Kanien'kehake to provide leadership and example to all who have failed. The children of the Kanien'kehake are the seventh generation.

PART 2

Spiritual Voices

Reconsidering Scripture in Late Industrial Society: Religious Traditions and the Natural Environment

Introduction by Thomas J. Burns
University of Oklahoma

The world's religions are, without exception, grounded in beliefs and practices from before the industrial era—before the overwhelming problems of anthropogenic environmental change reached truly global and life-threatening proportions. Of central concern here is how religious beliefs influence how people think about, and behave toward, the natural environment. In looking at canonical texts of the respective traditions, multiple interpretations are not only possible, but ubiquitous. In tracing the rise of environmental consciousness, it bears noting that the readings of the past and present are themselves a product, not only of the cultures in which they are written, but of the cultures in which they are read.

Reconsidering Scripture in Late Industrial Society

Humankind has entered an era where there are environmental problems, risks, and challenges greater in magnitude and complexity than at any time in human history. In the words of historian J.R. McNeill, the environmental problems we face at the dawn of the third millennium do constitute "*Something New Under the Sun.*" The very title of McNeill's book is a takeoff on an expression from the Old Testament (Ecclesiastes) holding that there is "nothing new under the sun." Yet McNeill and others question whether that notion is still true, noting that problems such as global environmental change, pollution, deforestation, and the destruction of habitats are rapidly approaching, or have already reached, a crisis state. The effect is so dramatic that some observers have come to refer to the current era as the Anthropocene age—characterized by humankind having profound effects on the planet of the magnitude that were caused in prior ages by natural phenomena such as the melting of glaciers.

In trying to understand how people make sense out of the world in which they live, including these pressing environmental challenges, it bears noting that religions often offer the dominant tropes for a culture (Burns and LeMoyne 2003). Individuals, including those with other than spiritual motives, will often use those religious ideas as a backdrop in which to package their own views in hopes of making them seem "reasonable" (Royal 1999). As with many or most issues throughout the ages, people can find something in scriptures, and in the tradition more generally, to back their claims. Of central concern here is how religious beliefs influence how people think about, and behave toward, the natural environment.

Yet the severity of many of the environmental problems of the world came into focus only in the post-industrial era. Scripture does not *directly* address industrial problems. Human institutions adapt over time, yet very slowly. Among the slowest of society's institutions to change are its religions. Part of the adaptation process is reading old scripture in the light of contemporary problems.

It bears emphasizing that this is *not* to say that scripture does not apply to those problems, and a case is easily made that it applies in myriad ways. Yet that application requires some careful consideration. To which problems, and to what particular aspects of those problems, do scriptures, or a set of passages in them, apply?

Attempts to adapt scripture are always subject to cultural considerations. Every text has a context, and the geography and history of the people producing it are huge considerations. Yet this fact can be lost in the attempt to "universalize" a scripture.

Recent thinkers, including process theologians such as John Cobb (1995, 1999; also see Bube 1988, Daly and Cobb 1994), Robert Fowler (1995), and Matthew Fox (1988) are attempting to seriously engage the environment *and* scripture. They come to very different—sometimes diametrically opposite—ways of reading the same canonical texts (e.g., the first three chapters of Genesis and the book of Ecclesiastes) than do, for example, more fundamentalist readings (Roskos 2007; Rossing 2005).

The Vedas have much to say about the environment, as does the Tao Te Ching. In fact, every tradition has much to say, and the messages are sometimes simple, sometimes complex, and seemingly contradictory. Scholars throughout the ages have added their interpretations, often to justify some action that may be markedly different from someone seemingly taking counsel from precisely the same text.

Many passages open up numerous avenues of discussion and interpretation. The Bible, for example, has numerous accounts of plagues. What are we to make of these? A number of contemporary scholars (e.g., Fretheim 1991) hold that plagues are themselves often the product of ecological disasters. This still, of course, begs the question of whether they are sent by God and God alone, perhaps to punish humankind, or if human practices have a hand in causing them.

It also bears noting that while there is a large and growing literature on religion and the environment (much of which is reviewed in this article), the preponderance of work that is published in the West focuses on Western religions (particularly Christianity). Yet this is evolving rapidly, as more scholars and researchers come to look at the endlessly fascinating and timely questions of how people in cultures from around the world are conscious of the environment and how much that consciousness is embedded in age-old wisdom traditions. While the work on the Western traditions is important, so is that focusing on Eastern and Indigenous Traditions. In this article, we consider the environment in the perspective of eight major wisdom traditions: Judaism, Christianity, Islam, Hinduism, Buddhism, Confucianism, Taoism, and Indigenous (or Native) Traditions.

At the end of the day, the important question remains how people informed by scripture will think about, and act toward, the environment. Let us now consider some of the formative influences on the Abrahamic Traditions and then turn East.

Looking at the Abrahamic Traditions

Because of the sheer number of people confessing some aspect of the Abrahamic faiths (Christianity accounts for about a third of the over seven billion people on the planet; when adding Muslims to the mix, the proportion rises to over half of the total world population) and the often (not always, but often enough to make a difference) intertwining of religion with the political and cultural powers of the day, these religious traditions bear particular scrutiny for their influences on people.

Yet they have humble origins, arising from among desert peoples. The trials and tribulations are embedded in circumstances faced by those people a time long ago. Even if, as is often the case, the vision is otherworldly, that other world is rich in images of the natural world as it was at the times of their origins.

We see in the Jewish and Christian traditions (which, in turn, heavily influenced Islam) an origin story with plenitude. Most notable in the Judeo-Christian tradition is the Garden of Eden, as accounted in the book of Genesis. God provided as much as humankind would need and more, but man and woman were, in return, to obey God. But early humankind, represented by Adam and Eve, did not follow God's admonition and were expelled from the Garden. Thus, very early on, there is an Edenic vision of plenitude juxtaposed with humankind's sinfulness and loss. Much in Christianity and Islam extend back to their ties with Judaism.

Of particular interest in this regard goes back to a singular event in the book of Genesis—God's covenant with Abraham. God promises Abraham his descendants will be as numerous as the stars and tells him to be fruitful and multiply. The sheer sizes of Christianity and Islam are at least partially due to their high fertility rates. Perhaps taking God's covenant with Abraham seriously, particularly the part about God's promise to make the descendants of Abraham as "numerous as the stars," birth rates among Christians (and even more so among Muslims, but not among Jews) are far above replacement levels and significantly higher than among most other religious traditions.

Judaism and Christianity are, of course, different religions, and for the most part, we discuss them separately here. Yet passages from the Hebrew Bible that are also in the Old Testament of the Christian Bible stand as foundational to both traditions. The first three chapters of the first book of the Bible, the book of Genesis, are central to both traditions. Perhaps the passage that is most studied, debated, misquoted, and taken out of context is Genesis 1:26–28.

This is the verse that says that humankind (or "man" in many versions, particularly those translated before industrial times) is to have "dominion" over the earth and its creatures. The specifics of how to envision dominion have been a matter of much thought and consideration by believers since then, as they draw on this passage and other scriptures to inform and guide their actions (Jobling 1977).

The third chapter of Genesis tells of the "fall" of humankind in partaking of the forbidden fruit of the tree of knowledge. Genesis 3:23 tells how God's wrath affects Adam and Eve as the first humans when they are cast out of the Garden of Eden. They, and all of their descendants, are to till the fields for a living after the expulsion.

The desert and shepherding images come up repeatedly in Judaism and Christianity (Hareuveni 1991). These themes are found in Islam as well (for discussion, see Johnston 2010). Jesus is the good shepherd; in the end, the sheep (those bound for heaven) will be separated from the goats (those going to hell). As Moses and the Jewish people wander in the desert for forty years in the book of Exodus, so Jesus, just prior to entering his public ministry at age thirty, goes into the desert for forty days to gird his otherworldliness. Muhammad's views, as well as that of his followers, particularly at the time of the writing of the Qur'an and the Hadiths, are profoundly affected by experiences in the desert.

Judaism and the Environment

Judaism has a view of the interconnectedness of humankind with nature. Yet it also has this sense of the specialness of humankind. Going back to what may be the most widely known scripture in the entire world, the first book of the Bible, Genesis, tells the Jewish version of God's creation of the world and its creatures. Along with the creation story itself, there is a vision of paradise on earth. The story of the Garden of Eden tells of a land of plenitude, freedom from hunger, and beautiful surroundings.

Judaism has a sense of *Tikkun Olam*, or healing a wounded world (Lerner 1990). Humankind moves toward restoring itself to God's grace as it strives to put together the pieces of a broken world (Berman and Waskow 1996). It is worth noting here that as important and central to the Jewish (and Christian and Islamic) imagination that the Garden of Eden is, the Abrahamic peoples lived in what was largely desert and arid land. As in any tradition coming from a specific place in the world, the visions of reality, the tropes and metaphors and thoughts to discuss and think about them, arise there.

Perhaps one of the most enduring of all visions is that of paradise. The Garden of Eden was the perfect place, lost because of the depraved and sinful nature of humankind. The Edenic vision, articulated most clearly in the book of Genesis, has had a profound effect not just on the Jewish people, but on the Christians and Muslims so influenced by Judaism and, by extension, on the world in general (Eisenberg 1998).

Starting with the fall from Eden early on, conditions are harsh. After the fall, at least one interpretation, and one very much in favor in the Protestant ethic, is that value and virtue come through labor and subduing the ground, but not *in* the ground itself. The verse in Genesis indicates that: "[B]y the sweat of your brow ye shall plow the fields..." The Bible refers to the wheat (the righteous tilled crop) and the chaff (the unrighteous "weeds" accruing from neglect of the hard work of tilling).

This may be an allegory for the gradual move from hunting and gathering to farming and shepherding as a chief way of obtaining subsistence (Hareuveni 1991). The conflict between hunters and farmers also comes up almost immediately in the Bible in the fratricidal story of one of the sons of Adam and Eve (Cain the farmer) slaying the other son (Abel the hunter).

Christianity and the Environment

We can find a number of strains of thought about environmental issues in Christianity. From the outset, it bears noting that the early chapters of Genesis have had every bit as much influence in Christianity as in Judaism. Christians struggle with the first few chapters of Genesis, particularly in terms of the Edenic vision and the fall from grace and with the question of humankind's dominion over the environment (Bonhoeffer 1997; Black 1970).

One of the central features of any cultural tradition is how issues are interpreted and prioritized (Burns 1999). This often lies under what is actually said, yet becomes crucial (Burns 2009; Brown 1989). While the scriptures do not change, these other social and cultural things do change, as does the pressing nature of environmental problems (Conradie 2009; Habel 2011).

Particularly since the theory of evolution came to supplant the Genesis account in the popular imagination, the scriptures came to be seen in a different light than before (for extended discussion, see Clough 2009, Richardson 2001). The tropes and frames of science and economics now exert a profound a pull on cultural mores, as does religion—but religion of the sort that is filtered through the lenses of these products of the modern age (Hallman 1992).

These passages from the early chapters of Genesis figure prominently in Christianity in another way, forming the basis for what becomes the doctrine of "original sin," articulated by St. Augustine and resurrected (no pun intended!) in the Protestant Reformation. The Swiss theologian John Calvin, for example, sees these passages as indicative of the "total depravity" of humans, redeemed not through any actions of their own, but only by the grace of an Almighty God.

This grace, or lack thereof is, in the hands of Protestant theologians and believers in the mold of Calvin, predestined. Predestination is a heretical idea in older strains of Christianity—notably Catholicism and Orthodoxy. The idea of the inherent sinfulness and fallenness of humankind has come to be a specter over many sects of Christianity, particularly of the Protestant variety.

At its worst, however, people have used this, ironically, to counsel some combination of wanton overuse of the natural world and cravenness about humankind taking action to help save the environment from even the worst human abuses. One popular variant holds that since God causes all things, concern for global warming and attempts to alleviate it, for example, are but further instances of humankind's misguided tendency to want to play God (Rossing 2005; Roskos 2007).

As sociologist Max Weber (1904–05) points out in his seminal work, *The Protestant Ethic and the Spirit of Capitalism*, many of these ideas came together to help bring about capitalism, particularly in the West. While even the prophetic Weber did not foresee the extent to which environmental problems would come to be so pressing, the methods of his analyses are amenable to understanding how capitalism and religion became so conflated. Christianity has been hugely influential on the world economy in general, as well as in economic and technological developments, as Weber

(1904–05/1958) points out, through a number of mechanisms, including facilitating the rise and application of formal rationality.

At its worst, people even came to conflate capitalism with the very will of God. The invisible hand of the market, as articulated by Adam Smith and his followers even to the present day, is but another of God's laws. Left to its own devices, the "law" of supply and demand comes to be seen as sacrosanct (Lux 1990).

Some historians (see, in particular, White 1942 and 1967; Whitney 1993) see the very roots of the current worldwide ecological crisis going back to the first chapters of Genesis and, more particularly, to the interpretation of those passages as establishing human dominion over the rest of the world. In this view, humankind is created in the image of God, has a soul, and is rational. In juxtaposition, the natural world is seen as incapable of rationality and is soulless. Humankind, in this view, is meant to rule over nature.

This "anthropomorphic dualism" between humankind and the rest of nature then leads to a number of related difficulties, including the view that technology is a means for dominating nature. Consider the fact that Francis Bacon, who many consider to be the father of rational science as it came to be practiced, at one point articulated the task of science as "…torturing Mother Nature for her secrets…" (Wybrow 1991).

In interrogating these views of historical Christianity, Lynn White (1942, 1967) does offer other possible interpretations of these biblical passages. Most notable is what White allows for seeing the "democracy" of creation, in which nature is respected and not exploited. He adduces the reading of these same passages from Genesis, but through the lenses of St. Francis of Assisi, as the ideal counter-interpretation of this anthropomorphic dualism.

It is important for those of us looking back into the far past to glean insights from the canonical texts and to be aware that multiple interpretations are not only possible, but ubiquitous. In tracing the rise of environmental consciousness, it bears noting that the readings of the past and present are themselves a product not only of the cultures in which they are written, but of the cultures in which they are read.

Islam and the Environment

Islam's most holy of scriptures, the Qur'an, clearly proclaims one universal, all-powerful God, Allah. It bears noting that the word Islam means something like "the peace that comes through submission to the Almighty." All of creation, including humankind and the natural world, are God's creation and subject to God's laws.

In contrast to Christianity, in which one of the persons of the Trinity (Jesus) takes a human form, or Hinduism, where an incarnation of God occasionally takes an earthly form that may be human-like at times and animal-like at others, Islam has no image of humankind as on a plane with God in any way or form.

This has some rather profound implications for attitudes to the environment. God "surrounds" all things, is in all things, is as distant as the heavens, and yet is as near as the veins in the neck of any live being. This leads to a view that the environment is, first and foremost, a creation of God that humankind at best should care for and not exploit (Chitlick 1986). Particularly in the more mystical Sufi movement within Islam, there is a prominent idea of one world where all are subject to the laws of God and worthy of dignity, but none more so than others (Chitlick 2000).

The values and scriptures of a people are heavily influenced by their historical geography. Going back to its earliest roots, Islam had a strong connection with the desert. As is the case in Judaism (and through its Old Testament foundations in Christianity), Abraham is an important historical figure in Islam. Every year, Muslims from the world over converge at Mecca (in modern-day Saudi Arabia) for their annual pilgrimage, or Hajj. One of the central rituals is partaking of the water of the Zamzam well, which provided respite and survival from a harsh and unforgiving desert for a thirsting Hagar and Ishmael (her son with Abraham). Water represents the mercy and life-giving power of the all-powerful God, Allah.

Water is an essential resource, and desert peoples are particularly aware of how it is never to be taken for granted. Perhaps stemming from this, Islam has, from the earliest times, had an elaborate set of laws and guidelines on water usage and water quality (Ahmad 1999). Humankind acts as a "vice-regent" or steward of God on earth. There is a sense that every one of God's creatures, including animals, have a right to water (Westcoat 1995), and humankind has an obligation to respect that right (Idris 1990).

As discussed earlier, Abrahamic religions account for just over half of the world's seven billion people. Compared with Christianity (which has about 2.4 billion believers) and Judaism (which has only approximately 15 million people worldwide), Islam has about 1.4 billion adherents. While fertility rates among Jews are low (with Orthodox Jews being an exception), Christianity and particularly Islam have fertility rates high above replacement levels. Thus, there is rapid population growth among Muslims.

In Islam, there is a sense that since God provides the resources of the earth and all are his subjects, everyone should be able to have enough of a share to maintain livelihood. While there are rich and poor, it is intended by God that everyone should be able to partake of what God has provided, without anyone taking too much (Asmal and Asmal 2000). While many in developed countries see high birth rates as creating population pressures and environmental overuse, Islam tends not to emphasize population increases as a threat to the environment. Going back to their earliest writings, Muslims historically have placed a higher priority on lessening greed and overuse of the resources (for discussion, see Anmar 2000).

As do all religions, Islam responds to environmental problems of the twenty-first century, often drawing on the scriptures of centuries past (Wersal 1995). As it does so, it finds within its tradition approaches to addressing these challenges.

Native Traditions and the Environment

Although many indigenous peoples had no direct contact with one another, particularly from another part of the earth in antiquity, we do find commonalities among Native Traditions, or indigenous religions, from around the world. It bears mentioning at the outset that almost always, these native religious practices arose in oral cultures, and, as such, there historically *are no sacred texts per se*. Rather, there are rich oral traditions that go far back in time. These oral traditions typically are not written down until there is contact with people with a written language (Smith 1994). Those people with a written language often have other resources at their disposal (larger armies, more technologically sophisticated weapons, etc.) that put indigenous cultures at a disadvantage. There is almost always an intrusion onto native lands, a contestation and taking of those lands (Schmink and Wood 1992, Olson 1990), sometimes genocide, and often a cultural cooptation (Witt and Wiles 2006). As an indigenous culture's rich oral traditions are cast into writing, the culture comes to be seen not so much on its own terms, but through the lenses and biases of the culture from which it learns (or perhaps is coerced) to become literate (Niedhardt 1972).

So as we consider native traditions, it is also necessary to consider the respective avenues of the written word, including those that may be considered sacred. Most commonly, there are writings *about* the traditions from outsiders or a collection of stories and myths that were long an oral tradition, now written in someone else's language. That said, we can find a number of emergent themes in native traditions, where humankind and the surrounding ecological environment are not separate. Rather, there is a continuity between them that is rarely found in industrial and post-industrial societies.

Time and place are central organizing concepts in native traditions, and it is important to consider how they tend to be quite different from how they are viewed in industrial and post-industrial societies. This is particularly true of time.

In modern society, we tend to see time as linear and historical. In virtually any conversation or discussion in modern society, we can give a year (2014 CE), and that concept has meaning. Likewise, we can discuss particular historical events, sacred or secular (e.g., the birth of Jesus, the first day of the French Revolution, etc.), and situate them as unique events along the continuum of time. Historical and religious scholars (Eliade 1954/1991) see this conception of time and unique historical events as largely an artifact of Hebrew, Greek, and Roman influences on what became the "historical" religions (notably, Judaism, Christianity, and Islam), which in turn profoundly affected the way an overall global culture of modernity came to unfold the way it did.

Yet this historical conception is in contrast with native traditions, which tend to see the world more in terms of "cosmos" rather than as "history" (Eliade 1954/1991). Indigenous religions tend to be tuned into the recreating, repeating aspects of time, such as the rising and setting of the sun and the moon, the food cycles and the seasons on which they depend, and the regular migration patterns of animals. Thus, their very conception of time is much more tied to the natural ecology than is the modern conception of time in terms of historical events measured against precisely calibrated clocks and written calendars.

There are profound differences in conceptions of place as well. In native traditions, there is virtually always a sacred place, which is a prominent part of the natural ecology. In particular, the sacred mountain is found in a wide variety of native cultures on virtually every continent (Bernbaum 1988; Cajette 1994).

Many native traditions have totemic beliefs that tie them back to the natural ecology of which they are a part (Durkheim 1912/2001). In this way, as well, indigenous people see themselves as part of the natural flora or fauna. A people may have a creation myth in which they are descended from a local plant or fruit, such as corn or sweet potatoes, or they may see themselves as a blood brother to a particular local animal, such as the caribou, the jaguar, or the turtle (Plant and Plant 1990). Throughout much of time, indigenous cultures have relied on shamans and other mystics to serve as a prophetic voice. The shamanic visions typically come as the shaman communes with nature in a profound way (Narby and Huxley 2001).

In sum, then, in native traditions from around the world, humankind is situated as an integral part of nature. Rather than being juxtaposed to, and in opposition to, nature, as is often the case in industrial and post-industrial societies, indigenous peoples tend not to see themselves as separate from the local or larger ecology (Rose 2005; Redford 1993).

Hinduism and the Environment

Particularly in juxtaposition to Western culture that was so heavily influenced by Christian culture, religions of India, particularly Hinduism and Buddhism (which began there, although it later branched out far and wide), did not see such a discontinuity between humankind and nature (for extended discussion, see Weber 1916/1958). Perhaps stemming from this conception of the oneness of all, Hinduism embraces a low-impact lifestyle, as does Buddhism.

There is a sense that everything is interconnected and that nothing happens in a vacuum. Humankind is profoundly dependent upon the land, the rivers, and the rain for its livelihood. Plants and animals are an integral part of that and play a prominent role in Hindu scripture (Banerjee 1980; Rambachan 1989; Sharma 1998).

Many of the rivers in India, particularly the Ganges, are seen as sacred (Alter 2001; Darian 1978). Yet the runoff, particularly from agricultural operations, is sometimes overwhelming. As such, the sacred Ganges has become polluted. Ironically, there is not a significant move to clean it up. This is perhaps an artifact of the tendency to trust the Gods to keep nature pristine and not to take human responsibility for it. While the particulars can be quite different, there are ironic parallels between what may be thought of as perverse aspects of the Hindu and Christian postures toward the natural world. Even as human activities pollute the river, there is a sense that acting to clean it up or keep it clean in the first place would be too much of an intrusion into the realm of the Gods (Chapple 1993).

In a related vein, there is a long and complex history of some kinds of environmental misuse, overuse, and degradation in Hindu culture. Even as there is a celebration of forests and nature (e.g., Dua 1999; Nugturen 2005), there is also a long history of deforestation and other types of depletion (Gadgill and Guha 1992; Erdosy 1998). Even as we can find a strong respect for nature, we also can see some aspects of the tradition that lead to passiveness, even in the face of profound and overwhelming environmental problems (Mawdsley 2005).

To be sure, there are trends and countertrends, all of which can, on some level, trace ideas back to the scriptures. Consider, for example, the *Chipko*, or "tree hugger," movement of the current century in which activists display a profound reverence for nature and often put themselves in harm's way to attempt to prevent deforestation and other disruptions in the natural ecology. This actually is based on timeless values (Shiva and Bandyopadhyay 1988; Sharma 1998).

The value of non-violence, or *ahimsa* (which, more literally, means "not killing") is important in Hinduism. Ahimsa is a value in a number of religious traditions, starting in Hinduism and being brought subsequently into Buddhism and particularly Jainism. Ahimsa was also a guiding principle in the Indian Independence Movement and a common theme in the work of its leader, Mahatma Gandhi.

There is a history of worship and veneration of the Gods, which orients people to have reverence for all of creation, including the natural ecology (Klostermaier 1991). There is a history of this going back to some of the earliest times, and it has been reflected in the canonical texts of Hinduism ever since. While there are, as with any major religions, differing interpretations, there is a discernible through-line in Hindu scripture that the natural environment is something to be revered.

Buddhism and the Environment

Buddhism does not privilege humankind in the sense of setting it apart from the rest of the living world. There is a sense among many Buddhists of loving the world as oneself. This is sometimes referred to as an ethic of non-dualism (Loy 2003).

The ethic of non-dualism is grounded in the view that everything in the universe is related. As such, human beings are not separate from each other or from the natural environment (Colt 1990). This way of being in the world can, by itself or in conjunction with other Buddhist values, serve as the basis of a broader environmental ethic. To see any part of the universe as separate from any other is an "illusion" (here, it is useful to understand that Eastern religions tend to use the word "illusion" in a way akin to the way Westerners would use the word "perception").

In Buddhism, as in Taoism and many of the Native Traditions, planetism trumps economism. Put another way, there is nothing in Buddhism that embraces human exemptionalism. It thus could be seen as lining up with the New Environmental Paradigm (although Buddhism predated the NEP by well over two millennia, so for Buddhists, there is nothing particularly new about it!). More broadly, the Buddhist ethic, along with the Taoist and many Native ethics, harmonizes well with the Gaia hypothesis (Aitken 1990), which holds that the entire earth and its atmosphere comprise what amounts to one large, complex system; a change to any part affects the whole.

Putting this worldview together with the Buddhist tradition of Right Livelihood (an aspect of The Eightfold Path, as articulated by the Buddha himself, and one of the core values of Buddhism; Aitken 1990), this orientation leads some Buddhists into environmental activism (Ikeda 1977). The Chipko movement (or "tree hugger" movement, which also attracts people of other religions, such as Hindus) stems from this, as do attempts at reforestation of environmentally degraded areas (Getz 1991).

Even for the majority who are not engaged directly in activism, there is a sense that even purchases made in the marketplace have an aggregate effect on the market. Buddhists tend to avoid buying something that requires making an impact on some other part of the planet (e.g., buying lumber from endangered redwood trees to make a hot tub, or driving a gas-guzzling SUV when a less impactful means of transportation would be an alternative). Even if s/he is not directly involved in the extraction of resources, it is more ethical not to create a demand for harmful products (Payuto 1994).

Many Buddhists, particularly Zen practitioners, do gardening as a meditative practice. As such, it attunes a person to the cycles of nature, and it also serves as a vehicle of discipline and mindfulness. Even among non-Zen practitioners, the Zen ideal of gardening sets something of a standard for mindfulness, the beauty of simplicity, and engaged practice (Barash 1973).

While there are some major exceptions (such as Theravada monks, who tend to eat only once a day and then only what they are given, which may include meat, as they beg for their daily food), many Buddhists do not eat meat, as the slaughter of animals adds to the suffering of sentient beings. This differs significantly from practices in cultures shaped by the Abrahamic traditions, such as Christianity (Waldau 2000). Buddhists see this as a practice of the value of ahimsa, or nonviolence (Balsys 2004).

Religions of China and the Environment

In the religions of China, Taoism and Confucianism both are embedded in practices and ways of seeing the world that pre-date their sacred texts. Confucianism became more popular in the cities and placed an emphasis on interpersonal human relations. Taoism remained more embedded in the countryside. Its highest virtues are found in the natural world, and it emphasizes blending with the forces of nature. Rather than controlling nature, it is important to live in harmony with it.

While there are some stark differences between Confucianism and Taoism, they can also be seen as two sides of a coin—*yang* and *yin*. They both emphasize certain virtues. For example, *te*, or the judicious use of power, is prominent in both. Te is one of the five ideals of Confucianism; it is so central to Taoism that we see it in the very title of its central text, the Tao Te Ching. The te aspect of the Tao Te Ching deals with the judicious use of power. In relation to the environment, if the *tao* emphasizes harmonizing with the environment (Cooper 2001), te comes close to the Western idea of stewardship (Ames 1989).

Yet there is another use of te in Taoism, and that has to do with combining the forces of nature in a way that the practitioner hopes will bring health and longevity. This recombining of elements, or alchemy, is a significant practice in a number of religious traditions, perhaps especially in Hinduism and Taoism (Eliade 1965).

All the forces that shape the universe are in every living being, and vice versa. The passive, feminine yin and active, assertive, yang energies, indeed the tao itself, are present everywhere. Everything must find its own balance, or equilibrium. Mother Nature will find ways to restore balance, and that process may not necessarily seem pleasant to the people affected. When snow falls on the ground, its whiteness attracts the light to melt it.

When greenhouse gases are put into the environment, Mother Nature will try to restore an overall balance. Humankind tries to control nature at its own peril. Rather, in practicing *wu wei*, an enlightened being seeks to blend with the natural environment. Not unlike a surfer riding a wave, a few inches one way or the other may mean the difference between a smooth, exhilarating ride or being dumped from the board and ground into the sand below. The smooth ride comes not from trying to control nature, but from harmonizing with it. These ideas, such as wu wei, te, and the tao itself, are integral parts of an overall Taoist ecological ethic (Goodman 1980; Ip 1983).

The natural environment is a preferred place of meditation and *Tai Chi*. Being close to the energies and flow of nature is highly preferable to the artificial, built environment.

Water metaphors abound in virtually all religious traditions (think of Christian baptism, for example), and they are all through the writings of both Taoism and Confucianism (Allan 1997).

Much as flowing water is constantly changing and the river is never exactly the same from one time to another, so the tao itself is a process of constant change (Fox 2005). In nature, as in the tao, there is a constant interplay between order and chaos (Girardot 1983).

Confucianism and the Environment

In many of the world's religions, there is an emphasis on gardening. In some ways, this is an allegory for the complex process of imposing human order on an otherwise chaotic nature. In Taoism, and particularly in Confucianism, there is a history of gardening as cultivating not only nature, but also the soul of the gardener (Valder 2002; Tucker 1994).

Confucius draws on many of the same concepts as Taoism. In some ways, he interprets them similarly to Taoism, and in some ways, he interprets them very differently. Significantly, Confucius was one of the foremost scholars to read and interpret the ancient I Ching, or "book of changes," which is profoundly embedded in the workings of the natural world. Confucian scholars, starting with Confucius himself, draw heavily on the ideas of the tao, and also of *chi*, or the vital energy that suffuses the universe (Berthong 2003; Black 1989).

Much of Confucian thought and social ethics are organized around the "Five Ideals." The first of these is *ren*, or the mandate to act with compassion and benevolence, first to other human beings, but also to animals and nature (Blakely 2003). Another of the ideals is te, which also figures prominently in Taoism, the central text for which (the Tao Te Ching) holds that ideal to be so important as to make it part of the title. Te in both traditions means power, but the power is to be used judiciously. If someone is in a position of authority, s/he is to use his or her power with restraint and to uplift the less powerful. Taken together, these ideals call for compassion and, in a sense, stewardship over animals and the natural environment.

Environmental historians find some of the roots of the environmental degradation in China (in Beijing in January 2014, for example, the particulate matter in the air was on the order of thirty times the maximum healthy level) as a latent consequence of some of the thought of Confucius himself (Economy 2004; Evin 2004).

Taoism and the Environment

There is a sense that nature, the *tao*, is made up of impersonal forces which, depending upon where someone or something is positioned relative to them and how they interpret them, have both benevolent and malevolent aspects (Berger 1999). In Taoism, it is important to harmonize to nature. In so doing, it is the person who should adapt to the forces of nature, rather than vice versa (Cheng 1986). There is a constant interplay between the individual and the environment of which s/he is a part (Lai 2003; Sylvan and Bennett 1988).

The world's religions come into contact with one another, and out of that interaction, there is often a syncretism, or dialectical blending of aspects of the respective traditions. The Tao Te Ching is now read not only by people in China, but by people from around the world. In fact, it is second only to the Bible in terms of the number of copies printed throughout the ages, even outpacing the Qur'an. The syncretism between Taoist and Western thought has informed both, as a new syncretism emerges that has profound implications for how people think about and act toward the environment (Clarke 2000; Christ the eternal tao).

Scholars of comparative religions do see some significant differences between the Taoist and Abrahamic interpretations of the relationship between humankind and nature. Huston Smith (1972), for example, sees Western monotheistic (or Abrahamic) religions, going back to the Genesis accounts, as distancing nature from humankind. In contrast, the Taoist concept is that all aspects of the tao are interconnected. Ideas like *chi* (the energy that animates a single body runs throughout the universe) and *wu wei* (cooperating with, rather than trying to control or subdue, the natural order of the universe) support the idea that humankind is part of, rather than distinct from, nature. In this important sense, Taoist and Native traditions come quite close in their worldviews and relationship with the natural ecology (Spiegel 2002).

References for Judaism:

1. Berman, Phyllis, and Arthur Waskow. *Tales of Tikkun: New Jewish Stories to Heal the Wounded World*. Northvale, NJ: Jason Aronson, 1996.
2. Eisenberg, Evan. *The Ecology of Eden*. New York: Alfred A. Knopf, 1998.
3. Hareuveni, Nogah. *Desert and Shepherd in Our Biblical Heritage*. Kiryat Ono, Israel: Neot Kedumin, 1991.
4. Jobling, David. "'And have Dominion…': The Interpretation of Genesis 1:28 in Philo Judaeus." *Journal of the Study of Judaism* 8, no. 1 (1977): 50–82.
5. Lerner, Michael. "Critical: Support for Earth Day." *Tikkun* 5, no. 2 (1990): 48–50.
6. Sacks, Jonathan. *Tradition in an Untraditional Age*. London: Valentine Mitchell, 1990.

References for Christianity:

1. Black, John. *The Dominion of Man: The Search for Ecological Responsibility*. Edinburgh: Edinburgh
2. University Press, 1970.
3. Bonhoeffer, Dietrich. *Creation and Fall: A Theological Exposition of Genesis 1-3*. In John W. DeGrauchy, ed., Douglas Stephen Bax, trans., Dietrich Boenhoeffer Works, Vol. 3. Minneapolis, MN: Fortress, 1997.
4. Brown, Richard Harvey. *Society as Text*. Chicago: University of Chicago Press, 1989.
5. Bube, Paul C. *Ethics in John Cobb's Process Theology*. Atlanta, GA: Scholars Press, 1988.
6. Burns, Thomas J. "Rhetoric as a Framework for Analyzing Cultural Constraint and Change." *Current Perspectives in Social Theory* 19 (1999) :165–185.
7. Burns, Thomas J. "Culture and the Natural Environment." In *Current Trends in Human Ecology*, edited by Priscila Lopes and Alpina Begossi, pp. 56–72. Newcastle upon Tyne, UK: Cambridge Scholars Press, 2009.
8. Burns, Thomas J., and Terri LeMoyne. "Epistemology, Culture and Rhetoric: Some Social Implications of Human Cognition." *Current Perspectives in Social Theory* 22 (2003): 71–97.
9. Clough, David. "All God's Creatures: Reading Genesis on Human and Non-Human Animals." In *Reading Genesis after Darwin*, edited by Stephen C. Barton and David Wilkinson, pp. 145–162. Oxford: Oxford University Press, 2009.

10. Cobb, John B., Jr. *Sustaining the Common Good: A Christian Perspective on the Global Economy*. Cleveland, OH: Pilgrim Press, 1995.

11. Cobb, John B., Jr. *The Earthist Challenge to Economism: A Theological Critique of the World Bank*. New York: St. Martin's Press, 1999.

12. Conradie, Ernst M. "Interpreting the Bible amidst Ecological Degradation." *Theology* 112 (May/June 2009): 199–207.

13. Daly, Herman E., and John B. Cobb, Jr. *For the Common Good: Redirecting the Economy toward Community, the Environment, and a Sustainable Future*, updated and expanded, 2e. Boston: Beacon, 1994..

14. Davis, John J. "Economic Growth vs. the Environment? The Need for New Paradigms in Economics, Business Ethics, and Evangelical Theology." *Evangelical Review of Theology* 26, no. 3 (2002.): 265–275.

15. Eckberg, Douglas L., and T. Jean Blocker. "Christianity, Environmentalism, and the Theological Problem of Environmentalism." *Journal for the Scientific Study of Religion* 35 (1996): 343–355.

16. Finger, Thomas N. *Evangelicals, Eschatology, and the Environment: The Scholars Circle 2*. Wynnewood, PA: Evangelical Environmental Network, 1999.

17. Fowler, Robert B. *The Greening of Protestant Thought*. Chapel Hill, NC: University of North Carolina Press, 1995.

18. Fox, Matthew. *The Coming of the Cosmic Christ: The Healing of Mother Earth and the Birth of a Global Renaissance*. San Francisco: Harper and Row, 1988.

19. Fretheim, Terence E. "The Plagues as Ecological Signs of Historical Disaster." *Journal of Biblical Literature* 110, no. 3 (1991): 385–396.

20. Habel, Norman C. *The Birth, the Curse, and the Greening of Earth: An Ecological Reading of Genesis 1-11*. Sheffield: Sheffield Academic Press, 2011.

21. Hallman, David G. *A Place in Creation: Ecological Visions in Science, Religion and Economics*. Toronto: United Church of Canada Publishing House, 1992.

22. Lux, Kenneth. *Adam Smith's Mistake: How a Moral Philosopher Invented Economics and Ended Morality*. Boston and London: Shambhala, 1990.

23. Richardson, B.J. *Christianity, Evolution and the Environment: Fitting It Together*. Sydney: UNSW Press, 2001.

24. Roskos, Nicole A. "Felling Sacred Groves: Appropriation of a Christian Tradition for Antienvironmentalism." In *Ecospirit: Religions and Philosophies for the Earth*, edited by Laurel Kearns and Catherine Keller, pp. 483–494. New York: Fordham University Press, 2007.

25. Rossing, Barbara. "For the Healing of the World: Reading Revelation Ecologically." In *From Every People and Nation: The Book of Revelation in Intercultural Perspective*, edited by David Rhoads, pp. 165–182. Minneapolis, MN: Fortress Press, 2005.

26. Royal, Robert. *The Virgin and the Dynamo: The Use and Abuse of Religion in the Environmental Debate*. Grand Rapids, MI.: Eerdmans, 1999.

27. Weber, Max. *The Protestant Ethic and the Spirit of Capitalism*. NY: Free Press, 1904-05/1958.

28. White, Lynn T., Jr. "Christian Myth and Christian History." *Journal of the History of Ideas* 3, no. 2 (1942): 145–158.

29. White, Lynn T., Jr. "The Historical Roots of Our Ecological Crisis." *Science* 155, no. 3767 (1967): 1203–1207.

30. Whitney, Elspeth. "Lynn White, Ecotheology, and History." *Environmental Ethics* 15, no. 2 (1993): 151–169.

31. Wybrow, Cameron. *The Bible, Baconianism, and Mastery over Nature: The Old Testament and Its Modern Misreading*. American University Studies: Series 7, Theology and Religion, vol. 112. New York: Peter Lang, 1991.

References for Islam:

1. Ahmad, Ali. "Islamic Water Law as an Antidote for Maintaining Water Quality." *University of Denver Water Law Review* 2, no. 2 (1999): 170–188.

2. Ammar, Nawal H. "An Islamic Response to the Manifest Ecological Crisis: Issues of Justice." In *Visions of a New Earth: Religious Perspectives on Population, Consumption, and Ecology,* edited by Harold Coward and Daniel C. Maguire, pp. 131–46. Albany, NY: State University of New York Press, 2000.

3. Asmal, Abdul Cader, and Mohammed Asmal. "An Islamic Perspective." In *Consumption, Population, and Sustainability: Perspectives from Science and Religion,* edited by Audrey Chapman, Rodney Peterson, and Barbara Smith-Moran, pp. 157–65. Washington, DC: Island Press, 2000.

4. Chitlick, William C. "God Surrounds All Things: An Islamic Perspective on the Environment." *The World and I* 1, no. 6 (1986): 671–678.

5. Chitlick, William C. *Sufism: A Short Introduction.* Oxford: Oneworld Publications, 2000.

6. Idris, Jaafar. "Is Man the Viceregent of God?" *Journal of Islamic Studies* 1 (1990): 99–110.

7. Johnston, David L. *Earth, Empire and Sacred Text: Muslims and Christians as Trustees of Creation.* London: Equinox, 2010.

8. Wersal, Lisa. "Islam and Environmental Ethics: Tradition Responds to Contemporary Challenges." *Zygon* 30, no. 3 (1995): 451–459.

9. Westcoat, James L., Jr. "The Right of Thirst for Animals in Islamic Law: A Comparative Approach." *Environment and Planning D: Society and Space* 13, no. 6 (1995): 637–654.

References for Native Traditions:

1. Bernbaum, Edwin. "Sacred Mountains." *Parabola* 13, no. 4 (1988): 12–18.

2. Cajette, Gregory A. *Look to the Mountain: An Ecology of Indigenous Education.* Durango, CO: Kivaki Press, 1994.

3. Durkheim, Emile. *The Elementary Forms of Religious Life,* translated by Carol Cosman. New York: Oxford University Press, 1912/2001.

4. Eliade, Mircea. *The Myth of the Eternal Return: Or, Cosmos and History.* Princeton, NJ: Princeton University Press, 1954/1991.

5. Narby, Jeremy, and Francis Huxley. *Shamans through Time: 500 Years on the Path to Knowledge.* New York: Putnam, 2001.

6. Niedhardt, John G. *Black Elk Speaks.* New York: Pocket, 1972.

7. Olson, Paul A., ed. *The Struggle for the Land: Indigenous Insight and Industrial Empire in the Semiarid World.* Lincoln, NE: University of Nebraska Press, 1990.

8. Plant, Christopher, and Judith Plant. *Turtle Talk: Voices for a Sustainable Future.* Philadelphia, PA: New Society Publishers, 1990.

9. Redford, Kent. "The Ecologically Noble Savage." *Cultural Survival Quarterly* 15, no. 1 (1993.): 46–48.

10. Rose, Deborah. "An Indigenous Philosophical Ecology: Situating the Human." *Australian Journal of Anthropology* 16, no. 3 (2005): 294–305.

11. Schmink, Marianne, and Charles H. Wood. *Contested Frontiers in Amazonia.* New York: Columbia University Press, 1992.

12. Smith, Huston. *The Illustrated World's Religions: A Guide to Our Wisdom Traditions*. San Francisco: Harper Collins, 1994.

13. Witt, Joseph, and David Wiles. "Nature in Asian Indigenous Traditions: A Survey Article." *Worldviews: Environment, Culture, Religion* 10, no. 1 (2006): 40–68.

References for Hinduism:

1. Alter, Stephen. *Sacred Waters: A Pilgrimage up the Ganges River to the Source of Hindu Culture*. New York: Harcourt, 2001.

2. Banerjee, Sures Chandra. *Flora and Fauna in Sanskrit Literature*. Calcutta: Naya Prokash, 1980.

3. Chapple, Christopher Key. *Nonviolence to Animals, Earth, and Self in Asian Traditions*. Albany, NY: SUNY Press, 1993.

4. Darian, Steven G. *The Ganges in Myth and History*. Honolulu: University of Hawaii Press, 1978.

5. Dua, Kamal Kumar. *Bhagavad Gita and the Environment*. Delhi, India: Koshal Book Depot, 1999.

6. Erdosy, George. "Deforestation in Pre- and Proto-Historic South Asia." In *Nature and the Orient: The Environmental History of South and Southeast Asia*, edited by Richard A. Grove, Vinita Damodaran, and Satpal Sangwan, pp. 51–69. Delhi: Oxford University Press, 1998.

7. Gadgill, Madhav, and Ramachandra Guha. *This Fissured Land: An Ecological History of India*. Delhi: Oxford University Press, 1992.

8. Klostermaier, Klaus. "Bhakti, Ahimsa, and Ecology." *Journal of Dharma* 16, no. 3 (1991): 246–254.

9. Mawdsley, Emma. "The Abuse of Religion and Ecology: The Vishva Hindu Parishad and Tehri Dam." *Worldviews: Environment, Culture and Religion* 9, no. 1 (2005): 1–24.

10. Nugturen, Albertina. *Belief, Bounty, and Beauty: Rituals around Sacred Trees in India*. Amsterdam: Brill, 2005.

11. Rambachan, Anatanand. "The Value of the World as the Mystery of God in the Advaita Vedanta." *Journal of Dharma* 14, no. 3 (1989): 287–297.

12. Sharma, Arvind. "Attitudes to Nature in the Early Upanishads." In *Purifying the Earthly Body of God: Religion and Ecology in Hindu India*, edited by Lance E. Nelson, pp. 51–60. Albany: SUNY Press, 1998.

13. Shiva, Vandana, and J. Bandyopadhyay. "The Chipko Movement." In *Deforestation: Social Dynamics in Watersheds and Mountain Ecosystems*, edited by J. Ives and D. Pitt, pp. 224–241. London: Routledge, 1998.

14. Weber, Max. *The Religion of India: The Sociology of Hinduism and Buddhism*. NY: Free Press, 1916/1958.

References for Buddhism:

1. Aitken, Robert. "Right Livelihood for the Western Buddhist." In *Dharma Gaia: A Harvest of Essays in Buddhism and Ecology*, edited by Allan H. Badiner, pp. 227–232. Berkeley, CA: Parallax Press. 1990.

2. Balsys, Bodo. *Ahimsa: Buddhism and the Vegetarian Ideal*. New Delhi: Munshiram Manoharlal, 2004.

3. Barash, David P. "The Ecologist as Zen Master." *American Midland Naturalist* 89, no. 1 (1973): 214–217.

4. Colt, Ames B. "Perceiving the World as Self: The Emergence of an Environmental Ethic." *Primary Point* 7, no. 2 (1990): 12–14.

5. Getz, Andrew. "A Natural Being: A Monk's Reforestation in Thailand." *Buddhist Peace Fellowship Newsletter*, Winter 1991: 24–25.

6. Ikeda, Daisaku. "Life and the Environment." In *Dialogue on Life*, vol. 2: 78–90. Tokyo: Nichiren Shoshu International Center, 1977.

7. Loy, David R. "Loving the World as Our Own Body: The Nondualist Ethic of Taoism, Buddhism and Deep Ecology." In *The Great Awakening: A Buddhist Social Theory*, pp. 171–194. Somerville, MA: Wisdom Publications. 2003.

8. Payuto, Prayudh. *Buddhist Economics: A Middle Way for the Marketplace*. Bangkok: Buddhadhamma Foundation, 1994.

9. Waldau, Paul. *The Specter of Speciesism: Buddhist and Christian Views of Animals*. Oxford: Oxford University Press, 2002.

References for the Religions of China:

1. Allan, Sarah. *The Way of Water and Sprouts of Virtue*. Albany, NY: State University of New York Press, 1997.

2. Berger, Anthony R. *Dark Nature in Classic Chinese Thought*. Victoria, BC: Centre for Studies in Religion and Society, University of Victoria, 1999.

3. Berthong, John. "Confucian Views of Nature." In *Nature across Cultures: Views of Nature and the Environment in Non-Western Cultures*, edited by Helaine Selin, pp. 373–392. The Hague and London: Kluwer, 2003.

4. Black, Alison H. *Man and Nature in the Philosophical Thought of Wang Fu-chih*. Seattle: University of Washington Press, 1989.

5. Blakely, Donald N. "Listening to Animals: The Confucian View of Animal Welfare." *Journal of Chinese Philosophy* 30, no. 2 (2003): 137–157.

6. Cheng, Chun-ying. "On the Environmental Ethics of the Tao and Ch'i." *Environmental Ethics* 8, no. 4 (1986): 351–370.

7. Clarke, John J. *The Tao of the West: Western Transformations of Taoist Thought*. New York: Routledge, 2000.

8. Cooper, David E. "Chuang Tzu." In *Fifty Key Thinkers on the Environment*, edited by Joy A. Palmer, pp. 7–12. New York: Routledge, 2001.

9. Economy, Elizabeth C. *The River Runs Black: The Environmental Challenge to China's Future*. New York: Cornell University Press, 2004.

10. Eliade, Mircea. *The Forge and the Crucible: The Origins and Structure of Alchemy*, 2e. Chicago: University of Chicago Press, 1965/1978.

11. Elvin, Mark. *The Retreat of the Elephants: An Environmental History of China*. New Haven, CT: Yale University Press, 2004.

12. Fox, Alan. "Process Ecology and the 'Ideal' Dao." *Journal of Chinese Philosophy* 32, no. 1 (2005): 47–57.

13. Girardot, Norman J. *Myth and Meaning in Early Taoism: The Theme of Chaos (Hun-tun)*. Berkeley, CA: University of California Press, 1983.

14. Goodman, Russell. "Taoism and Ecology." *Environmental Ethics* 2, no. 1 (1980): 73–80.

15. Ip, Po-keung. "Taoism and the Foundation of Environmental Ethics." *Environmental Ethics* 5, no. 4 (1983): 335–343.

16. Lai, Karyn L. "Conceptual Foundations for Environmental Ethics: A Daoist Perspective." *Environmental Ethics* 25, no. 3 (2003): 247–266.

17. Smith, Huston. "Tao Now: An Ecological Testament." In *Earth Might Be Fair: Reflections on Ethics, Religion, and Ecology*, edited by Ian G. Barbour, pp. 62–82. Englewood Cliffs, NJ: Prentice-Hall, 1972.

18. Spiegel, Richard. *The Last Word: The Taoist and Native American Philosophies as a Way of Living in Harmony with Nature*. Hod Hasharon, Israel: Astrolog Publishing, 2002.

19. Sylvan, Richard, and David Bennett. "Daoism and Deep Ecology." *Ecologist* 18, no. 4/5 (1988): 148–159.

20. Tucker, Mary Evelyn. "Ecological Themes in Taoism and Confucianism." In *Worldviews and Ecology: Religion, Philosophy, and the Environment*, edited by John Grimm and Mary Evelyn Tucker, pp. 150–160. Maryknoll, NY: Orbis, 1994.

21. Valder, Peter. *Gardens in China*. Portland, OR: Timber Press, 2002.

Genesis
Chapter 1

1 In the beginning God created the <u>heaven</u> and the earth. 2 And the earth was without form, and void; and <u>darkness</u> was upon the face of the <u>deep</u>. And the <u>Spirit</u> of God moved upon the face of the waters. 3 And God said, Let there be light: and there was light. 4 And God saw the light, that it was good: and God divided the light from the <u>darkness</u>. 5 And God called the light Day, and the <u>darkness</u> he called Night. And the evening and the morning were the first day. 6 And God said, Let there be a <u>firmament</u> in the midst of the waters, and let it divide the waters from the waters. 7 And God made the <u>firmament</u>, and divided the waters which were under the <u>firmament</u> from the waters which were above the <u>firmament</u>: and it was so. 8 And God called the <u>firmament</u> <u>Heaven</u>. And the evening and the morning were the second day. 9 And God said, Let the waters under the <u>heaven</u> be gathered together unto one place, and let the dry land appear: and it was so. 10 And God called the dry land Earth; and the gathering together of the waters called he Seas: and God saw that it was good. 11 And God said, Let the earth bring forth <u>grass</u>, the <u>herb</u> yielding seed, and the <u>fruit</u> tree yielding <u>fruit</u> after his kind, whose seed is in itself, upon the earth: and it was so. 12 And the earth brought forth <u>grass</u>, and <u>herb</u> yielding seed after his kind, and the tree yielding <u>fruit</u>, whose seed was in itself, after his kind: and God saw that it was good. 13 And the evening and the morning were the third day. 14 And God said, Let there be lights in the <u>firmament</u> of the <u>heaven</u> to divide the day from the night; and let them be for signs, and for <u>seasons</u>, and for days, and years: 15 And let them be for lights in the <u>firmament</u> of the <u>heaven</u> to give light upon the earth: and it was so. 16 And God made two great lights; the greater light to rule the day, and the lesser light to rule the night: he made the <u>stars</u> also. 17 And God set them in the <u>firmament</u> of the <u>heaven</u> to give light upon the earth, 18 And to rule over the day and over the night, and to divide the light from the <u>darkness</u>: and God saw that it was good. 19 And the evening and the morning were the fourth day. 20 And God said, Let the waters bring forth abundantly the moving <u>creature</u> that hath life, and fowl that may <u>fly</u> above the earth in the open <u>firmament</u> of <u>heaven</u>. 21 And God created great whales, and every living <u>creature</u> that moveth, which the waters brought forth abundantly, after their kind, and every winged fowl after his kind: and God saw that it was good. 22 And God blessed them, saying, Be fruitful, and multiply, and fill the waters in the seas, and let fowl multiply in the earth. 23 And the evening and the morning were the fifth day. 24 And God said, Let the earth bring forth the living <u>creature</u> after his kind, <u>cattle</u>, and creeping thing, and <u>beast</u>

of the earth after his kind: and it was so. 25 And God made the beast of the earth after his kind, and cattle after their kind, and every thing that creepeth upon the earth after his kind: and God saw that it was good. 26 And God said, Let us make man in our image, after our likeness: and let them have dominion over the fish of the sea, and over the fowl of the air, and over the cattle, and over all the earth, and over every creeping thing that creepeth upon the earth. 27 So God created man in his own image, in the image of God created he him; male and female created he them. 28 And God blessed them, and God said unto them, Be fruitful, and multiply, and replenish the earth, and subdue it: and have dominion over the fish of the sea, and over the fowl of the air, and over every living thing that moveth upon the earth. 29 And God said, Behold, I have given you every herb bearing seed, which is upon the face of all the earth, and every tree, in the which is the fruit of a tree yielding seed; to you it shall be for meat. 30 And to every beast of the earth, and to every fowl of the air, and to every thing that creepeth upon the earth, wherein there is life, I have given every green herb for meat: and it was so. 31 And God saw every thing that he had made, and, behold, it was very good. And the evening and the morning were the sixth day.

Genesis
Chapter 2

1 Thus the heavens and the earth were finished, and all the <u>host</u> of them. 2 And on the seventh day God ended his work which he had made; and he rested on the seventh day from all his work which he had made. 3 And God blessed the seventh day, and sanctified it: because that in it he had rested from all his work which God created and made. 4 These are the generations of the heavens and of the earth when they were created, in the day that the LORD God made the earth and the heavens, 5 And every plant of the field before it was in the earth, and every <u>herb</u> of the field before it grew: for the LORD God had not caused it to <u>rain</u> upon the earth, and there was not a man to till the ground. 6 But there went up a mist from the earth, and watered the whole face of the ground. 7 And the LORD God formed man of the <u>dust</u> of the ground, and breathed into his nostrils the breath of life; and man became a living soul. 8 And the LORD God planted a garden eastward in <u>Eden</u>; and there he put the man whom he had formed. 9 And out of the ground made the LORD God to grow every tree that is pleasant to the sight, and good for food; the tree of life also in the midst of the garden, and the tree of knowledge of good and evil. 10 And a river went out of <u>Eden</u> to water the garden; and from thence it was parted, and became into four heads…. And the fourth river is <u>Euphrates</u>. 15 And the LORD God took the man, and put him into the garden of <u>Eden</u> to <u>dress</u> it and to keep it. 16 And the LORD God commanded the man, saying, Of every tree of the garden thou mayest freely eat: 17 But of the tree of the knowledge of good and evil, thou shalt not eat of it: for in the day that thou eatest thereof thou shalt surely die. 18 And the LORD God said, It is not good that the man should be alone; I will make him an help meet for him. 19 And out of the ground the LORD God formed every <u>beast</u> of the field, and every fowl of the air; and brought them unto <u>Adam</u> to see what he would call them: and whatsoever <u>Adam</u> called every living <u>creature</u>, that was the name thereof. 20 And <u>Adam</u> gave names to all <u>cattle</u>, and to the fowl of the air, and to every <u>beast</u> of the field; but for <u>Adam</u> there was not found an help meet for him. 21 And the LORD God caused a <u>deep</u> sleep to fall upon <u>Adam</u>, and he slept: and he took one of his ribs, and closed up the <u>flesh</u> instead thereof; 22 And the rib, which the LORD God had taken from man, made he a woman, and brought her unto the man. 23 And <u>Adam</u> said, This is now bone of my bones, and <u>flesh</u> of my <u>flesh</u>: she shall be called Woman, because she was taken out of Man. 24 Therefore shall a man leave his father and his mother, and shall cleave unto his wife: and they shall be one <u>flesh</u>. 25 And they were both <u>naked</u>, the man and his wife, and were not ashamed.

Genesis
Chapter 3

1 Now the serpent was more subtil than any beast of the field which the LORD God had made. And he said unto the woman, Yea, hath God said, Ye shall not eat of every tree of the garden? 2 And the woman said unto the serpent, We may eat of the fruit of the trees of the garden: 3 But of the fruit of the tree which is in the midst of the garden, God hath said, Ye shall not eat of it, neither shall ye touch it, lest ye die. 4 And the serpent said unto the woman, Ye shall not surely die: 5 For God doth know that in the day ye eat thereof, then your eyes shall be opened, and ye shall be as gods, knowing good and evil. 6 And when the woman saw that the tree was good for food, and that it was pleasant to the eyes, and a tree to be desired to make one wise, she took of the fruit thereof, and did eat, and gave also unto her husband with her; and he did eat. 7 And the eyes of them both were opened, and they knew that they were naked; and they sewed fig leaves together, and made themselves aprons. 8 And they heard the voice of the LORD God walking in the garden in the cool of the day: and Adam and his wife hid themselves from the presence of the LORD God amongst the trees of the garden. 9 And the LORD God called unto Adam, and said unto him, Where art thou? 10 And he said, I heard thy voice in the garden, and I was afraid, because I was naked; and I hid myself. 11 And he said, Who told thee that thou wast naked? Hast thou eaten of the tree, whereof I commanded thee that thou shouldest not eat? 12 And the man said, The woman whom thou gavest to be with me, she gave me of the tree, and I did eat. 13 And the LORD God said unto the woman, What is this that thou hast done? And the woman said, The serpent beguiled me, and I did eat. 14 And the LORD God said unto the serpent, Because thou hast done this, thou art cursed above all cattle, and above every beast of the field; upon thy belly shalt thou go, and dust shalt thou eat all the days of thy life: 15 And I will put enmity between thee and the woman, and between thy seed and her seed; it shall bruise thy head, and thou shalt bruise his heel. 16 Unto the woman he said, I will greatly multiply thy sorrow and thy conception; in sorrow thou shalt bring forth children; and thy desire shall be to thy husband, and he shall rule over thee. 17 And unto Adam he said, Because thou hast hearkened unto the voice of thy wife, and hast eaten of the tree, of which I commanded thee, saying, Thou shalt not eat of it: cursed is the ground for thy sake; in sorrow shalt thou eat of it all the days of thy life; 18 Thorns also and thistles shall it bring forth to thee; and thou shalt eat the herb of the field; 19 In the sweat of thy face shalt thou eat bread, till thou return unto the ground; for out of it wast thou taken: for dust thou art, and unto dust shalt thou return. 20 And

Adam called his wife's name Eve; because she was the mother of all living. 21 Unto Adam also and to his wife did the LORD God make coats of skins, and clothed them. 22 And the LORD God said, Behold, the man is become as one of us, to know good and evil: and now, lest he put forth his hand, and take also of the tree of life, and eat, and live for ever: 23 Therefore the LORD God sent him forth from the garden of Eden, to till the ground from whence he was taken. 24 So he drove out the man; and he placed at the east of the garden of Eden Cherubims, and a flaming sword which turned every way, to keep the way of the tree of life.

Ecclesiastes
Chapter 3

1 To every thing there is a season, and a time to every purpose under the <u>heaven</u>: 2 A time to be born, and a time to die; a time to plant, and a time to pluck up that which is planted; 3 A time to kill, and a time to heal; a time to break down, and a time to build up; 4 A time to weep, and a time to laugh; a time to <u>mourn</u>, and a time to <u>dance</u>; 5 A time to cast away stones, and a time to gather stones together; a time to embrace, and a time to refrain from embracing; 6 A time to get, and a time to lose; a time to keep, and a time to cast away; 7 A time to rend, and a time to sew; a time to keep silence, and a time to speak; 8 A time to love, and a time to hate; a time of war, and a time of peace. 9 What profit hath he that worketh in that wherein he laboureth? 10 I have seen the travail, which God hath given to the sons of men to be exercised in it. 11 He hath made every thing beautiful in his time: also he hath set the world in their heart, so that no man can find out the work that God maketh from the beginning to the end. 12 I know that there is no good in them, but for a man to rejoice, and to do good in his life. 13 And also that every man should eat and <u>drink</u>, and enjoy the good of all his labour, it is the <u>gift</u> of God. 14 I know that, whatsoever God doeth, it shall be for ever: nothing can be put to it, nor any thing taken from it: and God doeth it, that men should fear before him. 15 That which hath been is now; and that which is to be hath already been; and God requireth that which is past. 16 And moreover I saw under the <u>sun</u> the place of judgment, that wickedness was there; and the place of <u>righteousness</u>, that iniquity was there. 17 I said in mine heart, God shall <u>judge</u> the righteous and the wicked: for there is a time there for every purpose and for every work. 18 I said in mine heart concerning the estate of the sons of men, that God might manifest them, and that they might see that they themselves are beasts. 19 For that which befalleth the sons of men befalleth beasts; even one thing befalleth them: as the one dieth, so dieth the other; yea, they have all one breath; so that a man hath no preeminence above a <u>beast</u>: for all is vanity. 20 All go unto one place; all are of the <u>dust</u>, and all turn to <u>dust</u> again. 21 Who knoweth the <u>spirit</u> of man that goeth upward, and the <u>spirit</u> of the <u>beast</u> that goeth downward to the earth? 22 Wherefore I perceive that there is nothing better, than that a man should rejoice in his own works; for that is his portion: for who shall bring him to see what shall be after him?

Gospel of Matthew
Chapter 6

…19 Lay not up for yourselves treasures upon earth, where moth and rust doth corrupt, and where thieves break through and steal: 20 But lay up for yourselves treasures in heaven, where neither moth nor rust doth corrupt, and where thieves do not break through nor steal: 21 For where your treasure is, there will your heart be also. 22 The light of the body is the eye: if therefore thine eye be single, thy whole body shall be full of light. 23 But if thine eye be evil, thy whole body shall be full of darkness. If therefore the light that is in thee be darkness, how great is that darkness! 24 No man can serve two masters: for either he will hate the one, and love the other; or else he will hold to the one, and despise the other. Ye cannot serve God and mammon. 25 Therefore I say unto you, Take no thought for your life, what ye shall eat, or what ye shall drink; nor yet for your body, what ye shall put on. Is not the life more than meat, and the body than raiment? 26 Behold the fowls of the air: for they sow not, neither do they reap, nor gather into barns; yet your heavenly Father feedeth them. Are ye not much better than they? 27 Which of you by taking thought can add one cubit unto his stature? 28 And why take ye thought for raiment? Consider the lilies of the field, how they grow; they toil not, neither do they spin: 29 And yet I say unto you, That even Solomon in all his glory was not arrayed like one of these. 30 Wherefore, if God so clothe the grass of the field, which to day is, and to morrow is cast into the oven, shall he not much more clothe you, O ye of little faith? 31 Therefore take no thought, saying, What shall we eat? or, What shall we drink? or, Wherewithal shall we be clothed? 32 (For after all these things do the Gentiles seek:) for your heavenly Father knoweth that ye have need of all these things. 33 But seek ye first the kingdom of God, and his righteousness; and all these things shall be added unto you. 34 Take therefore no thought for the morrow: for the morrow shall take thought for the things of itself. Sufficient unto the day is the evil thereof.

Gospel of Matthew
Chapter 13

1 The same day went Jesus out of the house, and sat by the sea side. 2 And great multitudes were gathered together unto him, so that he went into a ship, and sat; and the whole multitude stood on the shore. 3 And he spake many things unto them in parables, saying, Behold, a sower went forth to sow; 4 And when he sowed, some seeds fell by the way side, and the fowls came and devoured them up: 5 Some fell upon stony places, where they had not much earth: and forthwith they sprung up, because they had no deepness of earth: 6 And when the sun was up, they were scorched; and because they had no root, they withered away. 7 And some fell among thorns; and the thorns sprung up, and choked them: 8 But other fell into good ground, and brought forth fruit, some an hundredfold, some sixtyfold, some thirtyfold. 9 Who hath ears to hear, let him hear. 10 And the disciples came, and said unto him, Why speakest thou unto them in parables? 11 He answered and said unto them, Because it is given unto you to know the mysteries of the kingdom of heaven, but to them it is not given. 12 For whosoever hath, to him shall be given, and he shall have more abundance: but whosoever hath not, from him shall be taken away even that he hath. 13 Therefore speak I to them in parables: because they seeing see not; and hearing they hear not, neither do they understand. 14 And in them is fulfilled the prophecy of Esaias, which saith, By hearing ye shall hear, and shall not understand; and seeing ye shall see, and shall not perceive: 15 For this people's heart is waxed gross, and their ears are dull of hearing, and their eyes they have closed; lest at any time they should see with their eyes and hear with their ears, and should understand with their heart, and should be converted, and I should heal them. 16 But blessed are your eyes, for they see: and your ears, for they hear. 17 For verily I say unto you, That many prophets and righteous men have desired to see those things which ye see, and have not seen them; and to hear those things which ye hear, and have not heard them. 18 Hear ye therefore the parable of the sower. 19 When any one heareth the word of the kingdom, and understandeth it not, then cometh the wicked one, and catcheth away that which was sown in his heart. This is he which received seed by the way side. 20 But he that received the seed into stony places, the same is he that heareth the word, and anon with joy receiveth it; 21 Yet hath he not root in himself, but dureth for a while: for when tribulation or persecution ariseth because of the word, by and by he is offended. 22 He also that received seed among the thorns is he that heareth the word; and the care of this world, and the deceitfulness of riches, choke the word, and he becometh unfruitful.

23 But he that received seed into the good ground is he that heareth the word, and understandeth it; which also beareth fruit, and bringeth forth, some an hundredfold, some sixty, some thirty. 24 Another parable put he forth unto them, saying, The kingdom of heaven is likened unto a man which sowed good seed in his field: 25 But while men slept, his enemy came and sowed tares among the wheat, and went his way. 26 But when the blade was sprung up, and brought forth fruit, then appeared the tares also. 27 So the servants of the householder came and said unto him, Sir, didst not thou sow good seed in thy field? from whence then hath it tares? 28 He said unto them, An enemy hath done this. The servants said unto him, Wilt thou then that we go and gather them up? 29 But he said, Nay; lest while ye gather up the tares, ye root up also the wheat with them. 30 Let both grow together until the harvest: and in the time of harvest I will say to the reapers, Gather ye together first the tares, and bind them in bundles to burn them: but gather the wheat into my barn. 31 Another parable put he forth unto them, saying, The kingdom of heaven is like to a grain of mustard seed, which a man took, and sowed in his field: 32 Which indeed is the least of all seeds: but when it is grown, it is the greatest among herbs, and becometh a tree, so that the birds of the air come and lodge in the branches thereof. 33 Another parable spake he unto them; The kingdom of heaven is like unto leaven, which a woman took, and hid in three measures of meal, till the whole was leavened. 34 All these things spake Jesus unto the multitude in parables; and without a parable spake he not unto them: 35 That it might be fulfilled which was spoken by the prophet, saying, I will open my mouth in parables; I will utter things which have been kept secret from the foundation of the world. 36 Then Jesus sent the multitude away, and went into the house: and his disciples came unto him, saying, Declare unto us the parable of the tares of the field. 37 He answered and said unto them, He that soweth the good seed is the Son of man; 38 The field is the world; the good seed are the children of the kingdom; but the tares are the children of the wicked one; 39 The enemy that sowed them is the devil; the harvest is the end of the world; and the reapers are the angels. 40 As therefore the tares are gathered and burned in the fire; so shall it be in the end of this world. 41 The Son of man shall send forth his angels, and they shall gather out of his kingdom all things that offend, and them which do iniquity; 42 And shall cast them into a furnace of fire: there shall be wailing and gnashing of teeth. 43 Then shall the righteous shine forth as the sun in the kingdom of their Father. Who hath ears to hear, let him hear. 44 Again, the kingdom of heaven is like unto treasure hid in a field; the which when a man hath found, he hideth, and for joy thereof goeth and selleth all that he hath, and buyeth that field...

Gospel of John
Chapter 15

1 I am the true <u>vine</u>, and my Father is the <u>husbandman</u>. 2 Every <u>branch</u> in me that beareth not <u>fruit</u> he taketh away: and every <u>branch</u> that beareth <u>fruit</u>, he purgeth it, that it may bring forth more <u>fruit</u>. 3 Now ye are <u>clean</u> through the word which I have spoken unto you. 4 Abide in me, and I in you. As the <u>branch</u> cannot bear <u>fruit</u> of itself, except it abide in the <u>vine</u>; no more can ye, except ye abide in me. 5 I am the <u>vine</u>, ye are the branches: He that abideth in me, and I in him, the same bringeth forth much <u>fruit</u>: for without me ye can do nothing. 6 If a man abide not in me, he is cast forth as a <u>branch</u>, and is withered; and men gather them, and cast them into the fire, and they are burned. 7 If ye abide in me, and my words abide in you, ye shall ask what ye will, and it shall be done unto you. 8 Herein is my Father glorified, that ye bear much <u>fruit</u>; so shall ye be my disciples…

The Qur'an
Sūra XVI

In the name of God Most Gracious,
Most Merciful.

3. He has created the heavens
And the earth for just ends:
Far is He above having
The partners they ascribe to Him!

4. He has created man
From a sperm-drop;
And behold this same (man)
Becomes an open disputer!

5. And cattle He has created
For you (men): from them
Ye derive warmth,
And numerous benefits,
And of their (meat) ye eat.

6. And ye have a sense
Of pride and beauty in them
As ye drive them home
In the evening, and as ye
Lead them forth to pasture
In the morning.

7. And they carry your heavy loads
To lands that ye could not
(Otherwise) reach except with
Souls distressed: for your Lord
Is indeed Most Kind, Most Merciful

8. And (He has created) horses,
Mules, and donkeys, for you
To ride and use for show;
And He has created (other) things
Of which ye have no knowledge.

9. and unto God leads straight
The Way, but there are ways
That turn aside: if God
Had willed, He could have
Guided all of you.

10. It is He Who sends down
Rain from the sky:
From it ye drink,
And out of it (grows)
The vegetation on which
Ye feed your cattle.

11. With it He produces
For you corn, olives,
Date-palms, grapes,
And every kind of fruit:
Verily in this is a Sign
For those who give thought.

12. He has made subject to you
The Night and the Day;
The Sun and the Moon;
And the Stars are in subjection
By His Command: verily

In this are Signs
For men who are wise.

13. And the things on this earth
Which He has multiplied
In varying colours
(and qualities):
Verily in this is a Sign
For men who celebrate
The praises of God
(in gratitude).

14. It is He Who has made
The sea subject, that ye
May eat thereof flesh
That is fresh and tender,
And that ye may extract
Therefrom ornaments to wear;

And thou seest the ships
Therein that plough the waves,
That ye may seek (thus)
Of the bounty of God
And that ye may be grateful.

15. And He has set up
On the earth mountains
Standing firm, lest it should
Shake with you; and rivers
And roads; that ye
May guide yourselves;

16. And marks and sign-posts;
And by the stars
(Men) guide themselves.

The Golden Bough

BY JAMES FRAZER

THE WORSHIP of the oak tree or of the oak god appears to have been shared by all the branches of the Aryan stock in Europe. Both Greeks and Italians associated the tree with their highest god, Zeus or Jupiter, the divinity of the sky, the rain, and the thunder. Perhaps the oldest and certainly one of the most famous sanctuaries in Greece was that of Dodona, where Zeus was revered in the oracular oak. The thunder-storms which are said to rage at Dodona more frequently than anywhere else in Europe, would render the spot a fitting home for the god whose voice was heard alike in the rustling of the oak leaves and in the crash of thunder. Perhaps the bronze gongs which kept up a humming in the wind round the sanctuary were meant to mimic the thunder that might so often be heard rolling and rumbling in the coombs of the stern and barren mountains which shut in the gloomy valley. In Boeotia, as we have seen, the sacred marriage of Zeus and Hera, the oak god and the oak goddess, appears to have been celebrated with much pomp by a religious federation of states. And on Mount Lycaeus in Arcadia the character of Zeus as god both of the oak and of the rain comes out clearly in the rain charm practised by the priest of Zeus, who dipped an oak branch in a sacred spring. In his latter capacity Zeus was the god to whom the Greeks regularly prayed for rain. Nothing could be more natural; for often, though not always, he had his seat on the mountains where the clouds gather and the oaks grow. On the Acropolis at Athens there was an image of Earth praying to Zeus for rain. And in time of drought the Athenians themselves prayed, "Rain, rain, O dear Zeus, on the cornland of the Athenians and on the plains."

Again, Zeus wielded the thunder and lightning as well as the rain. At Olympia and elsewhere he was worshipped under the surname of Thunderbolt; and at Athens there was a sacrificial hearth of Lightning Zeus on the city wall, where some priestly officials watched for lightning over Mount Parnes at certain seasons of the year. Further, spots which had been struck by lightning were regularly fenced in by the Greeks and consecrated to Zeus the Descender, that is, to the god who came down in the flash from heaven. Altars were set up within these enclosures and sacrifices offered on them. Several such places are known from inscriptions to have existed in Athens.

Thus when ancient Greek kings claimed to be descended from Zeus, and even to bear his name, we may reasonably suppose that they also attempted to exercise his divine functions by making thunder and rain for the good of their people or the terror and confusion of their foes. In this respect the legend of Salmoneus probably reflects the pretensions of a whole class of petty sovereigns who reigned of old, each over his little canton, in the oak-clad highlands of Greece. Like their kinsmen the Irish kings, they were expected to be a source of fertility to the land and of fecundity to the cattle; and how could they fulfil these expectations better than by acting the part of their kinsman Zeus, the great god of the oak, the thunder, and the rain? They personified him, apparently, just as the Italian kings personified Jupiter.

In ancient Italy every oak was sacred to Jupiter, the Italian counterpart of Zeus; and on the Capitol at Rome the god was worshipped as the deity not merely of the oak, but of the rain and the thunder. Contrasting the piety of the good old times with the scepticism of an age when nobody thought that heaven was heaven, or cared a fig for Jupiter, a Roman writer tells us that in former days noble matrons used to go with bare feet, streaming hair, and pure minds, up the long Capitoline slope, praying to Jupiter for rain. And straightway, he goes on, it rained bucketsful, then or never, and everybody returned dripping like drowned rats. "But nowadays," says he, "we are no longer religious, so the fields lie baking."

When we pass from Southern to Central Europe we still meet with the great god of the oak and the thunder among the barbarous Aryans who dwelt in the vast primaeval forests. Thus among the Celts of Gaul the Druids esteemed nothing more sacred than the mistletoe and the oak on which it grew; they chose groves of oaks for the scene of their solemn service, and they performed none of their rites without oak leaves. "The Celts," says a Greek writer, "worship Zeus, and the Celtic image of Zeus is a tall oak." The Celtic conquerors, who settled in Asia in the third century before our era, appear to have carried the worship of the oak with them to their new home; for in the heart of Asia Minor the Galatian senate met in a place which bore the pure Celtic name of Drynemetum, "the sacred oak grove" or "the temple of the oak." Indeed the very name of Druids is believed by good authorities to mean no more than "oak men."

In the religion of the ancient Germans the veneration for sacred groves seems to have held the foremost place, and according to Grimm the chief of their holy trees was the oak. It appears to have been especially dedicated to the god of thunder, Donar or Thunar, the equivalent of the Norse Thor; for a sacred oak near Geismar, in Hesse, which Boniface cut down in the eighth century, went among the heathen by the name of Jupiter's oak (robur Jovis), which in old German would be Donares eih, "the oak of Donar." That the Teutonic thunder god Donar, Thunar, Thor was identified with the Italian thunder god Jupiter appears from our word Thursday, Thunar's day, which is merely a rendering of the Latin dies Jovis. Thus among the ancient Teutons, as among the Greeks and Italians, the god of the oak was also the god of the thunder. Moreover, he was regarded as the great fertilising power, who sent rain and caused the earth to bear fruit; for Adam of Bremen tells us that "Thor presides in the air; he it is who rules thunder and lightning, wind and rains, fine weather and crops." In these respects, therefore, the Teutonic thunder god again resembled his southern counterparts Zeus and Jupiter.

Amongst the Slavs also the oak appears to have been the sacred tree of the thunder god Perun, the counterpart of Zeus and Jupiter. It is said that at Novgorod there used to stand an image of Perun in the likeness of a man with a thunder-stone in his hand. A fire of oak wood burned day and night in his honour; and if ever it went out the attendants paid for their negligence with their lives. Perun seems, like Zeus and Jupiter, to have been the chief god of his people; for Procopius tells us that the Slavs "believe that one god, the maker of lightning, is alone lord of all things, and they sacrifice to him oxen and every victim…"

From the foregoing survey it appears that a god of the oak, the thunder, and the rain was worshipped of old by all the main branches of the Aryan stock in Europe, and was indeed the chief deity of their pantheon.

Celtic Folklore
The Religion of the Ancient Celts

BY J.A. MACCULLOUGH

In early thought everything was a person, in the loose meaning then possessed by personality, and many such "persons" were worshipped—earth, sun, moon, sea, wind, etc. This led later to more complete personification, and the sun or earth divinity or spirit was more or less separated from the sun or earth themselves. Some Celtic divinities were thus evolved, but there still continued a veneration of the objects of nature in themselves, as well as a cult of nature spirits or secondary divinities who peopled every part of nature. "Nor will I call out upon the mountains, fountains, or hills, or upon the rivers, which are now subservient to the use of man, but once were an abomination and destruction to them, and to which the blind people paid divine honours," cries Gildas. This was the true cult of the folk, the "blind people," even when the greater gods were organised, and it has survived with modifications in out-of-the-way places, in spite of the coming of Christianity...

The words suggest a belief in divine beings filling heaven, earth, sea, air, hills, glens, lochs, and rivers, and following human customs. A naïve faith, full of beauty and poetry, even if it had its dark and grim aspects! These powers or personalities had been invoked from time immemorial, but the invocations were soon stereotyped into definite formulæ. Such a formula is put into the mouth of Amairgen, the poet of the Milesians, when they were about to invade Erin, and it may have been a magical invocation of the powers of nature at the beginning of an undertaking or in times of danger:

> "I invoke the land of Ireland
>
> Shining, shining sea!
>
> Fertile, fertile mountain!
>
> Wooded vale!
>
> Abundant river, abundant in waters!
>
> Fish abounding lake!
>
> Fish abounding sea!
>
> Fertile earth!
>
> Irruption of fish! Fish there!
>
> Bird under wave! Great fish!
>
> Crab hole! Irruption of fish!
>
> Fish abounding sea!"

A similar formula was spoken after the destruction of Da Derga's Hostel by MacCecht on his finding water. He bathed in it and sang—

"Cold fountain! Surface of strand . . .
Sea of lake, water of Gara, stream of river
High spring well; cold fountain!"

The goddess Morrigan, after the defeat of the Fomorians, invokes the powers of nature and proclaims the victory to "the royal mountains of Ireland, to its chief waters, and its river mouths." It was also customary to take oaths by the elements—heaven, earth, sun, fire, moon, sea, land, day, night, etc., and these punished the breaker of the oath...

While the greater objects of nature were worshipped for themselves alone, the Celts also peopled the earth with spirits, benevolent or malevolent, of rocks, hills, dales, forests, lakes, and streams, and while greater divinities of growth had been evolved, they still believed in lesser spirits of vegetation, of the corn, and of fertility, connected, however, with these gods. Some of these still survive as fairies seen in meadows, woodlands, or streams, or as demoniac beings haunting lonely places. And even now, in French folk-belief, sun, moon, winds, etc., are regarded as actual personages. Sun and moon are husband and wife; the winds have wives; they are addressed by personal names and reverenced.

The Rig Veda
Book 10

1. HERBS that sprang up in time of old, three ages earlier than the Gods,—
Of these, whose hue is brown, will I declare the hundred powers and seven.
2 Ye, Mothers, have a hundred homes, yea, and a thousand are your growths.
Do ye who have a thousand powers free this my patient from disease.
3 Be glad and joyful in the Plants, both blossoming and bearing fruit,
Plants that will lead us to success like mares who conquer in the race.
4 Plants, by this name I speak to you, Mothers, to you the Goddesses:
Steed, cow, and garment may I win, win back thy very self, O man.
5 The Holy Fig tree is your home, your mansion is the Parna tree:
Winners of cattle shali ye be if ye regain for me this man.
6 He who hath store of Herbs at hand like Kings amid a crowd of men,—
Physician is that sage's name, fiend-slayer, chaser of disease.
7 Herbs rich in Soma, rich in steeds, in nourishments, in strengthening power,—
All these have I provided here, that this man may be whole again.
8 The healing virtues of the Plants stream forth like cattle from the stall,—
Plants that shall win me store of wealth, and save thy vital breath, O man.
9 Reliever is your mother's name, and hence Restorers are ye called.
Rivers are ye with wings that fly: keep far whatever brings disease.
10 Over all fences have they passed, as steals a thief into the fold.
The Plants have driven from the frame whatever malady was there.
11 When, bringing back the vanished strength, I hold these herbs within my hand,
The spirit of disease departs ere he can seize upon the life.
12 He through whose frame, O Plants, ye creep member by member, joint by joint,—
From him ye drive away disease like some strong arbiter of strife.
13 Fly, Spirit of Disease, begone, with the blue jay and kingfisher.
Fly with the wind's impetuousspeed, vanish together with the storm.
14 Help every one the other, lend assistance each of you to each,
All of you be accordant, give furtherance to this speech of mine.
15 Let fruitful Plants, and fruitless, those that blossom, and the blossomless,
Urged onward by Bṛhaspati, release us from our pain and grief;

16 Release me from the curse's plague and woe that comes from Varuṇa;
Free me from Yama's fetter, from sin and offence against the Gods.
17 What time, descending from the sky, the Plants flew earthward, thus they spake:
No evil shall befall the man whom while he liveth we pervade,
18 Of all the many Plants whose King is, Soma, Plants of hundred forms,
Thou art the Plant most excellent, prompt to the wish, sweet to the heart.
19 O all ye various Herbs whose King is Soma, that o'erspread the earth,
Urged onward by Bṛhaspati, combine your virtue in this Plant.
20 Unharmed be he who digs you up, unharmed the man for whom I dig:
And let no malady attack biped or quadruped of ours.
21 All Plants that hear this speech, and those that have departed far away,
Come all assembled and confer your healing power upon this Herb.
22 With Soma as their Sovran Lord the Plants hold colloquy and say:
O King, we save from death the man whose cure a Brahman undertakes.
23 Most excellent of all art thou, O Plant thy vassals are the trees.
Let him be subject to our power, the man who seeks to injure us.

Laws of Manu, Chapter I.

1. The great sages approached Manu, who was seated with a collected mind, and, having duly worshipped him, spoke as follows:2. 'Deign, divine one, to declare to us precisely and in due order the sacred laws of each of the (four chief) castes (varna) and of the intermediate ones…21. But in the beginning he assigned their several names, actions, and conditions to all (created beings), even according to the words of the Veda.22. He, the Lord, also created the class of the gods, who are endowed with life, and whose nature is action; and the subtile class of the Sadhyas, and the eternal sacrifice.23. But from fire, wind, and the sun he drew forth the threefold eternal Veda, called Rik, Yagus, and Saman, for the due performance of the sacrifice.24. Time and the divisions of time, the lunar mansions and the planets, the rivers, the oceans, the mountains, plains, and uneven ground.25. Austerity, speech, pleasure, desire, and anger, this whole creation he likewise produced, as he desired to call these beings into existence.26. Moreover, in order to distinguish actions, he separated merit from demerit, and he caused the creatures to be affected by the pairs (of opposites), such as pain and pleasure.27. But with the minute perishable particles of the five (elements) which have been mentioned, this whole (world) is framed in due order. 28. But to whatever course of action the Lord at first appointed each (kind of beings), that alone it has spontaneously adopted in each succeeding creation.29. Whatever he assigned to each at the (first) creation, noxiousness or harmlessness, gentleness or ferocity, virtue or sin, truth or falsehood, that clung (afterwards) spontaneously to it.30. As at the change of the seasons each season of its own accord assumes its distinctive marks, even so corporeal beings (resume in new births) their (appointed) course of action.31. But for the sake of the prosperity of the worlds he caused the Brahmana, the Kshatriya, the Vaisya, and the Sudra to proceed from his mouth, his arms, his thighs, and his feet.32. Dividing his own body, the Lord became half male and half female; with that (female) he produced Virag.33. But know me, O most holy among the twice-born, to be the creator of this whole (world), whom that male, Virag, himself produced, having performed austerities…36. They created… 38.Lightnings, thunderbolts and clouds, imperfect (rohita) and perfect rainbows, falling meteors, supernatural noises, comets, and heavenly lights of many kinds,39 (Horse-faced) Kinnaras, monkeys, fishes, birds of many kinds, cattle, deer, men, and carnivorous beasts with two rows of teeth,40. Small and large worms and beetles, moths, lice, flies, bugs, all stinging and biting insects and the several kinds of immovable things.41. Thus was this whole (creation), both the

immovable and the movable, produced by those high-minded ones by means of austerities and at my command, (each being) according to (the results of) its actions.42. But whatever act is stated (to belong) to (each of) those creatures here below, that I will truly declare to you, as well as their order in respect to birth.43. Cattle, deer, carnivorous beasts with two rows of teeth, Rakshasas, Pisakas, and men are born from the womb.44. From eggs are born birds, snakes, crocodiles, fishes, tortoises, as well as similar terrestrial and aquatic (animals).45. From hot moisture spring stinging and biting insects, lice, flies, bugs, and all other (creatures) of that kind which are produced by heat.46. All plants, propagated by seed or by slips, grow from shoots; annual plants (are those) which, bearing many flowers and fruits, perish after the ripening of their fruit;47. (Those trees) which bear fruit without flowers are called vanaspati (lords of the forest); but those which bear both flowers and fruit are called vriksha.48. But the various plants with many stalks, growing from one or several roots, the different kinds of grasses, the climbing plants and the creepers spring all from seed or from slips.49. These (plants) which are surrounded by multiform Darkness, the result of their acts (in former existences), possess internal consciousness and experience pleasure and pain.50. The (various) conditions in this always terrible and constantly changing circle of births and deaths to which created beings are subject, are stated to begin with (that of) Brahman, and to end with (that of) these (just mentioned immovable creatures).51. When he whose power is incomprehensible, had thus produced the universe and men, he disappeared in himself, repeatedly suppressing one period by means of the other.52. When that divine one wakes, then this world stirs; when he slumbers tranquilly, then the universe sinks to sleep…84. The life of mortals, mentioned in the Veda, the desired results of sacrificial rites and the (supernatural) power of embodied (spirits) are fruits proportioned among men according to (the character of) the age.85. One set of duties (is prescribed) for men in the Krita age, different ones in the Treta and in the Dvapara, and (again) another (set) in the Kali, in a proportion as (those) ages decrease in length.86. In the Krita age the chief (virtue) is declared to be (the performance of) austerities, in the Treta (divine) knowledge, in the Dvapara (the performance of) sacrifices, in the Kali liberality alone.87. But in order to protect this universe He, the most resplendent one, assigned separate (duties and) occupations to those who sprang from his mouth, arms, thighs, and feet.88. To Brahmanas he assigned teaching and studying (the Veda), sacrificing for their own benefit and for others, giving and accepting (of alms).89. The Kshatriya he commanded to protect the people, to bestow gifts, to offer sacrifices, to study (the Veda), and to abstain from attaching himself to sensual pleasures;90. The Vaisya to tend cattle, to bestow gifts, to offer sacrifices, to study (the Veda), to trade, to lend money, and to cultivate land.91. One occupation only the lord prescribed to the Sudra, to serve meekly even these (other) three castes.92. Man is stated to be purer above the navel (than below); hence the Self-existent (Svayambhu) has declared the purest (part) of him (to be) his mouth.93. As the Brahmana sprang from (Brahman's) mouth, as he was the first-born, and as he possesses the Veda, he is by right the lord of this whole creation.94. For the Self-existent (Svayambhu), having performed austerities, produced him first from his own mouth, in order that the offerings might be conveyed to the gods and manes and that this universe might be preserved.95. What created being can surpass him, through whose mouth the gods continually consume the sacrificial viands and the manes the offerings to the dead?96. Of created beings the most excellent are said to be those which are animated; of the animated, those which subsist by intelligence; of the intelligent, mankind; and of men, the Brahmanas;97. Of Brahmanas, those learned (in the Veda); of the learned, those who recognise (the necessity and the manner of performing the prescribed duties); of those who possess this knowledge, those who perform them; of the performers, those who know the Brahman.98. The very birth of a Brahmana is an eternal incarnation of the sacred law; for he is born to (fulfil) the sacred law, and becomes one with Brahman.99. A Brahmana, coming into existence, is born as the highest on earth, the lord of all created beings, for the protection of the treasury of the law.100. Whatever exists in the world is, the property of the Brahmana; on account of the excellence of his origin The Brahmana is, indeed, entitled to all.101. The Brahmana eats but his own food, wears but his own apparel, bestows but his own in alms; other mortals subsist through the benevolence of the Brahmana.

"The Parable of the Medicinal Herbs"
The Lotus Sutra

BY KUMĀRAJĪVA
translated BY BURTON WATSON

The Thus Come One, worthy of honor and
    reverence,
is profound and far-reaching in wisdom.
For long he remained silent regarding the
    essential,
in no hurry to speak of it at once.
If those who are wise hear of it
they can believe and understand it,
but those without wisdom will have doubts
    and regrets
and for all time will remain in error.
For this reason,
he adjusts to the person's power when
    preaching,
taking advantage of various causes
and enabling the person to gain a correct
    view.
You should understand
that it is like a great cloud
that rises up in the world
and covers it all over.
This beneficent cloud is laden with moisture;
the lightning gleams and flashes,
and the sound of thunder reverberates afar,
causing the multitude to rejoice.
The sun's rays are veiled and hidden,
a clear coolness comes over the land;
masses of darkness descend and spread—
you can almost touch them.
The rain falls everywhere,
coming down on all four sides.

Its flow and saturation are measureless,
reaching to every area of the earth,
to the ravines and valleys of the mountains
    and streams,
to the remote and secluded places where
    grow
plants, bushes, medicinal herbs,
trees large and small,
a hundred grains, rice seedlings,
sugar cane, grape vines.
The rain moistens them all,
none fails to receive its full share.
The parched ground is everywhere watered,
herbs and trees alike grow lush.
What falls from the cloud
is water of a single flavor,
but the plants and trees, thickets and groves,
each accept the moisture that is appropriate
    to its portion.
All the various trees,
whether superior, middling, or inferior,
take what is fitting for large or small,
and each is enabled to sprout and grow.
Root, stem, limb, leaf,
the glow and hue of flower and fruit—
one rain extends to them
and all are able to become fresh and glossy.
Whether their allotment
of substance, form, and nature is large or
    small,
the moistening they receive is one,

but each grows and flourishes in its own way.
The Buddha is like this
when he appears in the world,
comparable to a great cloud
that covers all things everywhere…
I appear in the world
like a great cloud
that showers moisture upon
all the dry and withered living beings,
so that all are able to escape suffering,
gain the joy of peace and security,
the joys of this world
and the joy of nirvana.
All you heavenly and human beings of this
   assembly,
listen carefully and with one mind! . . .
I bring fullness and satisfaction to the world,
like a rain that spreads its moisture
   everywhere.
Eminent and lowly, superior and inferior,
observers of precepts, violators of precepts,
those fully endowed with proper demeanor,
those not fully endowed,
those of correct views, of erroneous views,
of keen capacity, of dull capacity—
I cause the Dharma rain to rain on all equally,
never lax or neglectful.
When all the various living beings
hear my Law,
they receive it according to their power,
dwelling in their different environments.
Some inhabit the realm of human and
   heavenly beings,
of wheel-turning sage kings,
Shakra, Brahma and the other kings—

these are the inferior medicinal herbs.
Some understand the Law of no outflows,
are able to attain nirvana,
to acquire the six transcendental powers
and gain in particular the three
   understandings,
or live alone in mountain forests,
constantly practicing meditation…
Those who abide in peace in their transcendental powers,
turning the wheel of non-regression,
saving innumerable millions
of hundreds of thousands of living beings—
bodhisattvas such as these
I call the large trees.
The equality of the Buddha's preaching
is like a rain of a single flavor,
but depending upon the nature of the living
   being,
the way in which it is received is not uniform,
just as the various plants and trees
each receive the moisture in a different
   manner.
The Buddha employs this parable
As an expedient means to open up and reveal
   the matter,
using various kinds of words and phrases
and expounding the single Law,
but in terms of the Buddha wisdom
this is no more than one drop of the ocean.
I rain down the Dharma rain,
filling the whole world,
and this single-flavored Dharma
is practiced by each according to the
   individual's power…

Kumārajīva; trans. Burton Watson, Excerpt from "The Parable of the Medicinal Herbs," The Lotus Sutra, pp. 100-104. Copyright © 1993 by Columbia University Press. Reprinted with permission.

Analect's
Chapter 6

BY CONFUCIOUS
translated by JAMES LEGGE [1893]

… The Master said, "The wise find pleasure in water; the virtuous find pleasure in hills. The wise are active; the virtuous are tranquil. The wise are joyful; the virtuous are long-lived."…

Doctrine of the Mean

BY CONFUCIOUS
translated by JAMES LEGGE [1893]

500 BC

While there are no stirrings of pleasure, anger, sorrow, or joy, the mind may be said to be in the state of Equilibrium. When those feelings have been stirred, and they act in their due degree, there ensues what may be called the state of Harmony. This Equilibrium is the great root from which grow all the human actings in the world, and this Harmony is the universal path which they all should pursue.

Let the states of equilibrium and harmony exist in perfection, and a happy order will prevail throughout heaven and earth, and all things will be nourished and flourish.

The *Tao Te Ching*

BY LAO-TZU

5. Heaven and earth do not act from (the impulse of) any wish to be benevolent; they deal with all things as the dogs of grass are dealt with. The sages do not act from (any wish to be) benevolent; they deal with the people as the dogs of grass are dealt with…
May not the space between heaven and earth be compared to a bellows?…
'Tis emptied, yet it loses not its power;
'Tis moved again, and sends forth air the more.
Much speech to swift exhaustion lead we see;
Your inner being guard, and keep it free.

8. The highest excellence is like (that of) water. The excellence of water appears in its benefiting all things, and in its occupying, without striving (to the contrary), the low place which all men dislike. Hence (its way) is near to (that of) the Tao…

10. When the intelligent and animal souls are held together in one embrace, they can be kept from separating. When one gives undivided attention to the (vital) breath, and brings it to the utmost degree of pliancy, he can become as a (tender) babe. When he has cleansed away the most mysterious sights (of his imagination), he can become without a flaw…
The Tao) produces (all things) and nourishes them; it produces them and does not claim them as its own; it does all, and yet does not boast of it; it presides over all, and yet does not control them.
This is what is called 'The mysterious Quality' (of the Tao).

25. There was something undefined and complete, coming into existence before Heaven and Earth. How still it was and formless, standing alone, and undergoing no change, reaching everywhere and in no danger (of being exhausted)! It may be regarded as the Mother of all things.

I do not know its name, and I give it the designation of the Tao (the Way or Course). Making an effort (further) to give it a name… It passes on (in constant flow). Passing on, it becomes remote. Having become remote, it returns. Therefore the Tao is great; Heaven is great; Earth is great; and the (sage) king is also great. In the universe there are four that are great, and the (sage) king is one of them…Man takes his law from the Earth; the Earth takes its law from Heaven; Heaven takes its law from the Tao. The law of the Tao is its being what it is.

32. The Tao, considered as unchanging, has no name… Though in its primordial simplicity it may be small, the whole world dares not deal with (one embodying) it as a minister. If a feudal prince or the king could guard and hold it, all would spontaneously submit themselves to him.

Heaven and Earth (under its guidance) unite together and send down the sweet dew, which, without the directions of men, reaches equally everywhere as of its own accord…The relation of the Tao to all the world is like that of the great rivers and seas to the streams from the valleys.

43. The softest thing in the world dashes against and overcomes the hardest; that which has no (substantial) existence enters where there is no crevice. I know hereby what advantage belongs to doing nothing (with a purpose)…There are few in the world who attain to the teaching without words, and the advantage arising from non-action…

78. There is nothing in the world more soft and weak than water, and yet for attacking things that are firm and strong there is nothing that can take precedence of it;—for there is nothing (so effectual) for which it can be changed…
Every one in the world knows that the soft overcomes the hard, and the weak the strong, but no one is able to carry it out in practice.

PART 3

Voices of Early America

From Transcendental Musings to Abandoning the "Megamachine": Building the Foundation of the Modern Environmental Movement

Introduction by Rachel M. Gurney
Oklahoma State University

T he stark contrast between two competing ideologies of the natural world is illustrated by the settlement and westward expansion of the American frontier. While ancient Native American cultural norms support strong opposition to the wanton killing of wildlife, Christianity embraced no such prohibitions, and European settlers undertook an extensive transformation of the American landscape. Prior to contact, some thirty to one hundred million buffalo roamed from the Rocky Mountains to the Atlantic (Krech 1999). Buffalo kills increased rapidly through the first half of the nineteenth century and significantly gained momentum after the Civil War. Buffalo meat provided food for workers constructing the new transcontinental railroads; hides and tongues were shipped to national and international markets; and dwindling buffalo populations served the objective of depriving Plains Indians of their principle food source (LaDuke 1999). By 1887, no more than a few dozen small herds of buffalo, protected by various ranchers and Native American tribes, remained scattered across the West (O'Brien 2001). Disappearance of the buffalo forced wolves of the Great Plains and Rockies to search for a new food source, which they found in cattle. Buffalo hunters then turned their attention to the wolves. Between 1865 and 1895, hunters killed between one and two million wolves, eliminating them entirely in most states and reducing their populations to near-extinction in others (Lopez 1978). Left unrestrained, cattle ranching led to the demise of the tall-grass prairie, which cows graze much more intensely than their wild predecessors.

Overhunting for pelts in the late nineteenth century also led to the near-extinction of beavers, which previously thrived in virtually all waterways (Krech 1999). Their absence contributed to the decline of wetlands, which became increasingly polluted. The moving frontier line also brought extensive deforestation in order to meet growing demand for lumber by settlers, then business and industry. This resulted in the loss of tens of millions of acres of forest across all regions of the United States. Even oceans endured the wrath of expansion. American and Russian fleets killed over two hundred thousand sea otters on the Pacific coast, leading to their near-extinction by 1900 (Macdonald 1998). In addition, millions of whales met death by harpoons—some 1.5 million in the South Pacific alone (Scully 2002).

The achievements of industrial civilizations have long been the subject of boundless celebration; however, there have always been those who speak to the darker side of progress. Generations of discontented social critics, writers, artists, activists, and countless others have decried the destruction of nature and its wild inhabitants—building and sustaining the tradition of American environmental consciousness. By the second half of the nineteenth century, Americans began the painfully slow process of awakening to the costs of their rampant expansion and consumption—urging not for reform, but rather mourning the loss they had incurred. It was not until the end of the century that systematic efforts to preserve and manage natural resources began. Although some progress was made, early efforts for conservation and/or preservation were not widely successful. It was not until the last third of the twentieth century that environmental consciousness, driven largely by pragmatic concerns, would gain the momentum necessary to ignite a mass movement.

Less pragmatic, however, were the environmental musings of the mid-nineteenth century—sprouting from the fertile soil of romanticism, which provided an important source of veneration for nature and cultivated a culture of protest to the killing and ecological devastation. The most influential articulations of these early venerations arose from the transcendentalist tradition of New England, namely through the works of Ralph Waldo Emerson and Henry David Thoreau. Counter to the dominant frontier-capitalist mentality, Emerson and Thoreau wrote of soul and spirit—representing nature as altogether pristine, holy, and healing. Enchanted by these ideals, many American writers and artists enthusiastically embraced romanticism and often turned to nature for inspiration. However, the influence of these writers and wilderness advocates was limited during their time. It was not until the 1890s (the Progressive Era) that the political and spiritual heirs of Emerson and Thoreau began to apply greater pressure in national politics.

Grounded in the spiritual aspects of life, the New England interpretation of transcendentalism posited that in nature one could find the spirit of the Divine and continual renewal. This divine spirit, which Emerson termed the "Over-Soul" (1841), is present throughout nature and within every human being. Transcendentalists believed that one could access the power, wisdom, and beauty of this spirit by ridding oneself of the artifices of civilization. Emerson (1849) wrote:

> In the woods, is perpetual youth. Within these plantations of God, a decorum and sanctity reign, a perennial festival is dressed, and the guest sees not how he should tire of them in a thousand years. In the woods, we return to reason and faith. There I feel that nothing can befall me in life,—no disgrace, no calamity, (leaving me my eyes,) which nature cannot repair. Standing on the bare ground,—my head bathed by the blithe air, and uplifted into infinite space,—all mean egotism vanishes. I become a transparent eye-ball; I am nothing; I see all; the currents of the Universal Being circulate through me; I am part or particle of God.

While Emerson proselytized for humanity's union with nature, he did not reject industrialism and technology altogether. In fact, Emerson admitted that certain inventions brought some benefits; however, he also warned of the consequences of relying too heavily on machines and technology. It was balance Emerson sought, between nature and technology (provided it could be controlled)—a prevailing tenet of contemporary mainstream environmentalism. However, unlike Emerson and many of his time who believed in nature's ability to heal itself, contemporary environmentalists know all too well that human activity can indeed inflict irreversible damage on natural systems.

Thoreau, on the other hand, took a less complacent stance regarding the dominance of industry and technology. A staunch critic of the dehumanizing effects of industrial practices and the capitalist system they support, Thoreau wrote:

> The nation itself, with its so-called internal improvements, which, by the way are all external and superficial, is just an unwieldy and overgrown establishment, cluttered with furniture and tripped up by its own traps, ruined by luxury and heedless expense, by want of calculation and a worthy aim, as the million households in the land; and the only cure for it, as for them, is in a rigid economy, a stern and more than Spartan simplicity of life and elevation of purpose. It lives too fast. Men think that it is essential that the Nation have commerce, and export ice, and talk through a telegraph, and ride thirty miles an hour, without a doubt, whether they do or not; but whether we should live like baboons or like men, is a little uncertain. (Thoreau 1854)

Thoreau's words are a testament to the waste and despoilment he witnessed resulting from economic development, and he warned of much worse to come. To counterbalance the destructive force of an increasingly materialistic, urbanized society and the heavy burden placed on the human soul, Thoreau prescribed wilderness as the remedy. "[I]n Wildness is the preservation of the World," Thoreau (1862) declared—an enduring sentiment among many environmentalists today.

While praising the refreshing, redemptive qualities of nature, Thoreau was also among the first to admonish his fellow citizens that nature does not exist for their benefit alone, but for its own sake—valuing every animal and wild place in its own right, each with an individual spirit. Thoreau foreshadowed some of the concerns of contemporary environmentalists by raising the question of animal rights. Another dominant theme in Thoreau's work that has been adopted by the modern environmental movement is embodied in his contemplations regarding how life ought to be lived and what gives it meaning. Here Thoreau explains why he chose to live alone in a cabin at the edge of Walden Pond for two years:

> I went to the woods because I wished to live deliberately, to front only the essential facts of life, and see if I could not learn what it had to teach, and not, when I came to die, discover that I had not lived. I did not wish to live what was not life, living is so dear; nor did I wish to practise resignation, unless it was quite necessary. I wanted to live deep and suck out all the marrow of life, to live so sturdily and Spartan—like as to put to rout all that was not life, to cut a broad swath and shave close, to drive life into a corner, and Walden reduce it to its lowest terms, and, if it proved to be mean, why then to get the whole and genuine meanness of it, and publish its meanness to the world; or if it were sublime, to know it by experience, and be able to give a true account of it in my next excursion. (1854)

Many of Thoreau's contemporaries characterized him as elitist or impractical— unsympathetic to those who were living in any manner necessary to survive. However, Thoreau did not suggest that life should be lived primitively in wilderness; only that wilderness should be a part of human life. Today, Thoreau's compelling prose reminds us of how far we have strayed and what we must do to return to an authentic way of living.

Other than the recommendations prescribed by transcendentalists for reaching peace and harmony with nature, no plans had been rendered to reach such a goal, nor any systematic evaluations of the magnitude of environmental change. This remained for George Perkins Marsh, who studied and called attention to the pervasive destruction human activity was inflicting on nature in *Man and Nature: Or, Physical Geography as Modified by Human Action*, which continues to be a seminal book of American environmentalism. Marsh held many professions, including lawyer, teacher, naturalist, fish commissioner, congressman from Vermont, and U.S. ambassador to Turkey and Italy. A scholar with an enduring interest and love for nature, Marsh systematically evaluated historical and scientific records before reaching the conclusion that human activity was indeed having a damaging impact on much of the world. Marsh was the first to demonstrate that the cumulative impact of human activity could inflict widespread and permanent devastation on the earth. He argued that nature, if left undisturbed, is essentially stable. While natural occurrences of environmental degradation inflict superficial and temporary damage, human activity—intensified through the use of technology—has the potential to permanently transform the natural landscape. Marsh (1864) wrote, "But man is everywhere a disturbing agent. Wherever he plants his foot, the harmonies of nature are turned to discord." However, Marsh drew a distinction between the environmental impact of primitive hunter-gatherer societies (which caused relatively little damage) and that of industrial societies that, aided with technology, acquired greater capacity to alter the physical world.

Through his delineation of the impact of human activity on ecological systems, Marsh substantiated that humans, acting largely out of ignorance, ultimately harm themselves by corrupting the balance of nature.

> The ravages committed by man subvert the relations and destroy the balance which nature had established between her organized and her inorganic creations; and she avenges herself upon the intruder, by letting loose upon her defaced provinces destructive energies hitherto kept in check by organic forces destined to be his best auxiliaries, but which he has unwisely dispersed and driven from the field of action. (Marsh 1865)

The litany of offenses outlined in Marsh's work illustrates the pervasive and irreversible nature of man-made environmental degradation. To aid in addressing these impacts, Marsh called for intense study of human activity in the regions he identified as most affected. Although Marsh believed in the power of knowledge and science to remedy the imbalance between humans and nature, he also insisted that civilization must not wait for the slow and steady progress of exact science to teach it a better economy (1864).

Man and Nature was widely received in both the United States and Europe at the time of its publication in 1864, although it had virtually no immediate impact on environmental policies or practices in the U.S. The post-Civil War era of expansion and growth spawned a culture of ambivalence regarding the treatment of nature. For most of the nineteenth century, America was a nation not yet willing to admit the true cost of its development. Those who called attention to the waste and despoilment were accorded little notice or respect. Nevertheless, isolated acts of conservation and preservation of nature and its many lucrative resources grew more numerous as the century progressed.

By the end of the nineteenth century, central themes explored by Marsh in *Man and Nature* reemerged with greater political salience in the works of Gifford Pinchot and John Muir—two leaders responsible for writing the first pages of America's modern environmental history. Pinchot, serving as Theodore Roosevelt's chief forester, formulated robust policies to conserve public lands and resources for the present and future benefit of the nation. Conservation under Roosevelt was a vital tool of the progressive movement aimed at redressing social, economic, and political disparities resulting from industrialization, urbanization, and the concentration of power within the corporate realm. Roosevelt was also greatly influenced by John Muir, a naturalist and spokesman for the preservation of nature. Allies and frequent adversaries, Pinchot and Muir differed substantially on their perceived value of nature and approaches to protecting it.

Gifford Pinchot is often regarded (and considered himself to be) the "father of conservation." The early conservation movement represented an amalgam of sometimes disparate environmental traditions, including Pinchot's doctrine of "wise"/efficient use of natural resources; democratic values pertaining to ownership of, and responsibility for, public lands; Emerson and Thoreau's romantic-transcendental love of nature; and concern over threats to human and environmental health resulting from industrialization. Contrary to the preservation perception, Pinchot's concept of conservation was founded on the premise of scientific utilitarianism. Developed in the spirit of progressivism, the conservation movement viewed public land as a commons where natural resources were to be used in the interest of the general public (a concept that would later be expanded to include air and water). In his book *The Fight for Conservation*, Pinchot framed conservation not only as a moral issue, but an ultimate act of patriotism.

> The central thing for which Conservation stands is to make this country the best possible place to live in, both for us and for our descendants…. Conservation is the most democratic movement this country has known for a generation. It holds that the people have not only the right, but the duty to control the use of the natural resources, which are the great sources of prosperity. And it regards the absorption of these resources by the special interests, unless operations are under effective public control, as a moral wrong. Conservation is the application of common-sense to the common problems for the common good….
> (Pinchot 1920)

Perhaps Pinchot's greatest legacy while collaborating with Roosevelt was his ability to portray conservation as a democratic issue. For instance, Pinchot insisted that government control of forests was necessary to ensure the sustainable and efficient use of resources for the benefit of all people regardless of their social, economic, or political standing. Once established, this democratic principle would serve as a useful tool for scrutinizing the legitimacy of decisions pertaining to the use of public lands. In addition, Pinchot understood that in order to succeed, the scientific management of resources must be balanced with the assurance of commercial profits over the long term. While this balance has proven difficult to achieve as economic interests have continued to gnaw away at natural resources and public lands, frivolous consumption would never again be regarded as morally acceptable.

As Pinchot gained the understanding that all of nature is intrinsically linked and vital for the nation to thrive, his wise-use principle extended beyond the protection of forests—sparking a campaign of political resistance to the exploitation and misuse of additional natural resources. However, Pinchot was not concerned with preserving nature for its own sake, nor was he interested in protecting wildlife or preserving wild places for recreation. Although Theodore Roosevelt was moved by the spiritual qualities of nature and less concerned with its use, he and many others fervently adopted Pinchot's credo of conservation. Meanwhile, a different kind of credo was emerging on the national stage—adding complexity to the nation's evolving environmental consciousness with a campaign for the *preservation* of nature.

John Muir eloquently and effectively sounded the call for preservation of the nation's wild places. Much like Thoreau's transcendental love affair with nature, Muir, too, was converted by its many wonders. Seeing the natural world as sacred and finding a spiritual presence in every forest, valley, mountain, and desert, Muir often utilized religious language as a tool for influencing public opinion. Furthermore, Muir's writing frequently elicits insight into religious paradigms regarding nature and wildlife, as evident by this passage written while trekking through Florida's wilderness:

> Many good people believe that alligators were created by the Devil, thus accounting for their all-consuming appetite and ugliness. But doubtless these creatures are happy and fill the place assigned them by the great Creator of us all. Fierce and cruel they appear to us, but beautiful in the eyes of God. They, also, are his children, for He hears their cries, cares for them tenderly, and provides their daily bread. The antipathies existing in the Lord's great animal family must be wisely planned, like balanced repulsion and attraction in the mineral kingdom. How narrow we selfish, conceited creatures are in our sympathies! How blind to the rights of all the rest of creation! With what dismal irreverence we speak of our fellow mortals! Though alligators, snakes, etc., naturally repel us, they are not mysterious evils. They dwell happily in these flowery wilds, are part of God's family, unfallen, undepraved, and cared for with the same species of tenderness and love as is bestowed on angels in heaven or saints on earth. (Muir 1916)

Diverging greatly from the beliefs of early settlers—who utilized Christian dogma to support their dominance of wilderness and expansion across the country—Muir affirmed that the Creator grants *all* life an equal right to thrive. Ergo, to destroy life was not only immoral, but an affront to God.

Rather than through the domination and destruction of nature for human gain, Muir proposed alternative means for communing with nature. Like Thoreau, he believed that the preservation of the world could be found in wilderness, and he often wrote of its many healing attributes.

> Thousands of tired, nerve-shaken, over-civilized people are beginning to find out that going to the mountains is going home; that wildness is a necessity; and that mountain parks and reservations are useful not only as fountains of timber and irrigating rivers, but as fountains of life. (Muir 1901)

Like Thoreau (and unlike Pinchot), Muir believed that all of nature existed for its own sake—rather than for human utility—and should be honored and protected by humans willing to humble themselves with this truth. Furthermore, as a student of the new science of ecology, Muir was keening aware of the interconnectedness of natural systems. This strengthened his resolve to protect even the seemingly insignificant, and preserve that wilderness which remained intact and largely unspoiled by humans.

Muir was greatly troubled by the damage done to California's Yosemite by stockmen, lumbermen, and particularly sheep (or "hooved locusts" as he called them). Along with the editor of *Century Magazine*, Robert Underwood Johnson, Muir launched a spirited lobbying campaign with a series of articles aimed at persuading the federal government to protect Yosemite by designating the area a national park. During the course of the campaign, Johnson proposed to Muir that a permanent society be established to protect California's wild areas, and in 1892, Muir served as principal founder and first president of the Sierra Club. The burgeoning organization, founded upon the principles of preservationism, led the crusade for protecting what was left of America's wild landscape and served as a powerful force for establishing preservationism as a mainstay of the modern environmental movement. Intertwined with ecology, which emphasizes the interrelationship of living organisms within natural systems, the preservation movement aided efforts of existing wildlife organizations through the protection of wild areas serving as essential habitats. Out of this movement arose an intellectual and moral responsibility for the wellbeing of nature, a concept later defined by Aldo Leopold (1949) as "the land ethic."

In addition to catalyzing the preservation movement, Muir's literary contributions have proven capable of evoking radical change in perceptions of nature and informed generations of writers through fundamental rhetorical conventions. Readers converted by Muir's enchanting prose begin to revere the sanctity of nature, while even those who remain skeptical are moved to question their beliefs that nature exists only for human utility. By incorporating scientific references into lyrical descriptions of nature—rejecting the convention of separating science and spirituality—Muir portrayed nature as something awe-inspiring and very much alive. Rather than dry abstractions describing the natural world as an impersonal commodity, Muir drew his readers in with intimate accounts of intense, life-changing experiences—illustrating the aesthetic, spiritual, and moral qualities of wilderness.

Early in the twentieth century, Muir wrote in defense of Yosemite's Hetch Hetchy Valley, which was to be dammed to provide drinking water, and later electric power, for San Francisco's growing population. Demonstrating the use of religious language as a rhetorical tool of influence, Muir wrote, "These temple destroyers, devotees of ravaging commercialism, seem to have a perfect contempt for Nature, and, instead of lifting their eyes to the God of the mountains, lift them to the Almighty Dollar" (Muir 1912). The battle over how to manage the Hetch Hetchy Valley is perhaps the most renowned dispute in the history of American conservation, representing a crucial divergence within the modern environmental movement. To a point, conservationists (led by politician and forester Gifford Pinchot) and preservationists (led by mystic and naturalist John Muir) could take up a common cause protesting the wanton destruction of nature. Both called on the government to protect the nation's resources for present and future generations. However, Pinchot insisted that the land be utilized for human benefit, both wisely and efficiently, while Muir demanded that the land be protected from human assault.

Both Pinchot and Muir marshaled formidable allies in the clash over Hetch Hetchy; however, Roosevelt finally sided in favor of damming the valley, and Congress approved the project in 1913. Vestiges of this clash between conservationists and preservationists in the debate over Hetch Hetchy can be found in modern ideas and policies regarding the management of natural resource, such as the practice of "multiple use," which implies the maximum sustainable development of natural resources. While modern environmentalists still unite behind the preservationist tenets conceived by Muir and others, they also understand that public opinion may not favor the prohibition of economic growth for the sake of preserving pristine wilderness. This reality is reflected in the compromises many environmentalists make in accepting the exploitation of some wilderness for the protection of others.

Aldo Leopold, another key figure who informed modern America's approach to managing wilderness and its resources, is considered by many to be the "father of wildlife management." Conservationist, U.S. forester, philosopher, educator, author of the seminal book *A Sand County Almanac*, and a principal founder of The Wilderness Society (a leading organization in the protection of America's wild areas), Leopold played a pivotal role in shifting the paradigm underlying some of America's destructive environmental management policies and practices leading up to the 1920s. A Yale-educated forester and disciple of the emerging science of ecology, Leopold envisioned a prosperous union with nature that required humanity to adopt an entirely new set of principles for relating with the wild. Like many early environmentalists, Leopold was an avid hunter with a deep appreciation for the natural world. Beginning his career with the newly established U.S. Forest Service in 1909, Leopold initially accepted the principles of traditional game management, which required the killing of "bad" predators that preyed on "good" species sought by hunters. According to conventional thinking, fewer wolves (and other predators) meant more deer, and the Forest Service was responsible for managing public lands for the benefit of hunters.

Long regarded as fierce and menacing predators, the killing of wolves was awarded with bounties and public acclaim. However, two experiences, one spiritual and one scientific, compelled Leopold to reject the traditional approach to game management in favor of a more holistic one—abandoning moral categories of species as "good" or "bad" in recognition of the vital function each performs in an ecosystem. Leopold's spiritual awakening took place early in his career while hunting in the mountains of New Mexico. Spying a mother wolf and her pups, Leopold and his companions opened fire, then ran to the scene.

> We reached the old wolf in time to watch a fierce green fire dying in her eyes. I realized then, and have known ever since, that there was something new to me in those eyes—something known only to her and to the mountain. I was young then, and full of trigger-itch; I thought that because fewer wolves meant more deer, then no wolves would mean hunters' paradise. But after seeing the green fire die, I sensed that neither the wolf nor the mountain agreed with such a view. (Leopold 1949)

After his encounter with "the fierce green fire," Leopold perceived the relationship among predators, prey, and mountains much differently. He witnessed the deer population soar as a result of the extermination of wolves and mountain lions and the grave consequences this brought for life on the mountain. With no predators left to cull the herd, the plateau became unable to sustain it. A landscape, once covered in flourishing vegetation, lay barren—ravaged by starving animals and littered with the sun-bleached bones of deer.

> Such a mountain looks as if someone has given God a new pruning shears, and forbidden Him all other exercise.... I now suspect that just as a deer herd lives in mortal fear of its wolves, so does the mountain live in mortal fear of its deer. And perhaps with better cause, for while a buck pulled down by wolves can

be replaced in two or three years, a range pulled down by too many deer may fail of replacement in as many decades. (Leopold 1949)

These experiences led Leopold to draw two important conclusions contradictory to traditional approaches of wildlife management: (1) a species cannot be understood or managed in isolation from its habitat or co-existing species; and (2) in environments already dominated by human beings, humans have the responsibility to ensure that ecological systems remain balanced. Leopold insisted that humans are indeed part of the ecosystem, yet they had acquired the power to destroy it—threatening the entire system, including humanity itself. Well-meaning efforts to curb this threat would be futile without scientific understanding of the relationships existing within the system. Drawing inspiration from his failed attempt to protect deer through the extermination of their predators, Leopold wrote, "[T]oo much safety seems to yield only danger in the long run. Perhaps this is behind Thoreau's dictum: In wildness is the salvation of the world. Perhaps this is the hidden meaning in the howl of the wolf, long known among mountains, but seldom perceived among men" (Leopold 1949).

Perceiving nature through a scientific lens, Leopold concluded, was not enough to preserve the chain of life in a complex world where humans hold the power of life and death over entire ecosystems. In the late 1940s, Leopold elaborated upon the lessons he had learned and proposed a set of principles he called "the land ethic," designed to promote ethical behavior and requiring human beings to recognize their roles as members of an ecological community. "In short, a land ethic changes the role of *Homo sapiens* from conqueror of the land-community to plain member and citizen of it. It implies respect for his fellow-members, and also respect for the community as such" (Leopold 1949). Leopold argued that restricting "community" to incorporate only humans, disregarding all other species, was immoral and represented a failure to recognize humanity's dependence on nature. Within these terms, the virtue of human action could be measured by its impact on nature: "A thing is right when it tends to preserve the integrity, stability, and beauty of the biotic community. It is wrong when it tends otherwise" (Leopold 1949). Merging science and ethics, Leopold introduced concepts that illuminate the interrelationships of community—concepts now commonplace, working principles of modern environmentalism. The powerful prose contained in Leopold's *A Sand County Almanac* outlines many of the basic tenets of today's environmental movement, earning the title of one of the movement's sacred texts.

Prior to World War II, America's economy was relatively decentralized; however, rapid expansion of industrial capitalism during the war brought about the devastation of vast tracts of undeveloped land and the production of large quantities of toxic waste. This economic expansion, dominated by large firms, depended primarily on scientific and technological innovation. New techniques for manufacturing weaponry and other goods led to environmental degradation at an unprecedented rate, and the use of synthetic chemicals produced large-scale risks for humans and the natural world. By the 1950s, smog from automobile exhaust had become prevalent in major urban areas, and air quality advisories urging vulnerable populations to remain indoors were routine. Between 1940 and 1991, the annual production of synthetic organic chemicals (chemicals containing carbon atoms) skyrocketed, and some seventy thousand chemicals were in routine use—only a handful of which had been thoroughly evaluated and less than 10 percent tested for impact on the human nervous system (Kroll-Smith and Floyd 2000).

The heedless optimism and materialism immediately following World War II pushed environmental concerns off the national agenda. Although officials continued to pressure the government over issues of public health, the environmental agenda was largely ignored. The conservation policies of the New Deal suffered under the Eisenhower administration, which sought to turn federal lands and resources over for fiscal or political gain. During the 1960s, however, government slowly began to respond to the public's environmental concerns—evident by the establishment of the Land and Water Conservation Fund, the landmark Wilderness Protection Act and National Trails Act, and the existence of eleven environmental divisions within the Public Health Service. The clean air and water legislation of the 1960s set the stage for more substantial laws in the decade to come.

Throughout the 1960s, many apprised Americans of their foolish indifference to the misuse and deterioration of nature. A leader among them was Lewis Mumford. Historian, city planner, social commentator/philosopher, and writer, Mumford was one of the first to warn against the environmental dangers associated with population growth and expanding cities. Witnessing the rise of machine technocracy in modern society, Mumford saw a civilization overrun by what he termed the "megamachine"—an artificial creation that oppressed people, making them passive and purposeless. He was critical of Western civilizations' hubris in adopting the belief that the natural world could be controlled through science and technology and feared that succumbing to this myth would lead to catastrophe. Mumford begged the question, "What is the use of conquering nature if we fall prey to nature in the form of unbridled men?" (Mumford 1934). Our salvation, he proposed, lies in abandoning the "megamachine" for technology suited to the systems of nature and what he believed to be a more purposeful life.

This chapter charts the progression of the rise of early America's environmental consciousness through the passionate prose of some of its most noteworthy pioneers. Leaders and activists, these men were bricklayers of the foundation upon which the modern environmental movement now stands—reshaping perceptions, shifting paradigms, and inspiring action among numerous generations. Although influenced by European and Asian ideas, the modern environmental movement was essentially made in America—a response to witnessing the destructive transformation of a country previously unspoiled by Western civilization. Contrary to long-held belief, natural resources were not limitless after all (even in bountiful America), and heedless environmental destruction would no longer be deemed acceptable. Collectively, the work of these men calls our attention to America's shortsighted approach of expansion and consumption, and the false delineations made between humans and their environment—the health of each reflecting that of the other.

Environmentalism emerged a new concept in the nineteenth century, adhering to none of America's existing political categories. Nonetheless, the movement could be regarded as rather elitist—consisting primarily of wealthy, white, male Protestants. While women played a vital role at many levels, they were largely excluded from leadership positions for some time. Considered a venture of dedicated amateurs, the early environmental movement began what would become a tenacious campaign. However, amateurism proved inadequate for meeting the rising challenges posed by technology, urbanization, economic expansion, population growth, and the global market economy. In the next century, these challenges would threaten to overwhelm the movement, while for the first time in history, technology accorded humans the power to make the world uninhabitable for all species, including their own.

References

1. Emerson, Ralph Waldo. "The Over-Soul." in *Essays: First Series*. 1841.

2. ———."Nature." in *Nature; Addresses and Lectures*. 1849.

3. Krech, Shepard. *The Ecological Indian: Myth and History*. New York: W.W. Norton, 1999.

4. Kroll-Smith, Steve and H. Hugh Floyd. *Bodies in protest: Environmental Illness and the Struggle Over Medical Knowledge*. New York: NYU Press, 2000.

5. LaDuke, Winona. *All Our Relations: Native Struggles for Land and Life*. Cambridge, Massachusetts: South End Press, 1999.

6. Leopold, Aldo. *A Sand County Almanac*. New York: Oxford University Press, 1949.

7. Lopez, Barry. *Of Wolves and Men*. New York: Simon and Schuster, 1978.

8. Macdonald, Augustin. "Decline of the Sea Otter." In *Green Versus Gold: Sources in California's Environmental History*, edited by C. Merchant. Washington, DC: Island Press, 1998.

9. Marsh, George Perkins. *Man and Nature: Or, Physical Geography as Modified by Human Action*. New York: Charles Scribner, 1864.

10. Muir, John. "The Wild Parks and Forest Reservations of the West." In *Our National Parks*. San Francisco: Sierra Club, 1901.

11. ———."Hetch Hetchy Valley." In *The Yosemite*. New York: The Century Co., 1912.

12. ———."Through Florida Swamps and Forests." In *A Thousand-Mile Walk to the Gulf*, edited by W. F. Badè. Boston and New York: Houghton Mifflin Company, 1916.

13. Mumford, Lewis. *Technics and Civilization*. Chicago: University of Chicago Press, 1934.

14. Nash, Roderick Frazier. *The Rights of Nature: A History of Environmental Ethics*. Madison: University of Wisconsin Press, 1989.

15. O'Brien, Dan. *Buffalo for the Broken Heart: Restoring Life to a Black Hills Ranch*. New York: Random House, 2001.

16. Pinchot, Gifford. *The Fight for Conservation*. New York: Doubleday, Page & Company, 1920.

17. Scully, Matthew. *Dominion: The Power of Man, the Suffering of Animals, and the Call to Mercy*. New York: St. Martin's Press, 2002.

18. Thoreau, Henry David. "Where I Lived, and What I Lived For." In *Walden or Life in the Woods*. State College: Pennsylvania State University, 1854.

19. ———.*Walking*. 1862.

Nature
Chapter 1

BY RALPH WALDO EMERSON

To go into solitude, a man needs to retire as much from his chamber as from society. I am not solitary whilst I read and write, though nobody is with me. But if a man would be alone, let him look at the stars. The rays that come from those heavenly worlds, will separate between him and what he touches. One might think the atmosphere was made transparent with this design, to give man, in the heavenly bodies, the perpetual presence of the sublime. Seen in the streets of cities, how great they are! If the stars should appear one night in a thousand years, how would men believe and adore; and preserve for many generations the remembrance of the city of God which had been shown! But every night come out these envoys of beauty, and light the universe with their admonishing smile.

The stars awaken a certain reverence, because though always present, they are inaccessible; but all natural objects make a kindred impression, when the mind is open to their influence. Nature never wears a mean appearance. Neither does the wisest man extort her secret, and lose his curiosity by finding out all her perfection. Nature never became a toy to a wise spirit. The flowers, the animals, the mountains, reflected the wisdom of his best hour, as much as they had delighted the simplicity of his childhood. When we speak of nature in this manner, we have a distinct but most poetical sense in the mind. We mean the integrity of impression made by manifold natural objects. It is this which distinguishes the stick of timber of the wood-cutter, from the tree of the poet. The charming landscape which I saw this morning, is indubitably made up of some twenty or thirty farms. Miller owns this field, Locke that, and Manning the woodland beyond. But none of them owns the landscape. There is a property in the horizon which no man has but he whose eye can integrate all the parts, that is, the poet. This is the best part of these men's farms, yet to this their warranty-deeds give no title. To speak truly, few adult persons can see nature. Most persons do not see the sun. At least they have a very superficial seeing. The sun illuminates only the eye of the man, but shines into the eye and the heart of the child. The lover of nature is he whose inward and outward senses are still truly adjusted to each other; who has retained the spirit of infancy even into the era of manhood. His intercourse with heaven and earth, becomes part of his daily food. In the presence of nature, a wild delight runs through the man, in spite of real sorrows. Nature says,—he is my creature, and maugre all his impertinent griefs, he shall be glad with me. Not the sun or the summer alone, but every hour and season yields its tribute of delight; for every hour and change corresponds to and authorizes a different state of the mind, from breathless noon to grimmest midnight. Nature is a setting that fits equally well a comic or a mourning piece. In good health, the air is a cordial of incredible virtue. Crossing a bare common, in snow puddles, at twilight, under a clouded sky, without having in my thoughts any occurrence of special good fortune, I have enjoyed a perfect exhilaration. I am glad to the brink of fear. In the woods too, a man casts off his years, as the snake his slough, and at what period soever of life, is always a child. In the woods, is perpetual youth. Within these plantations of God, a decorum and sanctity reign, a perennial festival is dressed, and the guest sees not how he should tire of them in a thousand years. In the woods, we return to reason and faith. There I feel that nothing can befall me in life,—no disgrace, no calamity, (leaving me my eyes,) which nature cannot repair. Standing on the bare ground,—my head bathed by the blithe air, and uplifted into infinite space,—all mean egotism vanishes. I become a transparent eye-ball; I am nothing; I see all; the currents of the Universal Being circulate through me; I am part or particle of God. The name of the nearest friend sounds then foreign and accidental: to be brothers, to be acquaintances,—master or servant, is then a trifle and a disturbance. I am the lover of uncontained and immortal beauty. In the wilderness, I find something more dear and connate than in streets or villages. In the tranquil landscape, and especially in the distant line of the horizon, man beholds somewhat as beautiful as his own nature.

The greatest delight which the fields and woods minister, is the suggestion of an occult relation between man and the vegetable. I am not alone and unacknowledged. They nod to me, and I to them. The waving of the boughs in the storm, is new to me and old. It takes me by surprise, and yet is not unknown. Its effect is like that of a higher thought or a better emotion coming over me, when I deemed I was thinking justly or doing right.

Yet it is certain that the power to produce this delight, does not reside in nature, but in man, or in a harmony of both. It is necessary to use these pleasures with great temperance. For, nature is not always tricked in holiday attire, but the same scene which yesterday breathed perfume and glittered as for the frolic of the nymphs, is overspread with melancholy today. Nature always wears the colors of the spirit. To a man laboring under calamity, the heat of his own fire hath sadness in it. Then, there is a kind of contempt of the landscape felt by him who has just lost by death a dear friend. The sky is less grand as it shuts down over less worth in the population.

Excerpt from "Where I Lived, and What I Lived For,"
Walden, or Life in the Woods

BY HENRY DAVID THOREAU

I went to the woods because I wished to live deliberately, to front only the essential facts of life, and see if I could not learn what it had to teach, and not, when I came to die, discover that I had not lived. I did not wish to live what was not life, living is so dear; nor did I wish to practise resignation, unless it was quite necessary. I wanted to live deep and suck out all the marrow of life, to live so sturdily and Spartan—like as to put to rout all that was not life, to cut a broad swath and shave close, to drive life into a corner, and reduce it to its lowest terms, and, if it proved to be mean, why then to get the whole and genuine meanness of it, and publish its meanness to the world; or if it were sublime, to know it by experience, and be able to give a true account of it in my next excursion. For most men, it appears to me, are in a strange uncertainty about it, whether it is of the devil or of God, and have somewhat hastily concluded that it is the chief end of man here to "glorify God and enjoy him forever."

Still we live meanly, like ants; though the fable tells us that we were long ago changed into men; like pygmies we fight with cranes; it is error upon error, and clout upon clout, and our best virtue has for its occasion a superfluous and evitable wretchedness. Our life is frittered away by detail. An honest man has hardly need to count more than his ten fingers, or in extreme cases he may add his ten toes, and lump the rest. Simplicity, simplicity, simplicity! I say, let your affairs be as two or three, and not a hundred or a thousand; instead of a million count half a dozen, and keep your accounts on your thumb-nail. In the midst of this chopping sea of civilized life, such are the clouds and storms and quicksands and thousand-and one items to be allowed for, that a man has to live, if he would not founder and go to the bottom and not make his port at all, by dead reckoning, and he must be a great calculator indeed who succeeds. Simplify, simplify. Instead of three meals a day, if it be necessary eat but one; instead of a hundred dishes, five; and reduce other things in proportion. Our life is like a German Confederacy, made up of petty states, with its boundary forever fluctuating, so that even a German cannot tell you how it is bounded at any moment. The nation itself, with all its so-called internal improvements, which, by the way are all external and superficial, is just such an unwieldy and overgrown establishment, cluttered with furniture and tripped up by its own traps, ruined by luxury and heedless expense, by want of calculation and a worthy aim, as the million households in the land; and the only cure for it, as for them, is in a rigid economy, a stern and more than Spartan simplicity of life and elevation of purpose. It lives too fast.

Men think that it is essential that the Nation have commerce, and export ice, and talk through a telegraph, and ride thirty miles an hour, without a doubt, whether they do or not; but whether we should live like baboons or like men, is a little uncertain.

If we do not get out sleepers, and forge rails, and devote days and nights to the work, but go to tinkering upon our lives to improve them, who will build railroads? And if railroads are not built, how shall we get to heaven in season? But if we stay at home and mind our business, who will want railroads? We do not ride on the railroad; it rides upon us. Did you ever think what those sleepers are that underlie the railroad? Each one is a man, an Irishman, or a Yankee man. The rails are laid on them, and they are covered with sand, and the cars run smoothly over them. They are sound sleepers, I assure you. And every few years a new lot is laid down and run over; so that, if some have the pleasure of riding on a rail, others have the misfortune to be ridden upon. And when they run over a man that is walking in his sleep, a supernumerary sleeper in the wrong position, and wake him up, they suddenly stop the cars, and make a hue and cry about it, as if this were an exception. I am glad to know that it takes a gang of men for every five miles to keep the sleepers down and level in their beds as it is, for this is a sign that they may sometime get up again.

Why should we live with such hurry and waste of life? We are determined to be starved before we are hungry. Men say that a stitch in time saves nine, and so they take a thousand stitches today to save nine tomorrow. As for work, we haven't any of any consequence. We have the Saint Vitus' dance, and cannot possibly keep our heads still. If I should only give a few pulls at the parish bell-rope, as for a fire, that is, without setting the bell, there is hardly a man on his farm in the outskirts of Concord, notwithstanding that press of engagements which was his excuse so many times this morning, nor a boy, nor a woman, I might almost say, but would forsake all and follow that sound, not mainly to save property from the flames, but, if we will confess the truth, much more to see it burn, since burn it must, and we, be it known, did not set it on fire—or to see it put out, and have a hand in it, if that is done as handsomely; yes, even if it were the parish church itself. Hardly a man takes a halfhour's nap after dinner, but when he wakes he holds up his head and asks, "What's the news?" as if the rest of mankind had stood his sentinels. Some give directions to be waked every half-hour, doubt less for no other purpose; and then, to pay for it, they tell what they have dreamed. After a night's sleep the news is as indispensable as the breakfast. "Pray tell me anything new that has happened to a man anywhere on this globe"—and he reads it over his coffee and rolls, that a man has had his eyes gouged out this morning on the Wachito River; never dreaming the while that he lives in the dark unfathomed mammoth cave of this world, and has but the rudiment of an eye himself.

For my part, I could easily do without the post-office. I think that there are very few important communications made through it. To speak critically, I never received more than one or two letters in my life—I wrote this some years ago- that were worth the postage. The penny-post is, commonly, an institution through which you seriously offer a man that penny for his thoughts which is so often safely offered in jest. And I am sure that I never read any memorable news in a newspaper. If we read of one man robbed, or murdered, or killed by accident, or one house burned, or one vessel wrecked, or one steamboat blown up, or one cow run over on the Western Railroad, or one mad dog killed, or one lot of grasshoppers in the winter—we never need read of another. One is enough. If you are acquainted with the principle, what do you care for a myriad instances and applications? To a philosopher all news, as it is called, is gossip, and they who edit and read it are old women over their tea. Yet not a few are greedy after this gossip. There was such a rush, as

I hear, the other day at one of the offices to learn the foreign news by the last arrival, that several large squares of plate glass belonging to the establishment were broken by the pressure—news which I seriously think a ready wit might write a twelve-month, or twelve years, beforehand with sufficient accuracy. As for Spain, for instance, if you know how to throw in Don Carlos and the Infanta, and Don Pedro and Seville and Granada, from time to time in the right proportions—they may have changed the names a little since I saw the papers—and serve up a bull-fight when other entertainments fail, it will be true to the letter, and give us as good an idea of the exact state or ruin of things in Spain as the most succinct and lucid reports under this head in the newspapers: and as for England, almost the last significant scrap of news from that quarter was the revolution of 1649; and if you have learned the history of her crops for an average year, you never need attend to that thing again, unless your speculations are of a merely pecuniary character. If one may judge who rarely looks into the newspapers, nothing new does ever happen in foreign parts, a French revolution not excepted.

What news! how much more important to know what that is which was never old! "Kieou-he-yu (great dignitary of the state of Wei) sent a man to Khoung-tseu to know his news. Khoung-tseu caused the messenger to be seated near him, and questioned him in these terms: What is your master doing? The messenger answered with respect: My master desires to diminish the number of his faults, but he cannot come to the end of them. The messenger being gone, the philosopher remarked: What a worthy messenger! What a worthy messenger!" The preacher, instead of vexing the ears of drowsy farmers on their day of rest at the end of the weeknfor Sunday is the fit conclusion of an illspent week, and not the fresh and brave beginning of a new one-with this one other draggle-tail of a sermon, should shout with thundering voice, "Pause! Avast! Why so seeming fast, but deadly slow?"

Shams and delusions are esteemed for soundest truths, while reality is fabulous. If men would steadily observe realities only, and not allow themselves to be deluded, life, to compare it with such things as we know, would be like a fairy tale and the Arabian Nights' Entertainments. If we respected only what is inevitable and has a right to be, music and poetry would resound along the streets. When we are unhurried and wise, we perceive that only great and worthy things have any permanent and absolute existence, that petty fears and petty pleasures are but the shadow of the reality. This is always exhilarating and sublime. By closing the eyes and slumbering, and consenting to be deceived by shows, men establish and confirm their daily life of routine and habit everywhere, which still is built on purely illusory foundations. Children, who play life, discern its true law and relations more clearly than men, who fail to live it worthily, but who think that they are wiser by experience, that is, by failure. I have read in a Hindoo book, that "there was a king's son, who, being expelled in infancy from his native city, was brought up by a forester, and, growing up to maturity in that state, imagined himself to belong to the barbarous race with which he lived. One of his father's ministers having discovered him, revealed to him what he was, and the misconception of his character was removed, and he knew himself to be a prince. So soul," continues the Hindoo philosopher, "from the circumstances in which it is placed, mistakes its own character, until the truth is revealed to it by some holy teacher, and then it knows itself to be Brahme." I perceive that we inhabitants of New England live this mean life that we do because our vision does not penetrate the surface of things. We think that that is which appears to be. If a man should walk through this town and see only the reality, where, think you, would the "Milldam" go to? If he should give us an account of the realities he beheld there, we should not recognize the place in his description. Look at a meeting-house, or a court-house, or a jail, or a shop, or a dwelling-house, and say what that thing really is before a true gaze, and they would all go to pieces in your account of them. Men esteem truth remote, in the outskirts of the system, behind the farthest star, before Adam and after the last man. In eternity there is indeed something true and sublime. But all these times and places and occasions are now and here. God himself culminates in the present moment, and will never be more divine in the lapse of all the ages. And we are enabled to apprehend at all what is sublime and noble only by the perpetual instilling and drenching of the reality that surrounds us. The universe constantly and obediently answers to our conceptions; whether we travel fast or slow, the track is laid for us. Let us spend our lives in conceiving then. The poet or the artist never yet had so fair and noble a design but some of his posterity at least could accomplish it.

Let us spend one day as deliberately as Nature, and not be thrown off the track by every nutshell and mosquito's wing that falls on the rails. Let us rise early and fast, or break fast, gently and without perturbation; let company come and let company go, let the bells ring and the children cry—determined to make a day of it. Why should we knock under and go with the stream? Let us not be upset and overwhelmed in that terrible rapid and whirlpool called a dinner, situated in the meridian shallows. Weather this danger and you are safe, for the rest of the way is down hill. With unrelaxed nerves, with morning vigor, sail by it, looking another way, tied to the mast like Ulysses. If the engine whistles, let it whistle till it is hoarse for its pains. If the bell rings, why should we run? We will consider what kind of music they are like. Let us settle ourselves, and work and wedge our feet downward through the mud and slush of opinion, and prejudice, and tradition, and delusion, and appearance, that alluvion which covers the globe, through Paris and London, through New York and Boston and Concord, through Church and State, through poetry and philosophy and religion, till we come to a hard bottom and rocks in place, which we can call reality, and say, This is, and no mistake; and then begin, having a point d'appui, below freshet and frost and fire, a place where you might found a wall or a state, or set a lamp-post safely, or perhaps a gauge, not a Nilometer, but a Realometer, that future ages might know how deep a freshet of shams and appearances had gathered from time to time. If you stand right fronting and face to face to a fact, you will see the sun glimmer on both its surfaces, as if it were a cimeter, and feel its sweet edge dividing you through the heart and marrow, and so you will happily conclude your mortal career. Be it life or death, we crave only reality. If we are really dying, let us hear the rattle in our throats and feel cold in the extremities; if we are alive, let us go about our business.

Time is but the stream I go a-fishing in. I drink at it; but while I drink I see the sandy bottom and detect how shallow it is. Its thin current slides away, but eternity remains. I would drink deeper; fish in the sky, whose bottom is pebbly with stars. I cannot count one. I know not the first letter of the alphabet. I have always been regretting that I was not as wise as the day I was born. The intellect is a cleaver; it discerns and rifts its way into the secret of things. I do not wish to be any more busy with my hands than is necessary. My head is hands and feet. I feel all my best faculties concentrated in it. My instinct tells me that my head is an organ for burrowing, as some creatures use their snout and fore paws, and with it I would mine and burrow my way through these hills. I think that the richest vein is somewhere hereabouts; so by the divining-rod and thin rising vapors I judge; and here I will begin to mine.

Excerpt from Chapter 1
Man and Nature, or Physical Geography as Modified by Human Action

BY GEORGE PERKINS MARSH

It has been maintained by authorities as high as any known to modern science, that the action of man upon nature, though greater in *degree*, does not differ in *kind*, from that of wild animals. It appears to me to differ in essential character, because, though it is often followed by unforeseen and undesired results, yet it is nevertheless guided by a self-conscious and intelligent will aiming as often at secondary and remote as at immediate objects. The wild animal, on the other hand, acts instinctively, and, so far as we are able to perceive, always with a view to single and direct purposes. The backwoodsman and the beaver alike fell trees; the man that he may convert the forest into an olive grove that will mature its fruit only for a succeeding generation, the beaver that he may feed upon their bark or use them in the construction of his habitation. Human differs from brute action, too, in its influence upon the material world, because it is not controlled by natural compensations and balances. Natural arrangements, once disturbed by man, are not restored until he retires from the field, and leaves free scope to spontaneous recuperative energies; the wounds he inflicts upon the material creation are not healed until he withdraws the arm that gave the blow. On the other hand, I am not aware of any evidence that wild animals have ever destroyed the smallest forest, extirpated any organic species, or modified its natural character, occasioned any permanent change of terrestrial surface, or produced any disturbance of physical conditions which nature has not, of herself, repaired without the expulsion of the animal that had caused it.*

The form of geographical surface, and very probably the climate of a given country, depend much on the character of the vegetable life belonging to it. Man has, by domestication, greatly changed the habits and properties of the plants he rears; he has, by voluntary selection, immensely modified the forms and qualities of the animated creatures that serve him ; and he has, at the same time, completely rooted out many forms of both vegetable and animal being.† What is there, in the influence of brute life, that corresponds to this ? We have no reason to believe that in that portion of the American continent which, though peopled by many tribes of quadruped and fowl, remained

* There is a possible—but only a possible—exception in the case of the American bison. See note on that subject in chap. iii, *post*.

† Whatever may be thought of the modification of organic species by natural selection, there is certainly no evidence that animals have exerted upon any form of life an influence analogous to that of domestication upon plants, quadrupeds, and birds reared artificially by man; and this is as true of unforeseen as of purposely effected improvements accomplished by voluntary selection of breeding animals.

uninhabited by man, or only thinly occupied by purely savage tribes, any sensible geographical change had occurred within twenty centuries before the epoch of discovery and colonization, while, during the same period, man had changed millions of square miles, in the fairest and most fertile regions of the Old World, into the barrenest deserts.

The ravages committed by man subvert the relations and destroy the balance which nature had established between her organized and her inorganic creations; and she avenges herself upon the intruder, by letting loose upon her defaced provinces destructive energies hitherto kept in check by organic forces destined to be his best auxiliaries, but which he has unwisely dispersed and driven from the field of action. When the forest is gone, the great reservoir of moisture stored up in its vegetable mould is evaporated, and returns only in deluges of rain to wash away the parched dust into which that mould has been converted. The well-wooded and humid hills are turned to ridges of dry rock, which encumbers the low grounds and chokes the watercourses with its debris, and— except in countries favored with an equable distribution of rain through the seasons, and a moderate and regular inclination of surface—the whole earth, unless rescued by human art from the physical degradation to which it tends, becomes an assemblage of bald mountains, of barren, turfless hills, and of swampy and malarious plains. There are parts of Asia Minor, of Northern Africa, of Greece, and even of Alpine Europe, where the operation of causes set in action by man has brought the face of the earth to a desolation almost as complete as that of the moon ; and though, within that brief space of time which we call " the historical period," they are known to have been covered with luxuriant woods, verdant pastures, and fertile meadows, they are now too far deteriorated to be reclaimable by man, nor can they become again fitted for human use, except through great geological changes, or other mysterious influences or agencies of which we have no present knowledge, and over which we have no prospective control. The earth is fast becoming an unfit home for its noblest inhabitant, and another era of equal human crime and human improvidence, and of like duration with that through which traces of that crime and that improvidence extend, would reduce it to such a condition of impoverished productiveness, of shattered surface, of climatic excess, as to threaten the depravation, barbarism, and perhaps even extinction of the species.*

George Perkins Marsh, "Chapter 1," Man and Nature, or Physical Geography as Modified by Human Action, pp. 41-44. Copyright in the Public Domain.

Excerpt from Chapter 7
The Fight for Conservation

BY GIFFORD PINCHOT

The central thing for which Conservation stands is to make this country the best possible place to live in, both for us and for our descendants. It stands against the waste of the natural resources which cannot be renewed, such as coal and iron; it stands for the perpetuation of the resources which can be renewed, such as the food-producing soils and the forests; and most of all it stands for an equal opportunity for every American citizen to get his fair share of benefit from these resources, both now and hereafter.

Conservation stands for the same kind of practical common-sense management of this country by the people that every business man stands for in the handling of his own business. It believes in prudence and foresight instead of reckless blindness; it holds that resources now public property should not become the basis for oppressive private monopoly; and it demands the complete and orderly development of all our resources for the benefit of all the people, instead of the partial exploitation of them for the benefit of a few. It recognizes fully the right of the present generation to use what it needs and all it needs of the natural resources now available, but it recognizes equally our obligation so to use what we need that our descendants shall not be deprived of what they need.

Conservation has much to do with the welfare of the average man of to-day. It proposes to secure a continuous and abundant supply of the necessaries of life, which means a reasonable cost of living and business stability. It advocates fairness in the distribution of thebenefits which flow from the natural resources. It will matter very little to the average citizen, when scarcity comes and prices rise, whether he can not get what he needs because there is none left or because he can not afford to pay for it. In both cases the essential fact is that he can not get what he needs. Conservation holds that it is about as important to see that the people in general get the benefit of our natural resources as to see that there shall be natural resources left.

Conservation is the most democratic movement this country has known for a generation. It holds that the people have not only the right, but the duty to control the use of the natural resources, which are the great sources of prosperity. And it regards the absorption of these resources by the special interests, unless their operations are under effective public control, as a moral wrong. Conservation is the application of common-sense to the common problems for the common good, and I believe it stands nearer to the desires, aspirations, and purposes of the average man than any other policy now before the American people.

...It must be clear to any man who has followed the development of the Conservation idea that no other policy now before the American people is so thoroughly democratic in its essence and in its tendencies as the Conservation policy. It asserts that the people have the right and the duty, and that it is their duty no less than their right, to protect themselves against the uncontrolled monopoly of the natural resources which yield the necessaries of life. We are beginning to realize that the Conservation question is a question of right and wrong, as any question must be which may involve the differences between prosperity and poverty, health and sickness, ignorance and education, well-being and misery, to hundreds of thousands of families. Seen from the point of view of human welfare and human progress, questions which begin as purely economic often end as moral issues. Conservation is a moral issue because it involves the rights and the duties of our people—their rights to prosperity and happiness, and their duties to themselves, to their descendants, and to the whole future progress and welfare of this Nation.

Gifford Pinchot, "Chapter VII," The Fight for Conservation. Copyright in the Public Domain.

Excerpt from "The Wild Parks and Forest Reservations of the West"
Our National Parks

BY JOHN MUIR

"Keep not standing fix'd and rooted,
Briskly venture, briskly roam;
Head and hand, where'er thou foot it,
And stout heart are still at home.
In each land the sun does visit
We are gay, whate'er betide:
To give room for wandering is it
That the world was made so wide."

The tendency nowadays to wander in wildernesses is delightful to see. Thousands of tired, nerve-shaken, over-civilized people are beginning to find out that going to the mountains is going home; that wildness is a necessity; and that mountain parks and reservations are useful not only as fountains of timber and irrigating rivers, but as fountains of life. Awakening from the stupefying effects of the vice of over-industry and the deadly apathy of luxury, they are trying as best they can to mix and enrich their own little ongoings with those of Nature, and to get rid of rust and disease. Briskly venturing and roaming, some are washing off sins and cobweb cares of the devil's spinning in all-day storms on mountains; sauntering in rosiny pinewoods or in gentian meadows, brushing through chaparral, bending down and parting sweet, flowery sprays; tracing rivers to their sources, getting in touch with the nerves of Mother Earth; jumping from rock to rock, feeling the life of them, learning the songs of them, panting in whole-souled exercise, and rejoicing in deep, long-drawn breaths of pure wildness. This is fine and natural and full of promise. So also is the growing interest in the care and preservation of forests and wild places in general, and in the half wild parks and gardens of towns. Even the scenery habit in its most artificial forms, mixed with spectacles, silliness, and kodaks; its devotees arrayed more gorgeously than scarlet tanagers, frightening the wild game with red umbrellas,—even this is encouraging, and may well be regarded as a hopeful sign of the times.

All the Western mountains are still rich in wildness, and by means of good roads are being brought nearer civilization every year. To the sane and free it will hardly seem necessary to cross the continent in search of wild beauty, however easy the way, for they find it in abundance wherever they chance to be. Like Thoreau they see forests in orchards and patches of huckleberry brush, and oceans in ponds and drops of dew. Few in these hot, dim, strenuous times are quite sane or free; choked with care like clocks full of dust, laboriously doing so much good and making so much money,—or so little,—they are no longer good for themselves.

When, like a merchant taking a list of his goods, we take stock of our wildness, we are glad to see how much of even the most destructible kind is still unspoiled. Looking at our continent as scenery when it was all wild, lying between beautiful seas, the starry sky above it, the starry rocks beneath it, to compare its sides, the East and the West, would be like comparing the sides of a rainbow. But it is no longer equally beautiful. The rainbows of to-day are, I suppose, as bright as those that first spanned the sky; and some of our landscapes are growing more beautiful from year to year, notwithstanding the clearing, trampling work of civilization. New plants and animals are enriching woods and gardens, and many landscapes wholly new, with divine sculpture and architecture, are just now coming to the light of day as the mantling folds of creative glaciers are being withdrawn, and life in a thousand cheerful, beautiful forms is pushing into them, and new-born rivers are beginning to sing and shine in them. The old rivers, too, are growing longer, like healthy trees, gaining new branches and lakes as the residual glaciers at their highest sources on the mountains recede, while the rootlike branches in the flat deltas are at the same time spreading farther and wider into the seas and making new lands.

Under the control of the vast mysterious forces of the interior of the earth all the continents and islands are slowly rising or sinking. Most of the mountains are diminishing in size under the wearing action of the weather, though a few are increasing in height and girth, especially the volcanic ones, as fresh floods of molten rocks are piled on their summits and spread in successive layers, like the wood-rings of trees, on their sides. New mountains, also, are being created from time to time as islands in lakes and seas, or as subordinate cones on the slopes of old ones, thus in some measure balancing the waste of old beauty with new. Man, too, is making many far-reaching changes. This most influential half animal, half angel is rapidly multiplying and spreading, cover-ing the seas and lakes with ships, the land with huts, hotels, cathedrals, and clustered city shops and homes, so that soon, it would seem, we may have to go farther than Nansen to find a good sound solitude. None of Nature's landscape are ugly so long as they are wild; and much, we can say comfortingly, must always be in great part wild, particularly the sea and the sky, the floods of light from the stars, and the warm, unspoilable heart of the earth, infinitely beautiful, though only dimly visible to the eye of imagination. The geysers, too, spouting from the hot underworld; the steady, long-lasting glaciers on the mountains, obedient only to the sun; Yosemite domes and the tremendous grandeur of rocky cañons and mountains in general,—these must always be wild, for man can change them and mar them hardly more than can the butterflies that hover above them. But the continent's outer beauty is fast passing away, especially the plant part of it, the most destructible and most universally charming of all.

Excerpt from "Thinking Like a Mountain"
A Sand County Almanac

BY ALDO LEOPOLD

A deep chesty bawl echoes from rimrock to rimrock, rolls down the mountain, and fades into the far blackness of the uight. It is an outburst of wild defiant sorrow, and of contempt for all the adversities of the world.

Every living thing (and perhaps many a dead one as well) pays heed to that call. To the deer it is a reminder of the way of all flesh, to the pine a forecast of midnight scuffles and of blood upon the snow, to the coyote a promise of gleanings to come, to the cowman a threat of red ink at the bank, to the hunter a challenge of fang against bullet. Yet behind these obvious and immediate hopes and fears there lies a deeper meaning, known only to the mountain itself. Only the mountain has lived long enough to listen objectively to the howl of a wolf.

Those unable to decipher the hidden meaning know nevertheless that it is there, for it is felt in all wolf country, and distinguishes that country from all other land. It tingles in the spine of all who hear wolves by night, or who scan their tracks by day. Even without sight or sound of wolf, it is implicit in a hundred small events: the midnight whinny of a pack horse, the rattle of rolling rocks, the bound of a fleeing deer, the way shadows lie under the spruces. Only the ineducable tyro can fail to sense the presence or absence of wolves, or the fact that mountains have a secret opinion about them.

My own conviction on this score dates from the day I saw a wolf die. We were eating lunch on a high rimrock, at the foot of which a turbulent river elbowed its way. We saw what we thought was a doe fording the torrent, her breast awash in white water. When she climbed the bank toward us and shook out her tail, we realized our error: it was a wolf. A half-dozen others, evidently grown pups, sprang from the willows and all joined in a welcoming melee of wagging tails and playful maulings. What was literally a pile of wolves writhed and tumbled in the center of an open flat at the foot of our rimrock.

In those days we had never heard of passing up a chance to kill a wolf. In a second we were pumping lead into the pack, but with more excitement than accuracy: how to aim a steep downhill shot is always confusing. When our rifles were empty, the old wolf was down, and a pup was dragging a leg into impassable slide-rocks.

We reached the old wolf in time to watch a fierce green fire dying in her eyes. I realized then, and have known ever since, that there was something new to me in those eyes- something known only to her and to the mountain. I was young then, and full of trigger-itch; I thought that because fewer wolves meant more deer, that no wolves would mean hunters' paradise. But after seeing the green fire die, I sensed that neither the wolf nor the mountain agreed with such a view.

Since then I have lived to see state after state extirpate its wolves. I have watched the face of many a newly wolfless mountain, and seen the south-facing slopes wrinkle with a maze of new deer trails. I have seen every edible bush and seedling browsed, first to anaemic desuetude, and then to death. I have seen every edible tree defoliated to the height of a saddlehorn. Such a mountain looks as if someone had given God a new pruning shears, and forbidden Him all other exercise. In the end the starved bones of the hoped- for deer herd, dead of its own too-much, bleach with the bones of the dead sage, or molder under the high-lined junipers.

I now suspect that just as a deer herd lives in mortal fear of its wolves, so does a mountain live in mortal fear of its deer. And perhaps with better cause, for while a buck pulled down by wolves can be replaced in two or three years, a range pulled down by too many deer may fail of replacement in as many decades.

So also with cows. The cowman who cleans his range of wolves does not realize that he is taking over the wolf's job of trimming the herd to fit the range. He has not learned to think like a mountain. Hence we have dustbowls, and rivers washing the future into the sea.

We all strive for safety, prosperity, comfort, long life, and dullness. The deer strives with his supple legs, the cowman with trap and poison, the statesman with pen, the most of us with machines, votes, and dollars, but it all comes to the same thing: peace in our time. A measure of success in this is all well enough, and perhaps is a requisite to objective thinking, but too much safety seems to yield only danger in the long run. Perhaps this is behind Thoreau's dictum: In wildness is the salvation of the world. Perhaps this is the hidden meaning in the howl of the wolf, long known among mountains, but seldom perceived among men.

Aldo Leopold, "Thinking Like a Mountain," A Sand County Almanac, pp. 129-133. Copyright © 1949 by Oxford University Press. Reprinted with permission.

Excerpt from "The Land Ethic"
A Sand County Almanac

BY ALDO LEOPOLD

When god-like Odysseus returned from the wars in Troy, he hanged all on one rope a dozen slave-girls of his household whom he suspected of misbehavior during his absence.

This hanging involved no question of propriety. The girls were property. The disposal of property was then, as now, a matter of expediency, not of right and wrong. Concepts of right and wrong were not lacking from Odysseus' Greece: witness the fidelity of his wife through the long years before at last his black-prowed galleys clove the wine-dark seas for home. The ethical structure of that day covered wives, but had not yet been extended to human chattels. During the three thousand years which have since elapsed, ethical criteria have been extended to many fields of conduct, with corresponding shrinkages in those judged by expediency only.

The Ethical Sequence

This extension of ethics, so far studied only by philosophers, is actually a process in ecological evolution. Its sequences may be described in ecological as well as in philosophical terms. An ethic, ecologically, is a limitation on freedom of action in the struggle for existence. An ethic, philosophically, is a differentiation of social from anti-social conduct. These are two definitions of one thing. The thing has its origin in the tendency of interdependent individuals or groups to evolve modes of co-operation. The ecologist calls these symbioses. Politics and economics are advanced symbioses in which the original free-for-all competition has been replaced, in part, by co-operative mechanisms with an ethical content.

The complexity of co-operative mechanisms has increased with population density, and with the efficiency of tools. It was simpler, for example, to define the anti-social uses of sticks and stones in the days of the mastodons than of bullets and billboards in the age of motors.

The first ethics dealt with the relation between individuals; the Mosaic Decalogue is an example. Later accretions dealt with the relation between the individual and society. The Golden Rule tries to integrate the individual to society; democracy to integrate social organization to the individual.

There is as yet no ethic dealing with man's relation to land and to the animals and plants which grow upon it. Land, like Odysseus' slave-girls, is still property. The land-relation is still strictly economic, entailing privileges but not obligations.

The extension of ethics to this third element in human environment is, if I read the evidence correctly, an evolutionary possibility and an ecological necessity. It is the third step in a sequence. The first two have already been taken. Individual thinkers since the days of Ezekiel and Isaiah have asserted that the despoliation of land is not only inexpedient but wrong. Society, however, has not yet affirmed their belief. I regard the present conservation movement as the embryo of such an affirmation.

An ethic may be regarded as a mode of guidance for meeting ecological situations so new or intricate, or involving such deferred reactions, that the path of social expediency is not discernible to the average individual. Animal instincts are modes of guidance for the individual in meeting such situations. Ethics are possibly a kind of community instinct in-the-making.

The Community Concept

All ethics so far evolved rest upon a single premise: that the individual is a member of a community of interdependent parts. His instincts prompt him to compete for his place in that community, but his ethics prompt him also to co-operate (perhaps in order that there may be a place to compete for).

The land ethic simply enlarges the boundaries of the community to include soils, waters, plants, and animals, or collectively: the land.

This sounds simple: do we not already sing our love for and obligation to the land of the free and the home of the brave? Yes, but just what and whom do we love? Certainly not the soil, which we are sending helter-skelter downriver. Certainly not the waters, which we assume have no function except to turn turbines, float barges, and carry off sewage. Certainly not the plants, of which we exterminate whole communities without batting an eye. Certainly not the animals, of which we have already extirpated many of the largest and most beautiful species. A land ethic of course cannot prevent the alteration, management, and use of these 'resources,' but it does affirm their right to continued existence, and, at least in spots, their continued existence in a natural state. In short, a land ethic changes the role of *Homo sapiens* from conqueror of the land-community to plain member and citizen of it. It implies respect for his fellow-members, and also respect for the community as such.

In human history, we have learned (I hope) that the conqueror role is eventually self-defeating. Why? Because it is implicit in such a role that the conqueror knows, *ex cathedra*, just what makes the community clock tick, and just what and who is valuable, and what and who is worthless, in community life. It always turns out that he knows neither, and this is why his conquests eventually defeat themselves.

In the biotic community, a parallel situation exists. Abraham knew exactly what the land was for: it was to drip milk and honey into Abraham's mouth. At the present moment, the assurance with which we regard this assumption is inverse to the degree of our education.

The ordinary citizen today assumes that science knows what makes the community clock tick; the scientist is equally sure that he does not. He knows that the biotic mechanism is so complex that its workings may never be fully understood.

That man is, in fact, only a member of a biotic team is shown by an ecological interpretation of history. Many historical events, hitherto explained solely in terms of human enterprise, were actually biotic interactions between people and land. The characteristics of the land determined the facts quite as potently as the characteristics of the men who lived on it.

Consider, for example, the settlement of the Mississippi valley. In the years following the Revolution, three groups were contending for its control: the native Indian, the French and English traders, and the American settlers. Historians wonder what would have happened if the English at Detroit had thrown a little more weight into the Indian side of those tipsy scales which decided the outcome of the colonial migration into the cane-lands of Kentucky. It is time now to ponder the fact that the cane-lands, when subjected to the particular mixture of forces represented by the cow, plow, fire, and axe of the pioneer, became bluegrass. What if the plant succession inherent in this dark and bloody ground had, under the impact of these forces, given us some worthless sedge, shrub, or weed? Would Boone and Kenton have held out? Would there have been any overflow into Ohio, Indiana, Illinois, and Missouri? Any Louisiana Pur chase? Any transcontinental union of new states? Any Civil War?

Kentucky was one sentence in the drama of history. We are commonly told what the human actors in this drama tried to do, but we are seldom told that their success, or the lack of it, hung in large degree on the reaction of particular soils to the impact of the particular forces exerted by their occupancy. In the case of Kentucky, we do not even know where the bluegrass came from—whether it is a native species, or a stowaway from Europe.

Contrast the cane-lands with what hindsight tells us about the Southwest, where the pioneers were equally brave, resourceful, and persevering. The impact of occupancy here brought no bluegrass, or other plant fitted to withstand the bumps and buffetings of hard use. This region, when grazed by livestock, reverted through a series of more and more worthless grasses, shrubs, and weeds to a condition of unstable equilibrium. Each recession of plant types bred erosion; each increment to erosion bred a further recession of plants. The result today is a progressive and mutual deterioration, not only of plants and soils, but of the animal community subsisting thereon. The early settlers did not expect this: on the cienegas of New Mexico some even cut ditches to hasten it. So subtle has been its progress that few residents of the region are aware of it. It is quite invisible to the tourist who finds this wrecked landscape colorful and charming (as indeed it is, but it bears scant resemblance to what it was in 1848).

This same landscape was 'developed' once before, but with quite different results. The Pueblo Indians settled the Southwest in pre-Columbian times, but they happened *not* to be equipped with range livestock. Their civilization expired, but not because their land expired.

In India, regions devoid of any sod-forming grass have been settled, apparently without wrecking the land, by the simple expedient of carrying the grass to the cow, rather than vice versa. (Was this the result of some deep wisdom, or was it just good luck? I do not know.)

In short, the plant succession steered the course of history; the pioneer simply demonstrated, for good or ill, what successions inhered in the land. Is history taught in this spirit? It will be, once the concept of land as a community really penetrates our intellectual life.

The Ecological Conscience

Conservation is a state of harmony between men and land. Despite nearly a century of propaganda, conservation still proceeds at a snail's pace; progress still consists largely of letterhead pieties and convention oratory. On the back forty we still slip two steps backward for each forward stride. The usual answer to this dilemma is 'more conservation education.' No one will debate this, but is it certain that only the *volume* of education needs stepping up? Is something lacking in the *content* as well?

It is difficult to give a fair summary of its content in brief form, but, as I understand it, the content is substantially this: obey the law, vote right, join some organizations, and practice what conservation is profitable on your own land; the government will do the rest. Is not this formula too easy to accomplish anything worth-while? It defines no right or wrong, assigns no obligation, calls for no sacrifice, implies no change in the current philosophy of values. In respect of land-use, it urges only enlightened self-interest. Just how far will such education take us? An example will perhaps yield a partial answer.

By 1930 it had become clear to all except the ecologically blind that southwestern Wisconsin's topsoil was slipping seaward. In 1933 the farmers were told that if they would adopt certain remedial practices for five years, the public would donate CCC labor to install them, plus the necessary machinery and materials. The offer was widely accepted, but the practices were widely forgotten when the five-year contract period was up. The farmers continued only those practices that yielded an immediate and visible economic gain for themselves.

This led to the idea that maybe farmers would learn more quickly if they themselves wrote the rules. Accordingly the Wisconsin Legislature in 1937 passed the Soil Conservation District Law. This said to farmers, in effect: *We, the public, will furnish you free technical service and loan you specialized machinery, if you will write your own rules for land-use. Each county may write its own rules, and these will havf the force of law.* Nearly all the counties promptly organized to accept the proffered help, but after a decade of operation, *no county has yet written a single rule.* There has been visible progress in such practices as strip-cropping, pasture renovation, and soil liming, but none in fencing woodlots against grazing, and none in excluding plow and cow from steep slopes. The farmers, in short, have selected those remedial practices which were profitable anyhow, and ignored those which were profitable to the community, but not clearly profitable to themselves.

When one asks why no rules have been written, one is told that the community is not yet ready to support them; education must precede rules. But the education actually in progress makes no mention of obligations to land over and above those dictated by self-interest. The net result is that we have more education but less soil, fewer healthy woods, and as many floods as in 1937.

The puzzling aspect of such situations is that the existence of obligations over and above self-interest is taken for granted in such rural community enterprises as the betterment of roads, schools, churches, and baseball teams. Their existence is not taken for granted, nor as yet seriously discussed, in bettering the behavior of the water that falls on the land, or in the preserving of the beauty or diversity of the farm landscape. Land-use ethics are still governed wholly by economic self-interest, just as social ethics were a century ago.

To sum up: we asked the farmer to do what he conveniently could to save his soil, and he has done just that, and only that. The farmer who clears the woods off a 75 per cent slope, turns his cows into the clearing, and dumps its rainfall, rocks, and soil into the community creek, is still (if otherwise decent) a respected member of society. If he puts lime on his fields and plants his crops on contour, he is still entitled to all the privileges and emoluments of his Soil Conservation District. The District is a beautiful piece of social machinery, but it is coughing along on two cylinders because we have been too timid, and too anxious for quick success, to tell the farmer the true magnitude of his obligations. Obligations have no meaning without conscience, and the problem we face is the extension of the social conscience from people to land.

No important change in ethics was ever accomplished without an internal change in our intellectual emphasis, loyalties, affections, and convictions. The proof that conservation has not yet touched these foundations of conduct lies in the fact that philosophy and religion have not yet heard of it. In our attempt to make conservation easy, we have made it trivial.

Substitutes for a Land Ethic

When the logic of history hungers for bread and we hand out a stone, we are at pains to explain how much the stone resembles bread. I now describe some of the stones which serve in lieu of a land ethic.

One basic weakness in a conservation system based wholly on economic motives is that most members of the land community have no economic value. Wildflowers and songbirds are examples. Of the 22,000 higher plants and animals native to Wisconsin, it is doubtful whether more than 5 per cent can be sold, fed, eaten, or otherwise put to economic use. Yet these creatures are members of the biotic community, and if (as I believe) its stability depends on its integrity, they are entitled to continuance.

When one of these non-economic categories is threatened, and if we happen to love it, we invent subterfuges to give it economic importance. At the beginning of the century songbirds were supposed to be disappearing. Ornithologists jumped to the rescue with some distinctly shaky evidence to the effect that insects would eat us up if birds failed to control them. The evidence had to be economic in order to be valid.

It is painful to read these circumlocutions today. We have no land ethic yet, but we have at least drawn nearer the point of admitting that birds should continue as a matter of biotic right, regardless of the presence or absence of economic advantage to us.

A parallel situation exists in respect of predatory mammals, raptorial birds, and fish-eating birds. Time was when biologists somewhat overworked the evidence that these creatures preserve the health of game by killing weaklings, or that they control rodents for the farmer, or that they prey only on 'worthless' species. Here again, the evidence had to be economic in order to be valid. It is only in recent years that we hear the more honest argument that predators are members of the community, and that no special interest has the right to exterminate them for the sake of a benefit, real or fancied, to itself. Unfortunately this enlightened view is still in the talk stage. In the field the extermination of predators goes merrily on: witness the impending erasure of the timber wolf by fiat of Congress, the Conservation Bureaus, and many state legislatures.

Some species of trees have been 'read out of the party' by economics-minded foresters because they grow too slowly, or have too low a sale value to pay as timber crops: white cedar, tamarack, cypress, beech, and hemlock are examples. In Europe, where forestry is ecologically more advanced, the non-commercial tree species are recognized as members of the native forest community, to be preserved as such, within reason. Moreover some (like beech) have been found to have a valuable function in building up soil fertility. The interdependence of the forest and its constituent tree species, ground flora, and fauna is taken for granted.

Lack of economic value is sometimes a character not only of species or groups, but of entire biotic communities: marshes, bogs, dunes, and 'deserts' are examples. Our formula in such cases is to relegate their conservation to government as refuges, monuments, or parks. The difficulty is that these communities are usually interspersed with more valuable private lands; the government cannot possibly own or control such scattered parcels. The net effect is that we have relegated some of them to ultimate extinction over large areas. If the private owner were ecologically minded, he would be proud to be the custodian of a reasonable proportion of such areas, which add diversity and beauty to his farm and to his community.

In some instances, the assumed lack of profit in these 'waste' areas has proved to be wrong, but only after most of them had been done away with. The present scramble to reflood muskrat marshes is a case in point.

There is a clear tendency in American conservation to relegate to government all necessary jobs that private landowners fail to perform. Government ownership, operation, subsidy, or regulation is now widely prevalent in forestry, range management, soil and watershed management, park and wilderness conservation, fisheries management, and migratory bird management, with more to come. Most of this growth in governmental conservation is proper and logical, some of it is inevitable. That I imply no disapproval of it is implicit in the fact that I have spent most of my life working for it. Nevertheless the question arises: What is the ultimate magnitude of the enterprise? Will the tax base carry its eventual ramifications? At what point will governmental conservation, like the mastodon, become handicapped by its own dimensions? The answer, if there is any, seems to be in a land ethic, or some other force which assigns more obligation to the private landowner.

Industrial landowners and users, especially lumbermen and stockmen, are inclined to wail long and loudly about the extension of government ownership and regulation to land, but (with notable exceptions) they show little disposition to develop the only visible alternative: the voluntary practice of conservation on their own lands.

When the private landowner is asked to perform some unprofitable act for the good of the community, he today assents only with outstretched palm. If the act costs him cash this is fair and proper, but when it costs only forethought, open-mindedness, or time, the issue is at least debatable. The overwhelming growth of land-use subsidies in recent years must be ascribed, in large part, to the government's own agencies for conservation education: the land bureaus, the agricultural colleges, and the extension services. As far as I can detect, no ethical obligation toward land is taught in these institutions.

To sum up: a system of conservation based solely on economic self-interest is hopelessly lopsided. It tends to ignore, and thus eventually to eliminate, many elements in the land community that lack commercial value, but that are (as far as we know) essential to its healthy functioning. It assumes, falsely, I think, that the economic parts of the biotic clock will function without the uneconomic parts. It tends to relegate to government many functions eventually too large, too complex, or too widely dispersed to be performed by government.

An ethical obligation on the part of the private owner is the only visible remedy for these situations.

The Land Pyramid

An ethic to supplement and guide the economic relation to land presupposes the existence of some mental image of land as a biotic mechanism. We can be ethical only in relation to something we can see, feel, understand, love, or otherwise have faith in.

The image commonly employed in conservation education is 'the balance of nature.' For reasons too lengthy to detail here, this figure of speech fails to describe accurately what little we know about the land mechanism. A much truer image is the one employed in ecology: the biotic pyramid. I shall first sketch the pyramid as a symbol of land, and later develop some of its implications in terms of land-use.

Plants absorb energy from the sun. This energy flows through a circuit called the biota, which may be represented by a pyramid consisting of layers. The bottom layer is the soil. A plant layer rests on the soil, an insect layer on the plants, a bird and rodent layer on the insects, and so on up through various animal groups to the apex layer, which consists of the larger carnivores.

The species of a layer are alike not in where they came from, or in what they look like, but rather in what they eat. Each successive layer depends on those below it for food and often for other services, and each in turn furnishes food and services to those above. Proceeding upward, each successive layer decreases in numerical abundance. Thus, for every carnivore there are hundreds of his prey, thousands of their prey, millions of insects, uncountable plants. The pyramidal form of the system reflects this numerical progression from apex to base. Man shares an intermediate layer with the bears, raccoons, and squirrels which eat both meat and vegetables.

The lines of dependency for food and other services are called food chains. Thus soil-oak-deer-Indian is a chain that has now been largely converted to soil-corn-cow-farmer. Each species, including ourselves, is a link in many chains. The deer eats a hundred plants other than oak, and the cow a hundred plants other than corn. Both, then, are links in a hundred chains. The pyramid is a tangle of chains so complex as to seem disorderly, yet the stability of the system proves it to be a highly organized structure. Its functioning depends on the co-operation and competition of its diverse parts.

In the beginning, the pyramid of life was low and squat; the food chains short and simple. Evolution has added layer after layer, link after link. Man is one of thousands of accretions to the height and complexity of the pyramid. Science has given us many doubts, but it has given us at least one certainty: the trend of evolution is to elaborate and diversify the biota.

Land, then, is not merely soil; it is a fountain of energy flowing through a circuit of soils, plants, and animals. Food chains are the living channels which conduct energy upward; death and decay return it to the soil. The circuit is not closed; some energy is dissipated in decay, some is added by absorption from the air, some is stored in soils, peats, and long-lived forests; but it is a sustained circuit, like a slowly augmented revolving fund of life. There is always a net loss by downhill wash, but this is normally small and offset by the decay of rocks. It is deposited in the ocean and, in the course of geological time, raised to form new lands and new pyramids.

The velocity and character of the upward flow of energy depend on the complex structure of the plant and animal community, much as the upward flow of sap in a tree depends on its complex cellular organization. Without this complexity, normal circulation would presumably not occur. Structure means the characteristic numbers, as well as the characteristic kinds and functions, of the component species. This interdependence between the complex structure of the land and its smooth functioning as an energy unit is one of its basic attributes.

When a change occurs in one part of the circuit, many other parts must adjust themselves to it. Change does not necessarily obstruct or divert the flow of energy; evolution is a long series of self-induced changes, the net result of which has been to elaborate the flow mechanism and to lengthen the circuit. Evolutionary changes, however, are usually slow and local. Man's invention of tools has enabled him to make changes of unprecedented violence, rapidity, and scope.

One change is in the composition of floras and faunas. The larger predators are lopped off the apex of the pyramid; food chains, for the first time in history, become shorter rather than longer. Domesticated species from other lands are substituted for wild ones, and wild ones are moved to new habitats. In this world-wide pooling of faunas and floras, some species get out of bounds as pests and diseases, others are extinguished. Such effects are seldom intended or foreseen; they represent unpredicted and often untraceable readjustments in the structure. Agricultural science is largely a race between the emergence of new pests and the emergence of new techniques for their control.

Another change touches the flow of energy through plants and animals and its return to the soil. Fertility is the ability of soil to receive, store, and release energy. Agriculture, by overdrafts on the soil, or by too radical a substitution of domestic for native species in the superstructure, may derange the channels of flow or deplete storage. Soils depleted of their storage, or of the organic matter which anchors it, wash away faster than they form. This is erosion.

Waters, like soil, are part of the energy circuit. Industry, by polluting waters or obstructing them with dams, may exclude the plants and animals necessary to keep energy in circulation.

Transportation brings about another basic change: the plants or animals grown in one region are now consumed and returned to the soil in another. Transportation taps the energy stored in rocks, and in the air, and uses it elsewhere; thus we fertilize the garden with nitrogen gleaned by the guano birds from the fishes of seas on the other side of the Equator. Thus the formerly localized and self-contained circuits are pooled on a world-wide scale.

The process of altering the pyramid for human occupation releases stored energy, and this often gives rise, during the pioneering period, to a deceptive exuberance of plant and animal life, both wild and tame. These releases of biotic capital tend to becloud or postpone the penalties of violence.

***

This thumbnail sketch of land as an energy circuit conveys three basic ideas:

1. That land is not merely soil.
2. That the native plants and animals kept the energy circuit open; others may or may not.
3. That man-made changes are of a different order than evolutionary changes, and have effects more comprehensive than is intended or foreseen.

Excerpt from "Orientation"
Technics and Civilization

BY LEWIS MUMFORD

1. The Dissolution of "The Machine"

What we call, in its final results, "the machine," was not, we have seen, the passive by-product of technics itself, developing through small ingenuities and improvements and finally spreading over the entire field of social effort. On the contrary, the mechanical discipline and many of the primary inventions themselves were the result of deliberate effort to achieve a mechanical way of life: the motive in back of this was not technical efficiency but holiness, or power over other men. In the course of development machines have extended these aims and provided a physical vehicle for their fulfillment.

Now, the mechanical ideology, which directed men's minds toward the production of machines, was itself the result of special circumstances, special choices and interests and desires. So long as other values were uppermost, European technology had remained relatively stable and balanced over a period of three or four thousand years. Men produced machines partly because they were seeking an issue from a baffling complexity and confusion, which characterized both action and though: partly, too, because their desire for power, frustrated by the loud violence of other men, turned finally toward the neutral world of brute matter. Order had been sought before, again and again in other civilizations, in drill, regimentation, inflexible social regulations, the discipline of caste and custom: after the seventeenth century it was sought in a series of external instruments and engines. The Western European conceived of the machine because he wanted regularity, order, certainty, because he wished to reduce the movement of his fellows as well as the behavior of the environment to a more definite, calculable basis. But, more than an instrument of practical adjustment, the machine was, from 1750 on, a goal of desire. Though nominally designed to further the means of existence, the machine served the industrialist and the inventor and all the cooperating classes as an end. In a world of flux and disorder and precarious adjustment, the machine at least was seized upon as a finality.

If anything was unconditionally believe in and worshipped during the last two centuries, at least by the leaders and masters of society, it was the machine; for the machine and the universe were identified, linked together as they were by the formulae of the mathematical and physical sciences; and the service of the machine was the principal manifestation of faith and religion: the main motive of human action, and the source of most human goods. Only as a religion can one explain the compulsive nature of the urge toward mechanical development without regard for the actual outcome of the development in human relations themselves: even in departments where the results of mechanization were plainly disastrous, the most reasonable apologists nevertheless held that "the machine was here to stay"—by which they meant, not that history was irreversible, but that the machine itself was unmodifiable.

Today this unquestioned faith in the machine has been severely shaken. The absolute validity of the machine has become a conditioned validity: even Spengler, who has urged the men of his generation to become engineers and men of fact, regards that career as a sort of honorable suicide and looks forward to the period when the monuments of the machine civilization will be tangled masses of rusting iron and empty concrete shells. While for those of us who are more hopeful both of man's destiny and that of the machine, the machine is no longer the paragon of progress and the final expression of our desires: it is merely a series of instruments, which we will use in so far as they are serviceable to life at large, and which we will curtail where they infringe upon it or exist purely to support the adventitious structure of capitalism.

The decay of this absolute faith has resulted from a variety of causes. One of them is the fact that the instruments of destruction ingeniously contrived in the machine shop and the chemist's laboratory, have become in the hands of raw and dehumanized personalities a standing threat to the existence of organized society itself. Mechanical instruments of armament and offense, springing out of fear, have widened the grounds for fear among all the peoples of the world; and our insecurity against bestial, power-lusting men is too great a price to pay for relief from the insecurities of the natural environment. What is the use of conquering nature if we fall a prey to nature in the form of unbridled men? What is the use of equipping mankind with mighty powers to move and build and communicate, if the final result of this secure food supply and this excellent organization is to enthrone the morbid impulses of a thwarted humanity?

In the development of the neutral valueless world of science, and in the advance of the adaptive, instrumental functions of the machine, we have left to the untutored egoisms of mankind the control of the gigantic powers and engines technics has conjured into existence. In advancing too swiftly and heedlessly along the line of mechanical improvement we have failed to assimilate the machine and to coordinate it with human capacities and human needs; and by our social backwardness and our blind confidence that problems occasioned by the machine could be solved purely by mechanical means, we have outreached ourselves. When one subtracts from the manifest blessings of the machine the entire amount of energy and mind and time and resources devoted to the preparation for war—to say nothing of the residual burden of past wars—one realizes the net gain is dismayingly small, and with the advance of still more efficient means of inflicting death is becoming steadily smaller. Our failure here is the critical instance of a common failure all along the line.

The decay of the mechanical faith has, however, still another source: namely, the realization that the serviceability of machines has meant in the past serviceability to capitalist enterprise. We are now entering a phase of dissociation between capitalism and technics; and we begin to see with Thorstein Veblen that their respective interests, so far from being identical, are often at war, and that the human gains of technics have been forfeited by perversion in the interests of a pecuniary economy. We see in addition that many of the special gains in productivity which capitalism took credit for were in reality due to quite different agents—collective thought, cooperative action, and the general habits of order—virtues that have no necessary connection with capitalist enterprise. To perfect and extend the range of machines without perfecting and giving humane direction to the organs of social action and social control is to create dangerous tensions in the structure of society. Thanks to capitalism, the machine has been over-worked, over-enlarged, over-exploited because of the possibility of making money out of it. And the problem of integrating the machine in society is not merely a matter, as I have already pointed out, of making social institutions keep in step with the machine: the problem is equally one of altering the nature and the rhythm of the machine to fit the actual needs of the community. Whereas the physical sciences had first claim on the good minds of the past epoch, it is the biological and social sciences, and the political arts of industrial planning and regional planning and community planning that now most urgently need cultivation: one they begin to flourish they will awaken new interests and set new problems for the technologist. But the belief that the social dilemmas created by the machine can be solved merely by inventing more machines is today a sign of half-baked thinking which verges close to quackery.

These symptoms of social danger and decay, arising out of the very nature of the machine—its peculiar debts to warfare, mining, and finance—have weakened the absolute faith in the machine that characterized its earlier development.

At the same time, we have now reached appoint in the development of technology itself where the organic has begun to dominate the machine. Instead of simplifying the organic, to make it intelligibly mechanical, as was necessary for the great eotechnic and paleotechnic inventions, we have begun to complicate the mechanical, in order to make it more organic: therefore more effective, more harmonious with our living environment. For our skill, perfected on the finger exercises of the machine, would be bored by the mere repetition of the scales and such childlike imbecilities: supported by the analytic methods and the skills developed in creating the machine, we can now approach the larger tasks of synthesis. In short, the machine is serving independently, in its neotechnic phase, as a point for a fresh integration in thought and social life.

While in the past the machine was retarded by its limited historic heritage, by its inadequate ideology, by its tendency to deny the vital and the organic, it is now transcending these limitations. And indeed, as our machines and our apparatus become more subtle, and the knowledge derived with their aid becomes more delicate and penetrating, the simple mechanical analysis of the universe made by the earlier physicists ceases to represent anything in which the scientist himself is now interested. The mechanical world-picture is dissolving. The intellectual medium in which the machine once spawned so rapidly is being altered at the same time that the social medium—the point of application—is undergoing a parallel change. Neither of these changes is yet dominant; neither is automatic or inevitable. But one can now say definitely, as one could not fifty years ago, that there is a fresh gathering of forces on the side of life. The claims of life, once expressed solely by the Romantics and by the more archaic social groups and institutions of society, are now beginning to be represented at the very heart of technics itself. Let us trace out some of the implications of this fact.

PART 4

Voices from Science, Scholars & Intellectuals

Challenging Existing Assumptions: Human Exemptionalism & the Paradoxes of Modernity

Introduction by Beth Schaefer Caniglia
Regis University

T he next important phase of environmental consciousness is marked by the thinking of scientists, scholars, and intellectuals who confronted the mismatch between the scale and methods of capitalist development and the lives of plants, animals, and people in place. The primary benchmark of this era was the publication of *Silent Spring* by Rachel Carson, but the pieces we've chosen for this section are not always so directly traced to the findings of scientific research related to human and animal health. Instead, Rachel Carson's call to arms ushered in an era of rethinking humanity's place in the world—the slow evolution of a new paradigm of thinking about the value of nature, the dominance of humans over access to natural resources, and the logic of capitalism. In essence, this era rejects the practices of late modernity, especially the commodification of nature and the philosophy of human exemptionalism, and embarks on a systematic analysis of alternative approaches to harmonizing human systems with the natural world.

In a way, we find in these readings very similar concerns to those shared by the early American environmentalists. Though their concerns were driven by western expansion and the need to preserve natural places, the pervasive expansion of capitalism and its biophysical consequences were not halted by setting aside pieces of land. Instead, chemicals infiltrated water and air supplies in ways that flowed under and over fences. They found their way into streams, fish, birds, and human bodies. While at first their impacts were subtle and difficult to measure, with time and accumulation, scientists like Rachel Carson and back-to-the-landers like Wendell Berry began to notice the disappearance and mutations of particular bird, plant, and animal species, compelling them to seek the invisible causes. Science was forever changed as a result, and today we are still struggling to produce the correct tools and models that integrate the diverse scientific fields required to flesh out the ties between human and natural systems and overcome the old ideas of human exemptionalism.

Confronted with Rachel Carson's bellwether birds, a wide range of scientists, scholars, and intellectuals emerged in search of ways to rebuild human connections with the natural world. Inspired also by early environmentalists like Leopold, Walden, and Thoreau, these new approaches synthesized science with a sense of place, hoping to point out the blind spots of the existing, productivity-focused R&D world and mobilize people to protect the places where they live. A cacophony of approaches were advocated during this era: gardening, simple living, the study of animal emotions, deep ecology, and the development of the Gaia principle. In general, this era is marked by a movement to abandon the human exemptionalist paradigm and the philosophy of manifest destiny in favor of a new ecological paradigm, one that acknowledges that we have only one earth and we're all needed to steward the survival of that earth if she is to survive. All of the practices of late modernity are brought into question by these readings: the sustainability of capitalist development schemes, the safety and ethics of our current systems of growing and distributing food, the role of science and technology both as creators and solutions to environmental problems, and the design of contemporary living arrangements that alienate people from nature and the suffering of her creatures. Therefore, these readings attempt to convince us of the value of nature, the preciousness of her species, the benefits of taking time to connect to these living things, and the need to envision a more mutually beneficial relationship between humans and nature.

The Human Exemptionalist Paradigm

In our field, sociology, there was a call to acknowledge the central influence of the biophysical world on the social world, which created the subdiscipline of environmental sociology (Dunlap and Catton 1994). Our charge is to build integrated explanations for social and environmental consequences, explanations that bridge human and natural systems in ways that more accurately represent the true interdependence of societies and nature. To date, we have only begun to live up to this charge. Of course, environmental sociology isn't alone in its failure in this regard; the entire scientific enterprise that followed from the Enlightenment was built on a carefully crafted division of labor and schools of specialization that purposely separated the social and biophysical sciences.

Disciplines like botany, cell biology, chemistry, entomology, zoology, and animal science carved out their isolated pieces of nature, dissecting their parts of ecosystems into taxonomies meant to make them more intelligible. Likewise, disciplines like psychology, sociology, geography, history, and economics staked their claims to specific dimensions of the social world, each believing it alone held the key to understanding. The brilliance of Rachel Carson's work was its ability to capture the fundamental flaws present in the science of modernity. In very simple terms, she highlighted the vectors of chemical contamination:

> Strontium 90, released through nuclear explosions into the air, comes to earth in rain or drifts down as fallout, lodges in soil, enters into the grass or corn or wheat grown there, and in time takes up its abode in the bones of a human being, there to remain until his death. Similarly, chemicals sprayed on croplands or forests or gardens lie long in the soil, entering into living organisms, passing from one to another in a chain of poisoning and death. Or they pass mysteriously by underground streams until they emerge and, through the alchemy of air and sunlight, combine into new forms that kill vegetation, sicken cattle, and work unknown harm on those who drink from once pure wells. (Carson 2002)

Herein, Carson highlights complicated intersections between nuclear chemistry, the defense industry, agriculture, home gardens, groundwater, and animal and human food chains; at any step in the process, the chains can be broken, delayed, or change direction. She later summarizes succinctly: "This is an era of specialists, each of whom sees his own problems and is unaware or intolerant of the larger frame into which it fits."

Human exemptionalism and specialization in the sciences combine to produce unchecked technological exuberance (Volti 2009). Progress in one field can create problems in another, such as those Carson points out in the quotes above. The discovery of a chemical that eliminates insects that lower crop yields inadvertently causes birth defects in birds, cattle, or humans. We get so carried away to find solutions to one problem that we fail to consider potential negative consequences. Carson saw this need for technological exuberance to be tamed by the precautionary principle.

> I contend, furthermore, that we have allowed these chemicals to be used with little or no advance investigation of their effect on soil, water, wildlife, and man himself. Future generations are unlikely to condone our lack of prudent concern for the integrity of the natural world that supports all life. (Carson 2002)

A similar call to see a bigger picture than the one we're focused on is made by Daniel Quinn in his novel *Ishmael*. Here, he also highlights the ways exuberance overcomes precaution.

> Ah well, the vagaries of such foolish people are nothing to the Takers. They're pedaling away and having a wonderful time. They're not going to abandon *their* craft …But alas, a law is catching up to them…the law of gravity, and it's catching up to them…*at an accelerating rate.* (Quinn 1992; emphasis in the original)

Here, Quinn's protagonist, the gorilla Ishmael, uses the metaphor of a free-falling aircraft to describe humanity's ignorance of their unsustainable lifestyle. Because we're "pedaling away and having a wonderful time," we can't grasp the catastrophic end we're plunging toward. Like Carson before him, Quinn is begging us to look ahead at the inevitable consequences of the overindulgent production and consumption patterns of late modernity, which are fueled by a misplaced faith in science and technology to save the day.

A more holistic approach in the sciences is certainly needed to overcome the ways specialization prevents attention to the complexities of environmental problems. Recent studies in coupled human and natural systems (CHANS) attempt to merge biophysical and social variables into models designed to compare their effects on system vulnerabilities. Another approach is to search for a type of transcendent science under which all others should be subsumed. That is the approach taken by biologist Edward O. Wilson (1999) in his controversial book *Consilience*.

> It traverses the scales of space, time, and complexity to unite the disparate facts of the disciplines by consilience, the perception of a seamless web of cause and effect…The central idea of the consilience world view is that all tangible phenomena, from the birth of stars to the workings of social institutions, are based on material processes that are ultimately reducible, however long and tortuous the sequences, to the laws of physics.

Wilson argues that the physical material of the natural and social sciences is exactly the same; in fact, their frontiers intersect in numerous ways.

> The gaps of greatest potential include the final unification of physics, the reconstruction of living cells, the assembly of ecosystems, the coevolution of genes and culture, the physical basis of mind, and the deep origins of ethics and religion. If the consilience world view [*sic*] is correct, the traverse of the gaps will be a Magellanic voyage that eventually encircles the whole of reality.

Of course, we social scientists argue that social construction of reality is a product of social collectivities rather than reducible to "the physical basis of mind." Therefore, in the next section, we explore the ways scientists and intellectuals in this era challenge us to change the ways we perceive the world and humanity's role in it.

The Social Construction of the Environment: Do Animals Feel?

Quinn's *Ishmael* (1992) makes a powerful argument toward the end of the novel.

> As long as the people of your culture are convinced that the world belongs to them and that their divinely-appointed destiny is to conquer and rule it, then they are of course going to go on acting the way they've been acting for the past ten thousand years. They're going to go on treating the world as if it were a piece of human property and they're going to go on conquering it as if it were an adversary...You must change people's minds.

Clearly, the way people frame and perceive environmental problems is a central dilemma in contemporary debates (Snow and Benford 1988). Take, for example, the debate over whether climate change is real. Many argue that this debate, although settled among all but a few outlier scientists, has completely blocked the United States from creating policies to ameliorate this pressing environmental challenge (McCright and Dunlap 2010). Another example is the now-infamous bidding war to buy a single lobster that took place between Mary Tyler Moore and Rush Limbaugh. An ad purchased by PETA (People for the Ethical Treatment of Animals) featured an open letter from Mary Tyler Moore in which she wrote:

> Marine biologists report that lobsters are fascinating beings with complex social interactions, long child-hoods and awkward adolescences ... Like humans, they flirt with one another and have even been seen walking 'claw-in-claw!' And like humans, lobsters feel pain. (*New York Times*, 1995)

Rush Limbaugh was unable to purchase the lobster, even though he offered the highest bid, but that didn't stop him from dismissing the fact that lobsters and other invertebrates feel pain. Citing a study funded by the Norwegian government, Limbaugh stated:

> "The study ... written by a scientist at the University of Oslo suggests that lobsters and other invertebrates such as crabs, snails, and worms probably don't suffer even if lobsters do tend to thrash around in boiling water. The 39-page report says lobsters and crabs have some capacity of learning but it's unlikely that they

can feel pain." They have capacity for learning? Really? I've never seen one jump out of a pot yet. (Limbaugh, 2005)

Deep Ecology

Distinct from human exemptionalism, the era marked by the readings in this chapter can be credited for raising our awareness of how *similar* human and animal experiences and emotions can be. A deep appreciation of animal and plant emotions is often associated with deep ecology. Since the earliest records, scholars, theologians, and others staked powerful claims that humans were distinct from animals in terms of intelligence, consciousness, emotions, and even the physical experience of pain (Bekoff 2003; Narby 2006; Goodall 2011; Horowitz 2010; Uhl 2013; see also our section on religion and the environment). Scientific studies of animal intelligence, communication, and emotion advanced significantly during the last quarter of the twentieth century, producing findings that raise concerns about the ways capitalism and corporate food production systems raise and market animals as commodities. Jacky Turner and Joyce D'Silva (2006) edited a collection of essays on the topic, entitled *Animals, Ethics and Trade: The Challenge of Animal Sentience*. Citing several hundred scientific studies, their contributing authors argue that it is time to incorporate common sense into our treatment of livestock. Their argument is not that we should stop eating animal protein altogether; rather, they argue that ethics in the conditions under which animals are bred, raised, and killed should reflect acknowledgment of the most recent scientific data, which consistently proves that animals feel pain, joy, and fear, and even strongly suggests that animals can love.

This theme is discussed in our book by authors Masson and McCarthy (1995), who highlighted several examples of animal and insect behavior that looks like love.

> J.T. Moggridge tells the story of a trap-door spider he had collected and decided to preserve in alcohol. Moggridge shook the baby spiders off her back and dropped her into the alcohol. After a while, supposing her to be "dead to sense," he dropped her twenty-four babies in too. To his horror, the mother spider reached out her legs, folded the babies beneath her, and clasped them until she died. After this, Moggridge switched to the use of chloroform.

In another story, they tell of a giraffe mother who put herself in dire danger to protect her calf.

> Its [the giraffe calf's] mother tried to push the calf to run faster, but when she saw this would not work, she stood over it and faced the lion…The lion circled the giraffe, and the mother wheeled to face him. Whenever he got close, she kicked at him with her forelegs. After an hour, the lion gave up and left. The two giraffe rejoined the herd.

There is a theme in some of our readings that reflects the views of many contemporary animal scientists, those who work in contact with animals, and many pet owners that one need only be present and pay attention to see the signs that animals are deeply affected by their relationships with one another and with us. Our common sense and our experience tell us that we, too, are deeply affected by them. This sentiment extends beyond animals to the entire realm of nature, according to many scholars and intellectuals. In this section, Annie Dillard's (1974) work tells of the role that innocence plays in allowing us to fully see the power of a mountain, a puppy, a tree, or even a solar eclipse. Innocence, Dillard argued, is not restricted to babies and puppies. "It is not lost to us; the world is a better place than that…It is possible to pursue innocence as hounds pursue hares…". And innocence does not require us to give up our consciousness.

> Consciousness itself does not hinder living in the present…*Self*-consciousness, however, does hinder the experience of the present…So long as I lose myself in a tree, say, I can scent its leafy breath… But the second I become aware of myself at any of these activities… the tree vanishes, uprooted from the spot and flung out of sight as if it had never grown… What I call innocence is the spirit's unself-conscious state at any moment of pure devotion to any object. It is at once a receptiveness and total concentration.

Barry Lopez (2007) echoed Dillard's phrase in his introduction of *The Future of Nature*.

> I heard an unfamiliar voice this morning. The call of a bird I could not identify … I've studied birds here for thirty-seven years. I've been on this wooded slope in the rural mountains of western Oregon long enough to know, now, how vast is my innocence. Long enough to know how much will stay hidden, even from the most diligent observer.

Holistic Pragmatism

But what if animals do feel pain, loneliness, fear? What if we let ourselves feel for livestock animals the way we feel in private about our pets? How do we begin to make a change? Those answers have been addressed extensively by writers, hippies, dog and horse whisperers, scholars, and poets alike. They suggest that we need to reconnect with nature and especially reconnect our children with nature so they don't grow up without compassion for the full range of living creatures, plants, and places that reside outside of cities. We also desperately need to reconnect to the sources of our food so that we understand how much water it takes to feed a cow grain versus grass, so that we know that our meat was once a sentient being, so that we waste less and appreciate more, so that conservation becomes a practice of compassion rather than a form of denial.

Barbara Kingsolver (2007), her husband, and her daughter shared what their lives were like during the year they committed to eat locally and, where possible, grow their own food. Rather than romanticizing their garden and the turkeys they raised from chicks, the Kingsolver-Hopp family directly acknowledged that we all live from the death of other creatures every day. While the turkeys weren't pets, Lily's chickens were deeply loved: "You don't understand, Mama," she said, red-eyed. "I love my chickens as much as I love *you*." In the end, however, Lily agreed that they would only kill the mean ones for meat. In the selection included in our book, Kingsolver writes about their July garden, keeping them busy with weeds and producing gobs of crunchy, cool cucumbers: "Cucumbers became our all-day, all-summer snack of choice. We would try to get sick of them before winter". In the end, they concluded they grew too much squash, not enough garlic, yet overall enjoyed a pretty good food year.

Wendell Berry (2002) provides an interpretive lens for the pragmatic changes that are a part of holistic pragmatism. He says: "The changes that are required are fundamental changes in the way we are living."

> We have delegated all our vital functions and responsibilities to salesmen and agents and bureaus and experts of all sorts. We cannot feed or clothe ourselves, or entertain ourselves, or communicate with each other, or be charitable or neighborly or loving, or even respect ourselves, without recourse to a merchant or a corporation or a public-service organization or an agency of the government or a style-setter or an expert… Our model citizen is a sophisticate who before puberty understands how to produce a baby, but at the age of thirty will not know how to produce a potato".

This era of scholarship intellectual thinking encourages, above all, taking a closer look at nature. Environmental scientists like Rachel Carson use special instruments to measure the chemical load our production processes introduce to the natural world, but it wasn't those instruments that caught her attention. It was her own daily observations, her own wondering where all the birds had gone. While scientific instrumentation is useful in telling us about our natural world, it is not the only way of knowing. As Marc Bekoff writes in chapter 3 of *Animals, Ethics and Trade* (2006), intuition and common sense are equally useful when confronting the impacts of our contemporary, mediated relationships with nature and animals.

The solutions recommended require work, but they do not require us to cut ourselves off from the world and live in communes. They ask us to pay attention to the birds, the frogs, and the trees around us. They ask us to reclaim pragmatic knowledge regarding our basic needs, especially the way food is produced and animals are harvested. While some will choose to become vegetarians or back-to-the-landers, the scholars cited in this chapter suggest a moderate path—one that accepts animal emotions, preferences free-range and organic livestock operations and ethical forms of slaughter, and encourages us as consumers to reconnect the source of our meat to the living creatures whose lives were taken for our consumption. This path also encourages personal, school, and community gardens that reconnect us to the processes of seed germination, pollination, cooking, and canning. And it encourages us to more deeply appreciate the struggles of local, small farms and merchants whose livelihoods are threatened by large-scale industrial agriculture and an indifferent, ignorant group of consumers.

References

1. Bekoff, Marc. *Minding Animals: Awareness, Emotions, and Heart.* New York: Oxford University Press, 2003.
2. Berry, Wendell. *The Art of the Commonplace.* Berkeley, CA: Counterpoint, 2002.
3. Carson, Rachel. *Silent Spring.* New York: Mariner Books, 2002.
4. Dillard, Annie. *Pilgrim at Tinker Creek.* New York: HarperCollins, 1974.
5. Dunlap, Riley, and William Catton. "Struggling with Human Exemptionalism: The Rise, Decline and Revitalization of Environmental Sociology." *American Sociologist* 25 1994): 5–30.
6. Goodall, Jane. *Hope for Animals and Their World: How Endangered Species are Being Rescued from the Brink.* New York: Grand Central Publishers, 2011.

7. Horowitz, Alexandra. *Inside of a Dog: What Dogs See, Smell, and Know*. New York: Scribner, 2010.

8. Kingsolver, Barbara. *Animal, Vegetable, Miracle*. New York: HarperCollins, 2007.

9. Limbaugh, Rush. "Lobsters Are Idiots." http://www.rushlimbaugh.com/daily/2005/02/15/lobsters_are_idiots.

10. Lopez, Barry. *The Future of Nature*. Minneapolis: Milkweed Editions, 2007.

11. Masson, Jeffrey Moussaieff and Susan McCarthy. *When Elephants Weep: The Emotional Lives of Animals*. New York: Dell Publishing, 1995.

12. McCright, Aaron and Riley Dunlap. "Anti-Reflexivity: The American Conservation Movement's Success in Undermining Climate Science and Policy." *Theory, Culture, and Society* 27, no. 2–3 (2010): 1–34.

13. Moore, Mary Tyler. "New Animal Rights Cause Urges, 'Free the Lobsters!'" *New York Times*. http://www.nytimes.com/1995/12/31/us/new-animal-rights-cause-urges-free-the-lobsters.html.

14. Narby, Jeremy. *Intelligence in Nature*. New York: Penguin Publishers, 2006.

15. Quinn, Daniel. *Ishmael*. New York: Bantam, 1992.

16. Snow, David A. and Robert D. Benford. "Ideology, Frame Resonance and Participant Moblization." *International Social Movement Research* 1 (1988): 197–218.

17. Turner, Jacky and Joyce D'Silva, eds. *Animals, Ethics, and Trade: The Challenge of Animal Sentience*. New York: Routledge, 2006.

18. Uhl, Christopher. *Developing Ecological Consciousness: The End of Separation*. Lanham, MD: Rowman & Littlefield Publishers, 2013.

19. Volti, Rudi. *Society & Technological Change, 6th Edition*. Worth Publishers: New York, New York, 2009.

20. Wilson, Edward O. *Consilience*. New York: Vintage Books, 1998.

Silent Spring
The Obligation to Endure

BY RACHEL CARSON

The history of life on earth has been a history of interaction between living things and their surroundings. To a large extent, the physical form and the habits of the earth's vegetation and its animal life have been molded by the environment. Considering the whole span of earthly time, the opposite effect, in which life actually modifies its surroundings, has been relatively slight. Only within the moment of time represented by the present century has one species—man—acquired significant power to alter the nature of his world.

During the past quarter century this power has not only increased to one of disturbing magnitude but it has changed in character. The most alarming of all man's assaults upon the environment is the contamination of air, earth, rivers, and sea with dangerous and even lethal materials. This pollution is for the most part irrecoverable; the chain of evil it initiates not only in the world that must support life but in living tissues is for the most part irreversible. In this now universal contamination of the environment, chemicals are the sinister and little-recognized partners of radiation in changing the very nature of the world—the very nature of its life. Strontium 90, released through nuclear explosions into the air, comes to earth in rain or drifts down as fallout, lodges in soil, enters into the grass or corn or wheat grown there, and in time takes up its abode in the bones of a human being, there to remain until his death. Similarly, chemicals sprayed on croplands or forests or gardens lie long in soil, entering into living organisms, passing from one to another in a chain of poisoning and death. Or they pass mysteriously by underground streams until they emerge and, through the alchemy of air and sunlight, combine into new forms that kill vegetation, sicken cattle, and work unknown harm on those who drink from once pure wells. As Albert Schweitzer has said, "Man can hardly even recognize the devils of his own creation."

It took hundreds of millions of years to produce the life that now inhabits the earth—eons of time in which that developing and evolving and diversifying life reached a state of adjustment and balance with its surroundings. The environment, rigorously shaping and directing the life it supported, contained elements that were hostile as well as supporting. Certain rocks gave out dangerous radiation; even within the light of the sun, from which all life draws its energy, there were short-wave radiations with power to injure. Given time—time not in years but in millennia—life adjusts, and a balance has been reached. For time is the essential ingredient; but in the modern world there is no time.

The rapidity of change and the speed with which new situations are created follow the impetuous and heedless pace of man rather than the deliberate pace of nature. Radiation is no longer merely the background radiation of rocks, the bombardment of cosmic rays, the ultraviolet of the sun that have existed before there was any life on earth; radiation is now the unnatural creation of man's tampering with the atom. The chemicals to which life is asked to make its adjustment are no longer merely the calcium and silica and copper and all the rest of the minerals washed out of the rocks and carried in rivers to the sea; they are the synthetic creations of man's inventive mind, brewed in his laboratories, and having no counterparts in nature.

To adjust to these chemicals would require time on the scale that is nature's; it would require not merely the years of a man's life but the life of generations. And even this, were it by some miracle possible, would be futile, for the new chemicals come from our laboratories in an endless stream; almost five hundred annually find their way into actual use in the United States alone. The figure is staggering and its implications are not easily grasped—500 new chemicals to which the bodies of men and animals are required somehow to adapt each year, chemicals totally outside the limits of biologic experience.

Among them are many that are used in man's war against nature. Since the mid-1940's over 200 basic chemicals have been created for use in killing insects, weeds, rodents, and other organisms described in the modern vernacular as "pests"; and they are sold under several thousand different brand names.

These sprays, dusts, and aerosols are now applied almost universally to farms, gardens, forests, and homes—nonselective chemicals that have the power to kill every insect, the "good" and the "bad," to still the song of birds and the leaping of fish in the streams, to coat the leaves with a deadly film, and to linger on in soil—all this though the intended target may be only a few weeds or insects. Can anyone believe it is possible to lay down such a barrage of poisons on the surface of the earth without making it unfit for all life? They should not be called "insecticides," but "biocides."

The whole process of spraying seems caught up in an endless spiral. Since DDT was released for civilian use, a process of escalation has been going on in which ever more toxic materials must be found. This has happened because insects, in a triumphant vindication of Darwin's principle of the survival of the fittest, have evolved super races immune to the particular insecticide used, hence a deadlier one has always to be developed—and then a deadlier one than that. It has happened also because, for reasons to be described later, destructive insects often undergo a "flareback," or resurgence, after spraying, in numbers greater than before. Thus the chemical war is never won, and all life is caught in its violent crossfire.

Along with the possibility of the extinction of mankind by nuclear war, the central problem of our age has therefore become the contamination of man's total environment with such substances of incredible potential for harm—substances that accumulate in the tissues of plants and animals and even penetrate the germ cells to shatter or alter the very material of heredity upon which the shape of the future depends.

Some would-be architects of our future look toward a time when it will be possible to alter the human germ plasm by design. But we may easily be doing so now by inadvertence, for many chemicals, like radiation, bring about gene mutations. It is ironic to think that man might determine his own future by something so seemingly trivial as the choice of an insect spray.

All this has been risked—for what? Future historians may well be amazed by our distorted sense of proportion. How could intelligent beings seek to control a few unwanted species by a method that contaminated the entire environment and brought the threat of disease and death even to their own kind?

Yet this is precisely what we have done. We have done it, moreover, for reasons that collapse the moment we examine them. We are told that the enormous and expanding use of pesticides is necessary to maintain farm production. Yet is our real problem not one of *overproduction*? Our farms, despite measures to remove acreages from production and to pay farmers *not* to produce, have yielded such a staggering excess of crops that the American taxpayer in 1962 is paying out more than one billion dollars a year as the total carrying cost of the surplus-food storage program. And is the situation helped when one branch of the Agriculture Department tries to reduce production while another states, as it did in 1958, "It is believed generally that reduction of crop acreages under provisions of the Soil Bank will stimulate interest in use of chemicals to obtain maximum production on the land retained in crops."

All this is not to say there is no insect problem and no need of control. I am saying, rather, that control must be geared to realities, not to mythical situations, and that the methods employed must be such that they do not destroy us along with the insects.

The problem whose attempted solution has brought such a train of disaster in its wake is an accompaniment of our modern way of life. Long before the age of man, insects inhabited the earth—a group of extraordinarily varied and adaptable beings. Over the course of time since man's advent, a small percentage of the more than half a million species of insects have come into conflict with human welfare in two principal ways: as competitors for the food supply and as carriers of human disease.

Disease-carrying insects become important where human beings are crowded together, especially under conditions where sanitation is poor, as in time of natural disaster or war or in situations of extreme poverty and deprivation. Then control of some sort becomes necessary. It is a sobering fact, however, as we shall presently see, that the method of massive chemical control has had only limited success, and also threatens to worsen the very conditions it is intended to curb.

Under primitive agricultural conditions the farmer had few insect problems. These arose with the intensification of agriculture—the devotion of immense acreages to a single crop. Such a system set the stage for explosive increases in specific insect populations. Single-crop farming does not take advantage of the principles by which nature works; it is agriculture as an engineer might conceive it to be. Nature has introduced great variety into the landscape, but man has displayed a passion for simplifying it. Thus he undoes the built-in checks and balances by which nature holds the species within bounds. One important natural check is a limit on the amount of suitable habitat for each species. Obviously then, an insect that lives on wheat can build up its population to much higher levels on a farm devoted to wheat than on one in which wheat is intermingled with other crops to which the insect is not adapted.

The same thing happens in other situations. A generation or more ago, the towns of large areas of the United States lined their streets with the noble elm tree. Now the beauty they hopefully created is threatened with complete destruction as disease sweeps through the elms, carried by a beetle that would have only limited chance to build up large populations and to spread from tree to tree if the elms were only occasional trees in a richly diversified planting.

Another factor in the modern insect problem is one that must be viewed against a background of geologic and human history: the spreading of thousands of different kinds of organisms from their native homes to invade new territories. This worldwide migration has been studied and graphically described by the British ecologist Charles Elton in his recent book *The Ecology of Invasions*. During the Cretaceous Period, some hundred million years ago, flooding seas cut many land bridges between continents and living things found themselves confined in what Elton calls "colossal separate nature reserves." There, isolated from others of their kind, they developed many new species. When some of the land masses were joined again, about 15 million years ago, these species began to move out into new territories—a movement that is not only still in progress but is now receiving considerable assistance from man.

The importation of plants is the primary agent in the modern spread of species, for animals have almost invariably gone along with the plants, quarantine being a comparatively recent and not completely effective innovation. The United States Office of Plant Introduction alone has introduced almost 200,000 species and varieties of plants from all over the world. Nearly half of the 180 or so major insect enemies of plants in the United States are accidental imports from abroad, and most of them have come as hitchhikers on plants.

In new territory, out of reach of the restraining hand of the natural enemies that kept down its numbers in its native land, an invading plant or animal is able to become enormously abundant. Thus it is no accident that our most troublesome insects are introduced species.

These invasions, both the naturally occurring and those dependent on human assistance, are likely to continue indefinitely. Quarantine and massive chemical campaigns are only extremely expensive ways of buying time. We are faced, according to Dr. Elton, "with a life-and-death need not just to find new technological means of suppressing this plant or that animal"; instead we need the basic knowledge of animal populations and their relations to their surroundings that will "promote an even balance and damp down the explosive power of outbreaks and new invasions."

Much of the necessary knowledge is now available but we do not use it. We train ecologists in our universities and even employ them in our governmental agencies but we seldom take their advice. We allow the chemical death rain to fall as though there were no alternative, whereas in fact there are many, and our ingenuity could soon discover many more if given opportunity.

Have we fallen into a mesmerized state that makes us accept as inevitable that which is inferior or detrimental, as though having lost the will or the vision to demand that which is good? Such thinking, in the words of the ecologist Paul Shepard, "idealizes life with only its head out of water, inches above the limits of toleration of the corruption of its own environment . . . Why should we tolerate a diet of weak poisons, a home in insipid surroundings, a circle of acquaintances who are not quite our enemies, the noise of motors with just enough relief to prevent insanity? Who would want to live in a world which is just not quite fatal?"

Yet such a world is pressed upon us. The crusade to create a chemically sterile, insect-free world seems to have engendered a fanatic zeal on the part of many specialists and most of the so-called control agencies. On every hand there is evidence that those engaged in spraying operations exercise a ruthless power. "The regulatory entomologists . . . function as prosecutor, judge and jury, tax assessor and collector and sheriff to enforce their own orders," said Connecticut entomologist Neely Turner. The most flagrant abuses go unchecked in both state and federal agencies.

It is not my contention that chemical insecticides must never be used. I do contend that we have put poisonous and biologically potent chemicals indiscriminately into the hands of persons largely or wholly ignorant of their potentials for harm. We have subjected enormous numbers of people to contact with these poisons, without their consent and often without their knowledge. If the Bill of Rights contains no guarantee that a citizen shall be secure against lethal poisons distributed either by private individuals or by public officials, it is surely only because our forefathers, despite their considerable wisdom and foresight, could conceive of no such problem.

I contend, furthermore, that we have allowed these chemicals to be used with little or no advance investigation of their effect on soil, water, wildlife, and man himself. Future generations are unlikely to condone our lack of prudent concern for the integrity of the natural world that supports all life.

There is still very limited awareness of the nature of the threat. This is an era of specialists, each of whom sees his own problem and is unaware of or intolerant of the larger frame into which it fits. It is also an era dominated by industry, in which the right to make a dollar at whatever cost is seldom challenged. When the public protests, confronted with some obvious evidence of damaging results of pesticide applications, it is fed little tranquilizing pills of half truth. We urgently need an end to these false assurances, to the sugar coating of unpalatable facts. It is the public that is being asked to assume the risks that the insect controllers calculate. The public must decide whether it wishes to continue on the present road, and it can do so only when in full possession of the facts. In the words of Jean Rostand, "The obligation to endure gives us the right to know."

Consilience
To What End?

BY EDWARD O. WILSON

It is the custom of scholars when addressing behavior and culture to speak variously of anthropological explanations, psychological explanations, biological explanations, and other explanations appropriate to the perspectives of individual disciplines. I have argued that there is intrinsically only one class of explanation. It traverses the scales of space, time, and complexity to unite the disparate facts of the disciplines by consilience, the perception of a seamless web of cause and effect.

For centuries consilience has been the mother's milk of the natural sciences. Now it is wholly accepted by the brain sciences and evolutionary biology, the disciplines best poised to serve in turn as bridges to the social sciences and humanities. There is abundant evidence to support and none absolutely to refute the proposition that consilient explanations are congenial to the entirety of the great branches of learning.

The central idea of the consilience world view is that all tangible phenomena, from the birth of stars to the workings of social institutions, are based on material processes that are ultimately reducible, however long and tortuous the sequences, to the laws of physics. In support of this idea is the conclusion of biologists that humanity is kin to all other life forms by common descent. We share essentially the same DNA genetic code, which is transcribed into RNA and translated into proteins with the same amino acids. Our anatomy places us among the Old World monkeys and apes. The fossil record shows our immediate ancestor to be either *Homo ergaster* or *Homo erectus*. It suggests that the point of our origin was Africa about two hundred thousand years ago. Our hereditary human nature, which evolved during hundreds of millennia before and afterward, still profoundly affects the evolution of culture.

These considerations do not devalue the determining role of chance in history. Small accidents can have big consequences. The character of individual leaders can mean the difference between war and peace; one technological invention can change an economy. The main thrust of the consilience world view instead is that culture and hence the unique qualities of the human species will make complete sense only when linked in causal explanation to the natural sciences. Biology in particular is the most proximate and hence relevant of the scientific disciplines.

I know that such reductionism is not popular outside the natural sciences. To many scholars in the social sciences and humanities it is a vampire in the sacristy. So let me hasten to dispel the profane image that causes this reaction. As the century closes, the focus of the natural sciences has begun to shift away from the search for new fundamental laws and toward new kinds of synthesis—"holism," if you prefer—in order to understand complex systems. That is the goal, variously, in studies of the origin of the universe, the history of climate, the functioning of cells, the assembly of ecosystems, and the physical basis of mind. The strategy that works best in these enterprises is the construction of coherent cause-and-effect explanations across levels of organization. Thus the cell biologist looks inward and downward to ensembles of molecules, and the cognitive psychologist to patterns of aggregate nerve cell activity. Accidents, when they happen, are rendered understandable.

No compelling reason has ever been offered why the same strategy should not work to unite the natural sciences with the social sciences and humanities. The difference between the two domains is in the magnitude of the problem, not the principles needed for its solution. The human condition is the most important frontier of the natural sciences. Conversely, the material world exposed by the natural sciences is the most important frontier of the social sciences and humanities. The consilience argument can be distilled as follows: The two frontiers are the same.

The map of the material world, including human mental activity, can be thought a sprinkling of charted terrain separated by blank expanses that are of unknown extent yet accessible to coherent interdisciplinary research. Much of what I have offered in earlier chapters has been "gap analysis," a sketch of the position of the blank spaces, and an account of the efforts of scholars to explore them. The gaps of greatest potential include the final unification of physics, the reconstruction of living cells, the assembly of ecosystems, the coevolution of genes and culture, the physical basis of mind, and the deep origins of ethics and religion.

If the consilience world view is correct, the traverse of the gaps will be a Magellanic voyage that eventually encircles the whole of reality. But that view could be wrong: The exploration may be proceeding across an endless sea. The current pace is such that we may find out which of the two images is correct within a few decades. But even if the journey is Magellanic, and even if the boldest excursions of circumscription consequently taper off, so that the broad outline of material existence is well defined, we will still have mastered only an infinitesimal fraction of the internal detail. Exploration will go on in a profusion of scholarly disciplines. There are also the arts, which embrace not only all physically possible worlds but also all conceivable worlds innately interesting and congenial to the nervous system and thus, in the uniquely human sense, true.

Placed in this broader context—of existence coherent enough to be understood in a single system of explanation, yet still largely unexplored—the ambitions of the natural sciences might be viewed in a more favorable light by nonscientists. Nowadays, as polls have repeatedly shown, most people, at least in the United States, respect science but are baffled by it. They don't understand it, they prefer science fiction, they take fantasy and pseudoscience like stimulants to jolt their cerebral pleasure centers. We are still Paleolithic thrill seekers, preferring *Jurassic Park* to the Jurassic Era, and UFOs to astrophysics.

The productions of science, other than medical breakthroughs and the sporadic thrills of space exploration, are thought marginal. What really matters to humanity, a primate species well adapted to Darwinian fundamentals in body and soul, are sex, family, work, security, personal expression, entertainment, and spiritual fulfillment—in no particular order. Most people believe, I am sure erroneously, that science has little to do with any of these preoccupations. They assume that the social sciences and humanities are independent of the natural sciences and more relevant endeavors.

Who outside the technically possessed really needs to define a chromosome? Or understand chaos theory?

Science, however, is not marginal. Like art, it is a universal possession of humanity, and scientific knowledge has become a vital part of our species' repertory. It comprises what we know of the material world with reasonable certainty.

If the natural sciences can be successfully united with the social sciences and humanities, the liberal arts in higher education will be revitalized. Even the attempt to accomplish that much is a worthwhile goal. Profession-bent students should be helped to understand that in the twenty-first century the world will not be run by those who possess mere information alone. Thanks to science and technology, access to factual knowledge of all kinds is rising exponentially while dropping in unit cost. It is destined to become global and democratic. Soon it will be available everywhere on television and computer screens. What then? The answer is clear: synthesis. We are drowning in information, while starving for wisdom. The world henceforth will be run by synthesizers, people able to put together the right information at the right time, think critically about it, and make important choices wisely.

And this much about wisdom: In the long haul, civilized nations have come to judge one culture against another by a moral sense of the needs and aspirations of humanity as a whole. In thus globalizing the tribe, they attempt to formulate humankind's noblest and most enduring goals. The most important questions in this endeavor for the liberal arts are the meaning and purpose of all our idiosyncratic frenetic activity: *What are we, Where do we come from, How shall we decide where to go?* Why the toil, yearning, honesty, aesthetics, exaltation, love, hate, deceit, brilliance, hubris, humility, shame, and stupidity that collectively define our species? Theology, which long claimed the subject for itself, has done badly. Still encumbered by precepts based on Iron Age folk knowledge, it is unable to assimilate the great sweep of the real world now open for examination. Western philosophy offers no promising substitute. Its involuted exercises and professional timidity have left modern culture bankrupt of meaning.

The future of the liberal arts lies, therefore, in addressing the fundamental questions of human existence head on, without embarrassment or fear, taking them from the top down in easily understood language, and progressively rearranging them into domains of inquiry that unite the best of science and the humanities at each level of organization in turn. That of course is a very difficult task. But so are cardiac surgery and building space vehicles difficult tasks. Competent people get on with them, because they need to be done. Why should less be expected from the professionals responsible for education? The liberal arts will succeed to the extent that they are both solid in content and as coherent among themselves as the evidence allows. I find it hard to conceive of an adequate core curriculum in colleges and universities that avoids the cause-and-effect connections among the great branches of learning—not metaphor, not the usual second-order lucubrations on why scholars of different disciplines think this or that, but material cause and effect. There lies the high adventure for later generations, often mourned as no longer available. There lies great opportunity.

The legacy of the Enlightenment is the belief that entirely on our own we can know, and in knowing, understand, and in understanding, choose wisely. That self-confidence has risen with the exponential growth of scientific knowledge, which is being woven into an increasingly full explanatory web of cause and effect. In the course of the enterprise, we have learned a great deal about ourselves as a species. We now better understand where humanity came from, and what it is. *Homo sapiens,* like the rest of life, was self-assembled. So here we are, no one having guided us to this condition, no one looking over our shoulder, our future entirely up to us. Human autonomy having thus been recognized, we should now feel more disposed to reflect on where we wish to go.

In such an endeavor it is not enough to say that history unfolds by processes too complex for reductionistic analysis. That is the white flag of the secular intellectual, the lazy modernist equivalent of The Will of God. On the other hand, it is too early to speak seriously of ultimate goals, such as perfect green-belted cities and robot expeditions to the nearest stars. It is enough to get *Homo sapiens* settled down and happy before we wreck the planet. A great deal of serious thinking is needed to navigate the decades immediately ahead. We are gaining in our ability to identify options in the political economy most likely to be ruinous. We have begun to probe the foundations of human nature, revealing what people intrinsically most need, and why. We are entering a new era of existentialism, not the old absurdist existentialism of Kierkegaard and Sartre, giving complete autonomy to the individual, but the concept that only unified learning, universally shared, makes accurate foresight and wise choice possible.

In the course of all of it we are learning the fundamental principle that ethics is everything. Human social existence, unlike animal sociality, is based on the genetic propensity to form long-term contracts that evolve by culture into moral precepts and law. The rules of contract formation were not given to humanity from above, nor did they emerge randomly in the mechanics of the brain. They evolved over tens or hundreds of millennia because they conferred upon the genes prescribing them survival and the opportunity to be represented in future generations. We are not errant children who occasionally sin by disobeying instructions from outside our species. We are adults who have discovered which covenants are necessary for survival, and we have accepted the necessity of securing them by sacred oath.

The search for consilience might seem at first to imprison creativity. The opposite is true. A united system of knowledge is the surest means of identifying the still unexplored domains of reality. It provides a clear map of what is known, and it frames the most productive questions for future inquiry. Historians of science often observe that asking the right question is more important than producing the right answer. The right answer to a trivial question is also trivial, but the right question, even when insoluble in exact form, is a guide to major discovery. And so it will ever be in the future excursions of science and imaginative flights of the arts.

I believe that in the process of locating new avenues of creative thought, we will also arrive at an existential conservatism. It is worth asking repeatedly: Where are our deepest roots? We are, it seems, Old World, catarrhine primates, brilliant emergent animals, defined genetically by our unique origins, blessed by our newfound biological genius, and secure in our homeland if we wish to make it so. What does it all mean? This is what it all means. To the extent that we depend on prosthetic devices to keep ourselves and the biosphere alive, we will render everything fragile. To the extent that we banish the rest of life, we will impoverish our own species for all time. And if we should surrender our genetic nature to machine-aided ratiocination, and our ethics and art and our very meaning to a habit of careless discursion in the name of progress, imagining ourselves godlike and absolved from our ancient heritage, we will become nothing.

The Future of Nature
Introduction

BY BARRY LOPEZ

I heard an unfamiliar voice this morning; the call of a bird I could not identify. Birds calling are the conversations of neighbors. Not to know this voice urges me to leave my desk for a window where a pair of binoculars rests on the sill. The air is pale, the light flat. With the resolving power of the glasses I see snow slanting to the clearing below the house, particles fine as dust. A layer of fog wafts over the jade surface of the river, like an unfurled shroud, tattered and wind-buoyed.

I become so intent on the essence of the air I forget the unfamiliar call, until a flock of warbler-size birds bursts from the trees, a commotion tumbling through the lower branches of a red cedar, too far away to tell who they might be and then they're gone.

I've studied birds here for thirty-seven years. I've been on this wooded slope in the rural mountains of western Oregon long enough to know, now, how vast is my innocence. Long enough to know how much will stay hidden, even from the most diligent observer. 1 speak with my human neighbors about the particulars, because no one will ever know it all, and all of us together will never be able to explain the why of any of it. This isn't to wave away science or underestimate the sophisticated observation of Tsanchifin Kalapuya, earlier residents of this valley. It's to acknowledge—here, at least—the daily message: we don't know. Our plans for the future might go awry.

It is painful and old news that human life is in trouble. Fresh water, in ever-shortening supply for people around the world, is bottled in France to sell in America for more than the price of gasoline. A farrago of toxins, unsuspected and nameless, falls like mist over the dining table. Hormones designed to wrest market share for the manufacturer daily mock the integrity of the gamete. Corporations, nor content as individuals merely to vote through their lobbyists, now have them write bills for an obeisant Congress. Free market missionaries, long fractious over the democratic obligation to respect the commonweal's health and to heed lawful restraints, can now ignore the disintegration of human communities in any market (country) doing business with the World Trade Organization.

The great challenge of our time is an ethical and metaphysical one, not a call to new technologies. Do we have the courage to face the carnage that industrialization has wrought, to face, everywhere, the social blight of hypercapitalistic aggression? And, having come to grips with injustice and terracide, can we find the mind to act? Can we imagine a way out?

The outline of an answer is in the small flock of birds bursting and weaving through the pendant branches of the cedar just now, backlit by fog on the water. The event itself is not a Rosetta stone of some kind, a solution to the hieroglyphics of our predicament. The physical allure of the event, how it pulls the eye—the convergence of light, animation, and color, the fleetness of the moment, the mysterious identity of the actors—can be successfully plumbed; but more of this apparition lies outside the senses, beyond the province of the intellect. It is within the ambit of wisdom. The few seconds of the birds' passing continue to resonate within the imagination, which observes the separate, individual movement of each bird even as it regards the weave of the community through the forest. The imagination extends the event in time, filling in the before and after that is opaque to the senses. Where did they come from? Where are they going? It perceives the illuminated riverscape beneath an overcast sky together with the pale air as an orchestration of light, congruent with the trajectory of the birds. The imagination beholds the movement of the birds, the movement of the river, and the movement of the overcast sky as perfectly scaled within each other.

A community of birds, moving relentlessly through subdued light, in harmony with all else, does not need a destination to be beautiful. They do not need an explanation to have meaning. They do not have to serve a purpose. Merely by moving through, they instigate wonder. They stir possibility. A wave of anonymous energy, the fate of which bears directly on our own.

The largest positive social movement in the history of the world is afoot as I write these lines, a movement already apparent on the World Wide Web, but one that has not yet emerged in mainstream media. (Its best chronicler to date may be Paul Hawken, writing in *Blessed Unrest*, a portion of which appeared in a recent issue of *Orion*) It's the movement toward civil society.

In brief, by acting locally on issues of social and economic justice, civil society seeks to re-establish, broadly speaking, environmental and social integrity. Civil society effectively marginalizes the agendas of both government and business. Instead it seeks to establish civil alliances in order to address local and global problems. Through the establishment of such alliances, civil society comes to resemble "of, by, and for the people" writ large. According to Hawken, more than a million such human groups worldwide are now in regular contact with each other. Civil society has no staff, no address, no nation, no religion, no stake in commerce or policy making. Its concerns are the achievement and the enhancement of justice, the encouragement of reverence, and the rise of courageously outspoken communities.

In a glance out the window I see the birds, moving quickly through the cedar, are a civil society.

Ishmael
6

BY DANIEL QUINN

"You know that, as we sit here, we are in no sense defying the law of gravity. Unsupported objects fall toward the center of the earth, and the surfaces on which we're sitting are our supports."

"Right."

"The laws of aerodynamics don't provide us with a way of defying the law of gravity. I'm sure you understand that. They simply provide us with a way of using the air as a support. A man sitting in an airplane is subject to the law of gravity in exactly the way we're subject to it sitting here. Nevertheless the man sitting in the plane obviously enjoys a freedom we lack: the freedom of the air."

"Yes."

"The law we're looking for is like the law of gravity: There is no escaping it, but there is a way of achieving the equivalent of flight—the equivalent of freedom of the air. In other words, it is possible to build a civilization that flies."

I stared at him for a while, then I said, "Okay."

"You remember how the Takers went about trying to achieve powered flight. They didn't begin with an understanding of the laws of aerodynamics. They didn't begin with a theory based on research and carefully planned experimentation. They just built contraptions, pushed them off the sides of cliffs, and hoped for the best."

"True."

"All right. I want to follow one of those early trials in detail. Let's suppose that this trial is being made in one of those wonderful pedal–driven contraptions with flapping wings, based on a mistaken understanding of avian flight."

"Okay."

"As the flight begins, all is well. Our would–be airman has been pushed off the edge of the cliff and is pedaling away, and the wings of his craft are flapping like crazy. He's feeling wonderful, ecstatic. He's experiencing the freedom of the air. What he doesn't realize, however, is that this craft is aerodynamically incapable of flight. It simply isn't in compliance with the laws that make flight possible—but he would laugh if you told him this, He's never heard of such laws, knows nothing about them. He would point at those flapping wings and say, 'See? Just like a bird!' Nevertheless, whatever he thinks, he's not in flight. He's an unsupported object falling toward the center of the earth. He's not in flight, he's in free fall. Are you with me so far?"

"Yes."

"Fortunately—or, rather, unfortunately for our airman—he chose a very high cliff to launch his craft from. His disillusionment is a long way off in time and space. There he is in free fall, feeling wonderful and congratulating himself on his triumph. He's like the man in the joke who jumps out of a ninetieth–floor window on a bet. As he passes the tenth floor, he says to himself, 'Well, so far so good!'

"There he is in free fall, experiencing the exhilaration of what he takes to be flight. From his great height he can see for miles around, and one thing he sees puzzles him: The floor of the valley is dotted with craft just like his—not crashed, simply abandoned. 'Why,' he wonders, 'aren't these craft in the air instead of sitting on the ground? What sort of fools would abandon their aircraft when they could be enjoying the freedom of the air?' Ah well, the behavioral quirks of less talented, earthbound mortals are none of his concern. However, looking down into the valley has brought something else to his attention. He doesn't seem to be maintaining his altitude. In fact, the earth seems to be rising up toward him. Well, he's not very worried about that. After all, his flight has been a complete success up to now, and there's no reason why it shouldn't go on being a success. He just has to pedal a little harder, that's all.

"So far so good. He thinks with amusement of those who predicted that his flight would end in disaster, broken bones, and death. Here he is, he's come all this way, and he hasn't even gotten a bruise, much less a broken bone. But then he looks down again, and what he sees really disturbs him. The law of gravity is catching up to him at the rate of thirty–two feet per second per second—at an accelerating rate. The ground is now rushing up toward him in an alarming way. He's disturbed but far from desperate. 'My craft has brought me *this* far in safety,' he tells himself. 'I just have to keep going.' And so he starts pedaling with all his might. Which of course does him no good at all, because his craft simply isn't in accord with the laws of aerodynamics. Even if he had the power of a thousand men in his legs—ten thousand, a million—that craft is not going to achieve flight. That craft is doomed—and so is he unless he abandons it."

"Right. I see what you're saying, but I don't see the connection with what we're talking about here."

Ishmael nodded. "Here is the connection. Ten thousand years ago, the people of your culture embarked on a similar flight: a civilizational flight. Their craft wasn't designed according to any theory at all. Like our imaginary airman, they were totally unaware that there is a law that must be complied with in order to achieve civilizational flight. They didn't even wonder about it. They wanted the freedom of the air, and so they pushed off in the first contraption that came to hand: the Taker Thunderbolt.

"At first all was well. In fact, all was terrific. The Takers were pedaling away and the wings of their craft were flapping beautifully. They felt wonderful, exhilarated. They were experiencing the freedom of the air: freedom from restraints that bind and limit the rest of the biological community. And with that freedom came marvels—all the things you mentioned the other day: urbanization, technology, literacy, mathematics, science.

"Their flight could never end, it could only go on becoming more and more exciting. They couldn't know, couldn't even have guessed that, like our hapless airman, they were in the air but not in flight. They were in free fall, because their craft was simply not in compliance with the law that makes flight possible. But their disillusionment is far away in the future, and so they're pedaling away and having a wonderful time. Like our airman, they see strange sights in the course of their fall. They see the remains of craft very like their own—not destroyed, merely abandoned—by the Maya, by the Hohokam, by the Anasazi, by the peoples of the Hopewell cult, to mention only a few of those found here in the New World. 'Why,' they wonder, 'are these craft on the ground instead of in the air? Why would any people prefer to be earthbound when they could have the freedom of the air, as we do?' It's beyond comprehension, an unfathomable mystery.

"Ah well, the vagaries of such foolish people are nothing to the Takers. They're pedaling away and having a wonderful time. They're not going to abandon *their* craft. They're going to enjoy the freedom of the air forever. But alas, a law is catching up to them. They don't know such a law even exists, but this ignorance affords them no protection from its effects. This is a law as unforgiving as the law of gravity, and it's catching up to them in exactly the same way the law of gravity caught up to our airman: *at an accelerating rate.*

"Some gloomy nineteenth-century thinkers, like Robert Wallace and Thomas Robert Malthus, look down. A thousand years before, even five hundred years before, they would probably have noticed nothing. But now what they see alarms them. It's as though the ground is rushing up to meet them—as though they are going to crash. They do some figuring and say, 'If we go on this way, we're going to be in big trouble in the not-too-distant future.' The other Takers shrug their predictions off. 'We've come all this enormous way and haven't even received so much as a scratch. It's true the ground seems to be rising up to meet us, but that just means we'll have to pedal a little harder. Not to worry.' Nevertheless, just as was predicted, famine soon becomes a routine condition of life in many parts of the Taker Thunderbolt—and the Takers have to pedal even harder and more efficiently than before. But oddly enough, the harder and more efficiently they pedal, the worse conditions become. Very strange. Peter Farb calls it a paradox: 'Intensification of production to feed an increased population leads to a still greater increase in population.' 'Never mind,' the Takers said. 'We'll just have to put some people pedaling away on a reliable method of birth control. Then the Taker Thunderbolt will fly forever.'

"But such simple answers aren't enough to reassure the people of your culture nowadays. Everyone is looking down, and it's obvious that the ground is rushing up toward you—and rushing up faster every year. Basic ecological and planetary systems are being impacted by the Taker Thunderbolt, and that impact increases in intensity every year. Basic, irreplaceable resources are being devoured every year—and they're being devoured more greedily every year. Whole species are disappearing as a result of your encroachment—and they're disappearing in greater numbers every year. Pessimists—or it may be that they're realists—look down and say, 'Well, the crash may be twenty years off or maybe as much as fifty years off. Actually it could happen anytime. There's no way to be sure.' But of course there are optimists as well, who say, 'We must have faith in our craft. After all, it has brought us *this* far in safety. What's ahead isn't doom, it's just a little hump that we can clear if we all just pedal a little harder. Then we'll soar into a glorious, endless future, and the Taker Thunderbolt will take us to the stars and we'll conquer the universe itself.' But your craft isn't going to save you. Quite the contrary, it's your craft that's carrying you toward catastrophe. Five billion of you pedaling away—or ten billion or twenty billion—can't make it fly. It's been in free fall from the beginning, and that fall is about to end."

When Elephants Weep: The Emotional Lives of Animals
Love and Friendship

BY JEFFREY MOUSSAIEFF AND SUSAN McCARTHY

One evening in the 1930s Ma Shwe, a work elephant, and her three-month-old calf were trapped in rising floodwaters in the Upper Taungdwin River in Burma. Elephant handlers rushed to the river when they heard the calf screaming but could do nothing to help, for the steep banks were twelve to fifteen feet high. Ma Shwe's feet were still on the river bottom, but her calf was floating. Ma Shwe held the baby against her body; whenever she began to drift away, she used her trunk to pull the calf back against the current. The fast-rising water soon washed the calf away and Ma Shwe plunged downstream for fifty yards and retrieved it She pinned her calf against the bank with her head, then lifted it in her trunk, reared up on her hind legs, and placed it on a rocky ledge five feet above the water. Ma Shwe then fell back into the torrent and disappeared downstream.

The elephant handlers turned their attention to the calf, which could barely fit on the narrow ledge where it stood shivering, eight feet below. Half an hour later, J. H. Williams, the British manager of the elephant camp, was peering down at the calf wondering how to rescue her when he heard "the grandest sounds of a mother's love I can remember. Ma Shwe had crossed the river and got up the bank and was making her way back as fast as she could, calling the whole time—a defiant roar, but to her calf it was music. The two little ears, like little maps of India, were cocked forward listening to the only sounds that mattered, the call of her mother." When Ma Shwe saw her calf, safe on the other side of the river, her call changed to the rumble that elephants typically make when pleased. The two elephants were left where they were. By morning Ma Shwe had crossed the river, no longer in flood, and the calf was off the ledge.

Parental Love

The evolutionary approach suggests that parental love— watching over young—makes urgent sense. Parental care allows more young to survive. If parents protect their young, the young can grow bigger before they have to fend for themselves. A baboon can even inherit its mother's status in the troop and an adult female black bear can use her mother's territory while her mother is still occupying it. A young animal can learn survival practices while safely under the protection of its parent. Perhaps—this is debated —the parent even teaches it some of those things.

Not all creatures protect their young. A turtle lays eggs in the sand and departs. Presumably it would not recognize, let alone love, its offspring. But if an animal lays eggs and guards them, as crocodiles do, there must be something that motivates it to do so, and then prevents it from eating the young when they hatch. This might not necessarily be love—it could be brought about by such simple mechanisms as an inhibition against eating eggs and young crocodiles. But expressing care may be evidence of feeling love. Crocodiles also dig their young out of the nest when they hatch, guard the babies, carry them in their jaws, and respond vigorously to their distress calls. Females of a southeast Asian diadem butterfly apparently guard their eggs by standing over them. This probably increases their chances of survival. However, a female will sometimes continue this behavior even unto death, her rotted corpse standing guard over a batch of as yet unhatched eggs.

Mother wolf spiders not only tend their eggs but carry their babies on their backs. Perhaps the babies need to learn hunting skills. More likely, they just need protection while they grow. J. T. Moggridge tells the story of a trap-door spider he had collected and decided to preserve in alcohol. While he knew that spiders twitched for a long time after being put in alcohol, it was then believed that this was mere reflex action. Moggridge shook the baby spiders off her back and dropped her into alcohol. After a while, supposing her to be "dead to sense," he dropped her twenty-four babies in too. To his horror, the mother spider reached out her legs, folded the babies beneath her, and clasped them until she died. After this, Moggridge switched to the use of chloroform.

Can a spider love her babies? Was it a mere reflex that caused the trap-door spider to reach for her young? In this case it seems possible, but it is hard to be certain. One can imagine a simple instinct to draw close to anything that looks like a baby spider. Or she might have seized any objects that happened to be floating in the alcohol. A mother wolf spider is just as kind to strange baby wolf spiders as to her own. This might or might not be accompanied by an emotional state.

Does a spider love its eggs, something the writer John Crompton compares to loving a box of billiard balls? It is so hard to have insight into a spider's mind that it is almost impossible to guess, based on present knowledge. Yet spiders have evolved to produce complex venoms and digestive fluids, and spin silks of varying types from six different kinds of silk glands. Building a spider's web is an extremely complicated behavior. One can argue that a spider is not really a simple organism and that the development of maternal love might well be a shorter evolutionary step than web building. Perhaps one day we will know. What if it was discovered that when a mother wolf spider sees young spiders, her body is flooded with a hormone whose presence is associated with feelings of love in higher animals? Would that be evidence that the spider loves her young? What if it was a hormone peculiar to spiders? Would that mean it wasn't love?

When trying to comprehend the inner lives of creatures so unlike us, it is more useful and accurate to think not of a hierarchy with human beings at the top, but of a spectrum of creature commonality. A spider might have a rich inner life with a riot of emotions including some so different that using our own emotional range as a touchstone can only fail us.

While the question of whether a spider can feel parental love is baffling, there seems little doubt for "higher" animals. Their behavior is so complex that to dismiss it as the exclusive result of inhibitions, reflexes, and fixed action patterns is patently inadequate. Parental care manifests itself in feeding the young, washing them, playing with them, and protecting them from external dangers and from their own inexperience. Mammals, even "primitive" ones such as platypuses and spiny anteaters, suckle their young. The suckling mother is extremely vulnerable in a way that she will seldom allow herself to be with adult animals—in a way that many protective instincts would advise against.

Young mammals are safest in their own nests. In a series of classic experiments on rats, researchers put baby rats on cage floors. Mother rats, and in some cases females who were not mothers, proved zealous at retrieving the babies and bringing them into their nests. They would cross an electrified grid to get to the babies and retrieve unrelated babies as quickly as their own. Curious to see how long this would be kept up, the experimenters offered one rat no fewer than fifty-eight babies, every one of whom she picked up and crammed into her nest. "The female appeared to be as eager at the end of the experiment, which had to be interrupted because we had no more young at our disposal, as she had at the beginning." This behavior did not enhance her own survival. Similarly, when biologists climb up to ledges to band young thick-billed murres (penguinlike seabirds), most of the adults fly away in panic, but a few staunch birds sit tight. Frightened chicks whose own parents have flown off seek out the remaining adults. "It is not uncommon to see one motivated brooder vainly attempting to shelter a dozen or more chicks," seabird biologists have noted.

In contrast to the zealous rats and motivated murres, Nubian ibex who bear triplets instead of twins are reported to reject one fawn. Presumably the doe cannot produce milk for three, so if she kept them all, they would all be malnourished. This "lifeboat behavior" could also be a form of ethically responsible love. When most of a lioness's cubs die or are killed, she may abandon the last cub. Some biologists suggest that it is energetically inefficient for her to put the effort of raising a litter into just one cub, when she can breed again sooner if she does not, and that her "instinctive sense of investment" tells her so. What an instinctive sense of investment may be or feel like, and how it differs from making difficult, loving decisions under conditions of constraint, is not clear. Human parents have been known to take similar actions.

Pilgrim at Tinker Creek
The Present I

BY ANNIE DILLARD

Catch it if you can.

It is early March. I am dazed from a long day of interstate driving homeward; I pull in at a gas station in Nowhere, Virginia, north of Lexington. The young boy in charge ("Chick 'at oil?") is offering a free cup of coffee with every gas purchase. We talk in the glass-walled office while my coffee cools enough to drink. He tells me, among other things, that the rival gas station down the road, whose FREE COFFEE sign is visible from the interstate, charges you fifteen cents if you want your coffee in a Styrofoam cup, as opposed, I guess, to your bare hands.

All the time we talk, the boy's new beagle puppy is skidding around the office, sniffing impartially at my shoes and at the wire rack of folded maps. The cheerful human conversation wakes me, recalls me, not to a normal consciousness, but to a kind of energetic readiness. I step outside, followed by the puppy.

I am absolutely alone. There are no other customers. The road is vacant, the interstate is out of sight and earshot. I have hazarded into a new corner of the world, an unknown spot, a Brigadoon. Before me extends a low hill trembling in yellow brome, and behind the hill, filling the sky, rises an enormous mountain ridge, forested, alive and awesome with brilliant blown lights. I have never seen anything so tremulous and live. Overhead,, great strips and chunks of cloud dash to the northwest in a gold rush. At my back the sun is setting—how can I not have noticed before that the sun is setting? My mind has been a blank slab of black asphalt for hours, but that doesn't stop the sun's wild wheel. I set my coffee beside me on the curb; I smell loam on the wind; I pat the puppy; I watch the mountain.

My hand works automatically over the puppy's fur, following the line of hair under his ears, down his neck, inside his forelegs, along his hot-skinned belly.

Shadows lope along the mountain's rumpled flanks; they elongate like root tips, like lobes of spilling water, faster and faster. A warm purple pigment pools in each ruck and tuck of the rock; it deepens and spreads, boring crevasses, canyons. As the purple vaults and slides, it tricks out the unleafed forest and rumpled rock in gilt, in shape-shifting patches of glow. These gold lights veer and retract, shatter and glide in a series of dazzling splashes, shrinking, leaking, exploding. The ridge's bosses and hummocks sprout bulging from its side; the whole mountain looms miles closer; the light warms and reddens; the bare forest folds and pleats itself like living protoplasm before my eyes, like a running chart, a wildly scrawling oscillograph on the present moment. The air cools; the puppy's skin is hot. I am more alive than all the world.

This is it, I think, this is it, right now, the present, this empty gas station, here, this western wind, this tang of coffee on the tongue, and I am patting the puppy, I am watching the mountain. And the second I verbalize this awareness in my brain, I cease to see the mountain or feel the puppy. I am opaque, so much black asphalt. But at the same second, the second I know I've lost it, I also realize that the puppy is still squirming on his back under my hand. Nothing has changed for him. He draws his legs down to stretch the skin taut so he feels every fingertip's stroke along his furred and arching side, his flank, his flung-back throat.

I sip my coffee. I look at the mountain, which is still doing its tricks, as you look at a still-beautiful face belonging to a person who was once your lover in another country years ago: with fond nostalgia, and recognition, but no real feeling save a secret astonishment that you are now strangers. Thanks. For the memories. It is ironic that the one thing that all religions recognize as separating us from our creator—our very self-consciousness—is also the one thing that divides us from our fellow creatures. It was a bitter birthday present from evolution, cutting us off at both ends. I get in the car and drive home.

Catch it if you can. The present is an invisible electron; its lightning path traced faintly on a blackened screen is fleet, and fleeing, and gone.

That I ended this experience prematurely for myself--that I drew scales over my eyes between me and the mountain and gloved my hand between me and the puppy—is not the only point. After all, it would have ended anyway. I've never seen a sunset or felt a wind that didn't. The levitating saints came down at last, and their two feet bore real weight. No, the point is that not only does time fly and do we die, but that in these reckless conditions we live at all, and are vouchsafed, for the duration of certain inexplicable moments, to know it.

Stephen Graham startled me by describing this same gift in his antique and elegant book, *The Gentle Art of Tramping*. He wrote, "And as you sit on the hillside, or lie prone under the trees of the forest, or sprawl wet-legged on the shingly beach of a mountain stream, the great door, that does not look like a door, opens." That great door opens on the present, illuminates it as with, a multitude of flashing torches.

I had thought, because I had seen the tree with the lights in it, that the great door, by definition, opens on eternity. Now that I have "patted the puppy"—now that I have experienced the present purely through my senses—I discover that, although the door to the tree with the lights in it was opened *from* eternity, as it were, and shone on that tree eternal lights, it nevertheless opened on the real and present cedar. It opened on time: Where else? That Christ's incarnation occurred improbably, ridiculously, at such-and-such a time, into such-and-such a place, is referred to—with great sincerity even among believers—as "the scandal of particularity." Well, the "scandal of particularity" is the only world that I, in particular, know. What use has eternity for light? We're all up to our necks in this particular scandal. Why, we might as well ask, not a plane tree, instead of a bo? I never saw a tree that was no tree in particular; I never met a man, not the greatest theologian, who filled infinity, or even whose hand, say, was undifferentiated, fingerless, like a griddle cake, and not lobed and split just so with the incursions of time.

I don't want to stress this too much. Seeing the tree with the lights in it was an experience vastly different in quality as well as in import from patting the puppy. On that cedar tree shone, however briefly, the steady, inward flames of eternity; across the mountain by the gas station raced the familiar flames of the falling sun. But on both occasions I thought, with rising exultation, this is it, this is it; praise the lord; praise the land. Experiencing the present purely is being emptied and hollow; you catch grace as a man fills his cup under a waterfall.

Consciousness itself does not hinder living in the present. In fact, it is only to a heightened awareness that the great door to the present opens at all. Even a certain amount of interior verbalization is helpful to enforce the memory of whatever it is that is taking place. The gas station beagle puppy, after all, may have experienced those same moments more purely than I did, but he brought fewer instruments to bear on the same material, he had no data for comparison, and he profited only in the grossest of ways, by having an assortment of itches scratched.

Self-consciousness, however, does hinder the experience of the present. It is the one instrument that unplugs all the rest. So long as I lose myself in a tree, say, I can scent its leafy breath or estimate its board feet of lumber, I can draw its fruits or boil tea on its branches, and the tree stays tree. But the second I become aware of myself at any of these activities—looking over my own shoulder, as it were—the tree vanishes, uprooted from the spot and flung out of sight as if it had never grown. And time, which had flowed down into the tree bearing new revelations like floating leaves at every moment, ceases. It dams, stills, stagnates.

Self-consciousness is the curse of the city and all that sophistication implies. It is the glimpse of oneself in a storefront window, the unbidden awareness of reactions on the faces of other people—the novelist's world, not the poet's. I've lived there. I remember what the city has to offer: human companionship, major-league baseball, and a clatter of quickening stimulus like a rush from strong drugs that leaves you drained. I remember how you bide your time in die city, and think, if you stop to think, "next year ... I'll start living; next year ... I'll start my life." Innocence is a better world.

Innocence sees that this is it, and finds it world enough, and time. Innocence is not the prerogative of infants and puppies, and far less of mountains and fixed stars, which have no prerogatives at all. It is not lost to us; the world is a better place than that. Like any other of the spirit's good gifts, it is there if you want it, free for the asking, as has been stressed by stronger words than mine. It is possible to pursue innocence as hounds pursue hares: singlemindedly, driven by a kind of love, crashing over creeks, keening and lost in fields and forests, circling, vaulting over hedges and hills wide-eyed, giving loud tongue all unawares to the deepest, most incomprehensible longing, a root-flame in the heart, and that warbling chorus resounding back from the mountains, hurling itself from ridge to ridge over the valley, now faint, now clear, ringing the air through which the hounds tear, open-mouthed, the echoes of their own wails dimly knocking in their lungs.

What I call innocence is the spirit's unself-conscious state at any moment of pure devotion to any object. It is at once a receptiveness and total concentration. One needn't be, shouldn't be, reduced to a puppy. If you wish to tell me that the city offers galleries, I'll pour you a drink and enjoy your company while it lasts; but I'll bear with me to my grave those pure moments at the Tate (was it the Tate?) where I stood planted, open-mouthed, born, before that one particular canvas, that river, up to my neck, gasping, lost, receding into watercolor depth and depth to the vanishing point, buoyant, awed, and had to be literally hauled away. These are our few live seasons. Let us live them as purely as we can, in the present.

* * *

The color-patches of vision part, shift, and reform as I move through space in time. The present is the object of vision, and what I see before me at any given second is a full field of color patches scattered just so. The configuration will never be repeated. Living is moving; time is a live creek bearing changing lights. As I move, or as the world moves around me, the fullness of what I see shatters. This second of shattering is an *augenblick*, a particular configuration, a slant of light shot in the open eye. Goethe's Faust risks all if he should cry to the moment, the *augenblick*, "Verweile doch!" "Last forever!" Who hasn't prayed that prayer? But the *augenblick* isn't going to *verweile*. You were lucky to get it in the first place. The present is a freely given canvas. That it is constantly being ripped apart and washed downstream goes without saying; it is a canvas, nevertheless.

I like the slants of light; I'm a collector. That's a good one, I say, that bit of bank there, the snakeskin and the aquarium, that patch of light from the creek on bark. Sometimes I spread my fingers into a viewfinder; more often I peek through a tiny square or rectangle—a frame of shadow—formed by the tips of index fingers and thumbs held directly before my eye. Speaking of the development of *papier collé* in late Cubism, Picasso said, "We tried to get rid of *trompe-l'oeil* to find a *trompe-l'esprit*." Trompe-l'esprit! I don't know why the world didn't latch on to the phrase. Our whole life is a stroll—or a forced march—through a gallery hung in trompes-l'esprit.

By mid-month we were getting a dozen tomatoes a day, that many cucumbers, our first eggplants, and squash in unmentionable quantities. A friend arrived one morning as I was tag-teaming with myself to lug two full bushel-baskets of produce into the house. He pronounced a biblical benediction: "The harvest is bountiful and the labors few."

I agreed, of course, but the truth is I still had to go back to the garden that morning to pull about two hundred onions—our year's supply. They had bulbed up nicely in the long midsummer days and were now waiting to be tugged out of the ground, cured, and braided into the heavy plaits that would hang from our kitchen mantel and infuse our meals all through the winter. I also needed to pull beets that day, pick about a bushel of green beans, and slip paper plates under two dozen ripening melons to protect their undersides from moisture and sowbugs. In another week we would start harvesting these, along with sweet corn, peppers, and okra. The harvest was bountiful and the labors were blooming endless.

However high the season, it was important for us to remember we were still just gardeners feeding ourselves and occasional friends, not commercial farmers growing food as a livelihood. That is a whole different set of chores and worries. But in our family's "Year of Local," the distinction did blur for us somewhat. We had other jobs, but when we committed to the project of feeding ourselves (and reporting, here, the results), that task became a significant piece of our family livelihood. Instead of the normal modern custom of working for money that is constantly exchanged for food, we worked directly for food, skipping all the middle steps. Basically this was about efficiency, I told myself—and I still do, on days when the work seems as overwhelming as any second job. But most of the time that job provides rewards far beyond the animal-vegetable paycheck. It gets a body outside for some part of every day to work the heart, lungs, and muscles you wouldn't believe existed, providing a healthy balance to desk jobs that might otherwise render us chair potatoes. Instead of needing to drive to the gym, we walk up the hill to do pitchfork free weights, weed-pull yoga, and Hoe Master. No excuses. The weeds could win.

It is also noiseless in the garden: phoneless, meditative, and beautiful. At the end of one of my more ragged afternoons of urgent faxes from magazine editors or translators, copy that must be turned around on a dime, incomprehensible contract questions, and baffling requests from the IRS that are all routine parts of my day job, I relish the short commute to my second shift. Nothing is more therapeutic than to walk up there and disappear into the yellow-green smell of the tomato rows for an hour to address the concerns of quieter, more manageable colleagues. Holding the soft, viny limbs as tender as babies' wrists, I train them to their trellises, tidy the mulch at their feet, inhale the oxygen of their thanks.

Like our friend David who meditates on Creation while cultivating, I feel lucky to do work that lets me listen to distant thunder and watch a nest of baby chickadees fledge from their hole in the fencepost into the cucumber patch. Even the smallest backyard garden offers emotional rewards in the domain of the little miracle. As a hobby, this one could be considered bird-watching with benefits.

Every gardener I know is a junkie for the experience of being out there in the mud and fresh green growth. Why? An astute therapist might diagnose us as codependent and sign us up for Tomato-Anon meetings. We love our gardens so much it hurts. For their sake we'll bend over till our backs ache, yanking out fistfuls of quackgrass by the roots as if we are tearing out the hair of the world. We lead our favorite hoe like a dance partner down one long row and up the next, in a dance marathon that leaves us exhausted. We scrutinize the yellow beetles with black polka dots that have suddenly appeared like chickenpox on the bean leaves. We spend hours bent to our crops as if enslaved, only now and then straightening our backs and wiping a hand across our sweaty brow, leaving it striped with mud like some child's idea of war paint. What is it about gardening that is so addicting?

That longing is probably mixed up with our DNA. Agriculture is the oldest, most continuous livelihood in which humans have engaged. It's the line of work through which we promoted ourselves from just another primate to Animal-in-Chief. It is the basis for successful dispersal from our original home in Africa to every cold, dry, high, low, or clammy region of the globe. Growing food was the first activity that gave us enough prosperity to stay in one place, form complex social groups, tell our stories, and build our cities. Archaeologists have sturdy evidence that plant and animal domestication both go back 14,000 years in some parts of the world—which makes farming substantially older than what we call "civilization" in any place. All the important crops we now eat were already domesticated around five thousand years ago. Early humans independently followed the same impulse wherever they found themselves, creating small agricultural economies based on the domestication of whatever was at hand: wheat, rice, beans, barley, and corn on various continents, along with sheep in Iraq (around 9000 bc), pigs in Thailand (8000 bc), horses in the Ukraine (5000 bc), and ducks in the Americas (pre-Inca). If you want to know which came first, the chicken-in-every-pot or the politician, that's an easy answer.

Hunter-gatherers slowly gained the skills to control and increase their food supply, learned to accumulate surplus to feed family groups through dry or cold seasons, and then settled down to build towns, cities, empires, and the like. And when centralization collapses on itself, as it inevitably does, back we go to the family farm. The Roman Empire grew fat on the fruits of huge, corporate, slave-driven agricultural operations, to the near exclusion of any small farms by the end of the era. But when Rome crashed and burned, its urbanized citizenry scurried out to every nook and cranny of Italy's mountains and valleys, returning once again to the work of feeding themselves and their families. They're still doing it, famously, to this day.

Where our modern dependence on corporate agriculture is concerned, some signs suggest we might play out our hand a little smarter than Rome did. Industrialized Europe has lately developed suspicions of the centralized food supply, precipitated by mad cow disease and genetically modified foods. The European Union—through government agencies and enforceable laws—is now working to preserve its farmlands, its local food economies, and the authenticity and survival of its culinary specialties.

Here in the United States we are still, statistically speaking, in the thrall of drive-through dining, but we're not unaware that things have gone wrong with our food and the culture of its production. Sociologists write about "the Disappearing Middle," referring to both middle America and mid-sized operators: whole communities in the heartland left alarmingly empty after a decades-old trend toward fewer, bigger commodity farms. We are quicker to address our problems with regional rather than national solutions. Local agencies throughout the Midwest are devising their own answers, mandating the purchase of locally grown organic food in schools, jails, and other public facilities. Policies in many states aim to bring younger people to farming, a profession whose average age is currently about fifty-five. About 15 percent of U.S. farms are now run by women—up from 5 percent in 1978. The booming organic and market-garden industries suggest that consumers are capable of defying a behemoth industry and embracing change. The direct-sales farming sector is growing. Underneath our stylish clothing it seems we are still animals, retaining some vestigial desire to sniff around the water hole and the food supply.

In the forum of media and commerce, the notion of returning to the land is still reliably stereotyped as a hare-brained hippie enterprise. But image probably doesn't matter much to people who wear coveralls to work and have power meetings with a tractor. In a" nation pouring its resources into commodity agriculture—corn and soybeans everywhere and not a speck fit to eat—*back to the land* is an option with a permanent, quiet appeal. The popularity of gardening is evidence of this; so is the huge growth of U.S. agritourism, including U-pick operations, subscription farming, and farm-based restaurants or bed-and-breakfasts. Many of us who aren't farmers or gardeners still have some element of farm nostalgia in our family past, real or imagined: a secret longing for some connection to a life where a rooster crows in the yard.

Animal, Vegetable, Miracle

BY BARBARA KINGSOLVER

By mid-month we were getting a dozen tomatoes a day, that many cu¬cumbers, our first eggplants, and squash in unmentionable quantities. A friend arrived one morning as I was tag-teaming with myself to lug two full bushel-baskets of produce into the house. He pronounced a biblical benediction: "The harvest is bountiful and the labors few."

I agreed, of course, but the truth is I still had to go back to the garden that morning to pull about two hundred onions—our year's supply. They had bulbed up nicely in the long midsummer days and were now waiting to be tugged out of the ground, cured, and braided into the heavy plaits that would hang from our kitchen mantel and infuse our meals all through the winter. I also needed to pull beets that day, pick about a bushel of green beans, and slip paper plates under two dozen ripening melons to protect their undersides from moisture and sowbugs. In another week we would start harvesting these, along with sweet com, peppers, and okra. The harvest was bountiful and the labors were blooming endless.

However high the season, it was important for us to remember we were still just gardeners feeding ourselves and occasional friends, not commercial farmers growing food as a livelihood. That is a whole differ¬ent set of chores and worries. But in our family's "Year of Local," the dis¬tinction did blur-for us somewhat. We had other jobs, but when we committed to the project of feeding ourselves (and reporting, here, the results), that task became a significant piece of our family livelihood. In¬stead of the normal modern custom of working for money that is con-stantly exchanged for food, we worked directly for food, skipping all the middle steps. Basically this was about efficiency, I told myself—and I still do, on days when the work seems as overwhelming as any second job. But most of the time that job provides rewards far beyond the animal-vegetable paycheck. It gets a body outside for some part of every day to work the heart, lungs, and muscles you wouldn't believe existed, providing a healthy balance to desk jobs that might otherwise render us chair potatoes. In¬stead of needing to drive to the gym, we walk up the hill to do pitchfork free weights, weed-pull yoga, and Hoe Master. No excuses. The weeds could win.

It is also noiseless in the garden: phoneless, meditative, and beautiful. At the end of one of my more ragged afternoons of urgent faxes from magazine editors or translators, copy that must be turned around on a dime, incomprehensible contract questions, and baffling requests from the IRS that are all routine parts of my day job, I relish the short commute to my second shift. Nothing is more therapeutic than to walk up there and disappear into the yellow-green smell of the tomato rows for an hour to address the concerns of quieter, more manageable colleagues. Holding the soft, viny limbs as tender as babies' wrists, I train them to their trel¬lises, tidy the mulch at their feet, inhale the oxygen of their thanks.

Like our friend David who meditates on Creation while cultivating, I feel lucky to do work that lets me listen to distant thunder and watch a nest of baby chickadees fledge from their hole in the fencepost into the cucumber patch. Even the smallest backyard garden offers emotional re¬wards in the domain of the little miracle. As a hobby, this one could be considered bird-watching with benefits.

Every gardener I know is a junkie for the experience of being out there in the mud and fresh green growth. Why? An astute therapist might diag¬nose us as codependent and sign us up for Tomato-Anon meetings. We love our gardens so much it hurts. For their sake we'll bend over till our backs ache, yanking out fistfuls of quackgrass by the roots as if we are tearing out the hair of the world. We lead our favorite hoe like a dance partner down one long row and up the next, in a dance marathon that leaves us exhausted. We scrutinize the yellow beetles with black polka dots that have suddenly appeared like chickenpox on the bean leaves. We spend hours bent to our crops as if enslaved, only now and then straight¬ening our backs and wiping a hand across our sweaty brow, leaving it striped with mud like some child's idea of war paint. What is it about gar¬dening that is so addicting?

That longing is probably mixed up with our DNA. Agriculture is the oldest, most continuous liveli-hood in which humans have engaged. It's the line of work through which we promoted ourselves from just another primate to Animal-in-Chief. It is the basis for successful dispersal from our original home in Africa to every cold, dry, high, low, or clammy region of the globe. Growing food was the first activity that gave us enough pros¬perity to stay in one place, form complex social groups, tell our stories, and build our cities. Archaeologists have sturdy evidence that plant and animal domestication both go back 14,000 years in some parts of the world—which makes farming substantially older than what we call "civi¬lization" in any place. All the important crops we now eat were already domesticated around five thousand years ago. Early humans indepen¬dently fol-lowed the same impulse wherever they found themselves, creat¬ing small agricultural economies based on the domestication of whatever was at hand: wheat, rice, beans, barley, and corn on vari-ous continents, along with sheep in Iraq (around 9000 BC), pigs in Thailand (8000 BC), horses in the Ukraine (5000 BC), and ducks in the Americas (pre-Inca). If you want to know which came first, the chicken-in-every-pot or the politi¬cian, that's an easy answer.

Hunter-gatherers slowly gained the skills to control and increase their food supply, learned to accumulate surplus to feed family groups through dry or cold seasons, and then settled down to build towns, cities, empires, and the like. And when centralization collapses on itself, as it inevitably does, back we go to the family farm. The Roman Empire grew fat on the fruits of huge, corporate, slave-driven agricultural operations, to the near exclusion of any small farms by the end of the era. But when Rome crashed and burned, its urbanized citizenry scurried out to every nook and cranny of Italy's mountains and valleys, returning once again to the work of feeding themselves and their families. They're still doing it, fa-mously, to this day.

Where our modern dependence on corporate agriculture is concerned, some signs suggest we might play out our hand a little smarter than Rome did. Industrialized Europe has lately developed suspicions of the central¬ized food supply, precipitated by mad cow disease and genetically modi¬fied foods. The European Union—through government agencies and enforceable laws—is now working to preserve its farmlands, its local food economies, and the authenticity and survival of its culinary specialties.

Here in the United States we are still, statistically speaking, in the thrall of drive-through dining, but we're not unaware that things have gone wrong with our food and the culture of its production. Sociologists write about "the Disappearing Middle," referring to both middle America and mid-sized operators: whole communities in the heartland left alarm¬ingly empty after a decades-old trend toward fewer, bigger commodity farms. We are quicker to address our problems with regional rather than national solutions. Local agencies throughout the Midwest are devising their own answers, mandating the purchase of locally grown organic, food in schools, jails, and other public facilities. Policies in many states aim to bring younger people to farming, a profession whose average age is cur¬rently about fifty-five. About 15 percent of U.S. farms are now run by women—up from 5 percent in 1978. The booming organic and market- garden industries suggest that consumers are capable of defying a behe¬moth industry and embracing change. The direct-sales farming sector is growing. Underneath our stylish clothing it seems we are still animals, retaining some vestigial desire to sniff around the water hole and the food supply.

In the forum of media and commerce, the notion of returning to the land is still reliably stereo-typed as a hare-brained hippie enterprise. But image probably doesn't matter much to people who wear coveralls to work and have power meetings with a tractor. In a' nation pouring its resources into commodity agriculture—corn and soybeans everywhere and not a speck fit to eat—back to the land is an option with a permanent, quiet ap¬peal. The popularity of gardening is evidence of this; so is the huge growth of U.S. agritourism, including U-pick operations, subscription farming, and farm-based restaurants or bed-and-breakfasts. Many of us who aren't farmers or gardeners still have some element of farm nostalgia in our fam¬ily past, real or imagined: a secret longing for some connection to a life where a rooster crows in the yard.

The Art of Commonplace
Think Little

BY WENDELL BERRY

First there was Civil Rights, and then there was the War, and now it is the Environment. The first two of this sequence of causes have already risen to the top of the nation's consciousness and declined somewhat in a remarkably short time. I mention this in order to begin with what I believe to be a justifiable skepticism. For it seems to me that the Civil Rights Movement and the Peace Movement, as popular causes in the electronic age, have partaken far too much of the nature of fads. Not for all, certainly, but for too many they have been the fashionable politics of the moment. As causes they have been undertaken too much in ignorance; they have been too much simplified; they have been powered too much by impatience and guilt of conscience and short-term enthusiasm, and too little by an authentic social vision and long-term conviction and deliberation. For most people those causes have remained almost entirely abstract; there has been too little personal involvement, and too much involvement in organizations that were insisting that *other* organizations should do what was right.

There is considerable danger that the Environment Movement will have the same nature: that it will be a public cause, served by organizations that will self-righteously criticize and condemn other organizations, inflated for a while by a lot of public talk in the media, only to be replaced in its turn by another fashionable crisis. I hope that will not happen, and I believe that there are ways to keep it from happening, but I know that if this effort is carried on solely as a public cause, if millions of people cannot or will not undertake it as a *private* cause as well, then it is *sure* to happen. In five years the energy of our present concern will have petered out in a series of public gestures-and no doubt in a series of empty laws—and a great, and perhaps the last, human opportunity will have been lost.

It need not be that way. A better possibility is that the movement to preserve the environment will be seen to be, as I think it has to be, not a digression from the civil rights and peace movements, but the logical culmination of those movements. For I believe that the separation of these three problems is artificial. They have the same cause, and that is the mentality of greed and exploitation. The mentality that exploits and destroys the natural environment is the same that abuses racial and economic minorities, that imposes on young men the tyranny of the military draft, that makes war against peasants and women and children with the indifference of technology. The mentality that destroys a watershed and then panics at the threat of flood is the same mentality that gives institutionalized insult to black people and then panics at the prospect of race riots. It is the same mentality that can mount deliberate warfare against a civilian population and then express moral shock at the logical consequence of such warfare at My Lai. We would be fools to believe that we could solve any one of these problems without solving the others.

To me, one of the most important aspects of the environmental movement is that it brings us not just to another public crisis, but to a crisis of the protest movement itself. For the environmental crisis should make it dramatically clear, as perhaps it has not always been before, that there is no public crisis that is not also private. To most advocates of civil rights, racism has seemed mostly the fault of someone else. For most advocates of peace the war has been a remote reality, and the burden of the blame has seemed to rest mostly on the government. I am certain that these crises have been more private, and that we have each suffered more from them and been more responsible for them, than has been readily apparent, but the connections have been difficult to see. Racism and militarism have been institutionalized among us for too long for our personal involvement in those evils to be easily apparent to us. Think, for example, of all the Northerners who assumed—until black people attempted to move into *their* neighborhoods that racism was a Southern phenomenon. And think how quickly—one might almost say how naturally—among some of its members the peace movement has spawned policies of deliberate provocation and violence.

*   *   *

But the environmental crisis rises closer to home. Every time we draw a breath, every time we drink a glass of water, every time we eat a bite of food we are suffering from it. And more important, every time we indulge in, or depend on, the wastefulness of our economy-and our economy's first principle is waste-we are *causing* the crisis. Nearly every one of us, nearly every day of his life, is contributing *directly* to the ruin of this planet. A protest meeting on the issue of environmental abuse is not a convocation of accusers, it is a convocation of the guilty. That realization ought to clear the smog of self-righteousness that has almost conventionally hovered over these occasions, and let us see the work that is to be done.

In this crisis it is certain that every one of us has a public responsibility. We must not cease to bother the government and the other institutions to see that they never become comfortable with easy promises. For myself, I want to say that I hope never again to go to Frankfort to present a petition to the governor on an issue so vital as that of strip mining, only to be dealt with by some ignorant functionary-as several of us were not so long ago, the governor himself being "too busy" to receive us. Next time I will go prepared to wait as long as necessary to see that the petitioners' complaints and their arguments are heard *fully*—and by the governor. And then I will hope to find ways to keep those complaints and arguments from being forgotten until something is done to relieve them. The time is past when it was enough merely to elect our officials. We will have to elect them and then go and *watch* them and keep our hands on them, the way the coal companies do. We have made a tradition in Kentucky of putting self-servers, and worse, in charge of our vital interests. I am sick of it. And I think that one way to change it is to make Frankfort a less comfortable place. I believe in American political principles, and I will not sit idly by and see those principles destroyed by sorry practice. I am ashamed and deeply distressed that American government should have become the chief cause of disillusionment with American principles.

And so when the government in Frankfort again proves too stupid or too blind or too corrupt to see the plain truth and to act with simple decency, I intend to be there, and I trust that I won't be alone. I hope, moreover, to be there, not with a sign or a slogan or a button, but with the facts and the arguments. A crowd whose discontent has risen no higher than the level of slogans is *only* a crowd. But a crowd that understands the reasons for its discontent and knows the remedies is a vital community, and it will have to be reckoned with. I would rather go before the government with two men who have a competent understanding of an issue, and who therefore deserve a hearing, than with two thousand who are vaguely dissatisfied.

But even the most articulate public protest is not enough. We don't live in the government or in institutions or in our public utterances and acts, and the environmental crisis has its roots in our *lives*. By the same token, environmental health will also be rooted in our lives. That is, I take it, simply a fact, and in the light of it we can see how superficial and foolish we would be to think that we could correct what is wrong merely by tinkering with the institutional machinery. The changes that are required are fundamental changes in the way we are living.

*   *   *

What we are up against in this country, in any attempt to invoke private responsibility, is that we have nearly destroyed private life. Our people have given up their independence in return for the cheap seductions and the shoddy merchandise of so-called "affluence." We have delegated all our vital functions and responsibilities to salesmen and agents and bureaus and experts of all sorts. We cannot feed or clothe ourselves, or entertain ourselves, or communicate with each other, or be charitable or neighborly or loving, or even respect ourselves, without recourse to a merchant or a corporation or a public-service organization or an agency of the government or a style-setter or an expert. Most of us cannot think of dissenting from the opinions or the actions of one organization without first forming a new organization. Individualism is going around these days in uniform, handing out the party line on individualism. Dissenters want to publish their personal opinions over a thousand signatures.

The Confucian *Great Digest* says that the "chief way for the production of wealth" (and he is talking about real goods, not money) is "that the producers be many and that the mere consumers be few...." But even in the much-publicized rebellion of the young against the materialism of the affluent society, the consumer mentality is too often still intact: the standards of behavior are still those of kind and quantity, the security sought is still the security of numbers, and the chief motive is still the consumer's anxiety that he is missing out on what is "in." In this state of total consumerism—which is to say a state of helpless dependence on things and services and ideas and motives that we have forgotten how to provide ourselves—all meaningful contact between ourselves and the earth is broken. We do not understand the earth in terms either of what it offers us or of what it requires of us, and I think it is the rule that people inevitably destroy what they do not understand. Most of us are not directly responsible for strip mining and extractive agriculture and other forms of environmental abuse. But we are guilty nevertheless, for we connive in them by our ignorance. We are ignorantly dependent on them. We do not know enough about them; we do not have a particular enough sense of their danger. Most of us, for example, not only do not know how to produce the best food in the best way—we don't know how to produce any kind in any way. Our model citizen is a sophisticate who before puberty understands how to produce a baby, but who at the age of thirty will not know how to produce a potato. And for this condition we have elaborate rationalizations, instructing us that dependence for everything on somebody else is efficient and economical and a scientific miracle. I say, instead, that it is madness, mass produced. A man who understands the weather only in terms of golf is participating in a chronic public insanity that either he or his descendants will be bound to realize as suffering. I believe that the death of the world is breeding in such minds much more certainly and much faster than in any political capital or atomic arsenal.

For an index of our loss of contact with the earth we need only look at the condition of the American farmer—who must in our society, as in every society, enact man's dependence on the land, and his responsibility to it. In an age of unparalleled affluence and leisure, the American farmer is harder pressed and harder worked than ever before; his margin of profit is small, his hours are long; his outlays for land and equipment and the expenses of maintenance and operation are growing rapidly greater; he cannot compete with industry for labor; he is being forced more and more to depend on the use of destructive chemicals and on the wasteful methods of haste and anxiety. As a class, farmers are one of the despised minorities. So far as I can see, farming is considered marginal or incidental to the economy of the country, and farmers, when they are thought of at all, are thought of as hicks and yokels, whose lives do not fit into the modem scene. The average American farmer is now an old man whose sons have moved away to the cities. His knowledge, and his intimate connection with the land, are about to be lost. The small independent farmer is going the way of the small independent craftsmen and storekeepers. He is being forced off the land into the cities, his place taken by absentee owners, corporations, and machines. Some would justify all this in the name of efficiency. As I see it, it is an enormous social and economic and cultural blunder. For the small farmers who lived on their farms *cared* about their land. And given their established connection to their land—which was often hereditary and traditional as well as economic—they could have been encouraged to care for it more competently than they have so far. The corporations and machines that replace them will never be bound to the land by the sense of birthright and continuity, or by the love that enforces care. They will be bound by the rule of efficiency, which takes thought only of the volume of the year's produce, and takes no thought of the slow increment of the life of the land, not measurable in pounds or dollars, which will assure the livelihood and the health of the coming generations.

If we are to hope to correct our abuses of each other and of other races and of our land, and if our effort to correct these abuses is to be more than a political fad that will in the long run be only another form of abuse, then we are going to have to go far beyond public protest and political action. We are going to have to rebuild the substance and the integrity of private life in this country. We are going to have to gather up the fragments of knowledge and responsibility that we have parceled out to the bureaus and the corporations and the specialists, and we are going to have to put those fragments back together again in our own minds and in our families and households and neighborhoods. We need better government, no doubt about it. But we also need better minds, better friendships, better marriages, better communities. We need persons and households that do not have to wait upon organizations, but can make necessary changes in themselves, on their own.

✻   ✻   ✻

For most of the history of this country our motto, implied or spoken, has been Think Big. I have come to believe that a better motto, and an essential one now, is Think Little. That implies the necessary change of thinking and feeling, and suggests the necessary work. Thinking Big has led us to the two biggest and cheapest political dodges of our time: plan-making and law-making. The lotus-eaters of this era are in Washington, D.C., Thinking Big. Somebody comes up with a problem, and somebody in the government comes up with a plan or a law. The result, mostly, has been the persistence of the problem, and the enlargement and enrichment of the government.

But the discipline of thought is not generalization; it is detail, and it is personal behavior. While the government is "studying" and funding and organizing its Big Thought, nothing is being done. But the citizen who is willing to Think Little, and, accepting the discipline of that, to go ahead on his own, is already solving the problem. A man who is trying to live as a neighbor to his neighbors will have a lively and practical understanding of the work of peace and brotherhood, and let there be no mistake about it—he is *doing* that work. A couple who make a good marriage, and raise healthy, morally competent children, are serving the world's future more directly and surely than any political leader, though they never utter a public word. A good farmer who is dealing with the problem of soil erosion on an acre of ground has a sounder grasp of that problem and *cares* more about it and is probably doing more to solve it than any bureaucrat who is talking about it in general. A man who is willing to undertake the discipline and the difficulty of mending his own ways is worth more to the conservation movement than a hundred who are insisting merely that the government and the industries mend *their* ways.

PART 5

Global Voices
The North-South Divide: Environmental Justice,
Development & Corporate Hegemony

Introduction by Beth Schaefer Caniglia
Regis University

While the voices of intellectuals, scholars, and scientists were relatively moderate in their tone, global voices of concern about the environment tend to be more radical. Global social movements, international intergovernmental organizations, and many national governments have converged around the concepts of sustainable development, the precautionary principle, and environmental justice as ways to frame contemporary environmental problems. The concept of sustainable development is broad, but there is general agreement that the term indicates development that does not compromise the ability for future generations to develop and comprises three pillars: environment, economy, and equity. The authors featured in this section address the interdependence of these three pillars of sustainable development, bringing their own arguments to bear to frame the causes and solutions of environmental problems around the world.

Some of the general themes that mark global perspectives on environmental problems include resource exploitation in developing nations for use in industrialized nations; local livelihoods in the largely agricultural communities of the global South; health issues that surround water quality, pollution, and poverty; the commodification of traditional knowledge as a form of stealing from the developing world; and, in general, the domination of countries, communities, and individual lives by corporations. As you see, the philosophical questions regarding whether animals feel or whether conservation or preservation is a better alternative to protect endangered species are far off the radar screen of most of these authors. Instead, basic livelihoods, health, knowledge and technology transfer, local economic development, corrupt governance systems, and corporate exploitation top the list of concerns. As Maurice Strong states in his opening statement of the 1992 United Nations Conference on Environment and Development:

Central to the issues we are going to have to deal with are: patterns of production and consumption in the industrialized world that are undermining the Earth's life-support system …The concentration of population growth in the developing countries and economic growth in the industrialized nations has deepened, creating imbalances which are unsustainable, either in environmental or economic terms … Environment must be integrated into every aspect of our economic policy and decision-making as well as the culture and value systems which motivate economic behavior.

The dichotomy of North-South has been a feature of most writing on the global climate change movement and the climate justice movement. Scholars have universally argued that social movements from the global South face considerable barriers to effective participation in global movements. Southern NGOs often lack the financial resources to travel to the cites of international meetings, and those who can participate often suffer from slow learning curves since their governments don't typically mirror the parliamentarian structure of the UN. Finally, English-language dominance at UN meetings presents challenges that the industrialized North movements do not have to face (Caniglia 2010). Recent literature also reminds us that people in the global South often orient themselves toward their national governments and international corporations quite differently than activists and citizens from the Northern industrialized nations (Doyle and MacGregor 2013).

While many activists from the global North align their movements toward moderate changes in individual behaviors (as we have illustrated), "nearly all environmental movements in the global South still seem to cling to ideas from the Left … [and] tend to be framed as "the people" versus either a large transnational corporation or the state" (Doyle and MacGregor 2013). This tends to place activists from the global South on the margins of the global environmental movement and results in the use of more outsider tactics like protests, boycotts, and other anti-capitalist displays. Reformist approaches aren't easily embraced by activists in the global South, especially when their own governments are authoritarian or corrupt; in fact, it is a blatant sign of defeat in some parts of the global South to work in cooperation with the state or large corporations, particularly movements in Latin America. Post-colonialism viewpoints, like those of many African movements, also tend to place social distance between the framing and tactics chosen by movements in the global South and the industrialized North and global movements. We see these motivations clearly in the Nobel acceptance speech of Kenyan environmental activist Wangari Maathai (2004):

As I was growing up, I witnessed forests being cleared and replaced by commercial plantations, which destroyed local biodiversity and the capacity of the forests to conserve water … in 1977, when we started the Green Belt Movement, I was partly responding to needs identified by rural women, namely lack of firewood, clean drinking water, balanced diets, shelter and income.

This was due to the degradation of their immediate environment as well as the introduction of commercial farming, which replaced the growing of household food crops … I came to understand that when the environment is destroyed, plundered or mismanaged, we undermine our quality of life and that of future generations.

The global South does not experience their lives as post-Industrial Revolution; rather, industrialization is either marching forward with severe environmental impacts or it is a noticeably absent option for upward mobility and improved quality of life. The "injustices of international economic arrangements," in the words of Maathai, characterize a fundamental disconnect between the industrialization of the North and the poverty, unemployment, and exploitation of the people and natural resources of the South. This story is the central theme of Vandana Shiva's (2000) work on international food justice and biopiracy.

> …As small farms and small farmers are pushed to extinction, as monocultures replace biodiverse crops, as farming is transformed from the production of nourishing and diverse foods into the creation of markets for genetically engineered seeds, herbicides, and pesticides. As farmers are transformed from producers into the consumers of corporate-patented agricultural products, as markets are destroyed locally and nationally but expanded globally, the myth of "free trade" and the global economy becomes a means for the rich to rob the poor of their right to food and even their right to life. For the vast majority of the world's people—70 percent—earn their livelihoods by producing food … In contrast, in the industrialized countries, only 2 percent of the population are farmers.

Shiva highlights particular ways that industrial agriculture has led to the monopolization of seeds, mono-cropping over local biodiversity, and replacing local culture with the culture of capitalism:

> Imported soybeans' takeover of the Indian market is a clear example of the imperialism on which globalization is built. One crop exported from a single country by one or two corporations replaced hundreds of foods and food producers, destroying biological and cultural diversity, and economic and political democracy. Small mills are now unable to serve small farmers and poor consumers with low-cost, healthy, and culturally appropriate edible oils. Farmers are robbed of their freedom to choose what they grow, and consumers are being robbed of their freedom to choose what they eat.

Echoing Shiva's understanding of local plants as culture, Wangari Maathai (2004) states in her Nobel Prize acceptance speech: "The Green Belt Movement explores the concept of cultural biodiversity, especially with respect to indigenous seeds and medicinal plants."

To understand the position of activists in the developing world, we must closely evaluate the interdependence of development, environmental resources, and culture, sometimes referred to as the tie between people, prosperity, and the planet. Regardless of the site chosen for agricultural development, mono-cropping impacts biodiversity and makes the land more vulnerable to disease. These findings are unquestioned at this point. Mono-cropping is also partially to blame for the collapse of pollinating species like bees and butterflies, and it generally requires greater inputs of water and other chemicals. Those chemicals are costly, sometimes too costly for small-scale and subsistence farmers from the developing countries. While government officials are often excited by the opportunities of large-scale industrial agriculture, small-scale farmers can't compete and remain independent; they often have to sell or lease their land to become part of the new export market, and local forms of agriculture all but disappear due to the competition. Local people lose their traditional foods and their relationship with food production, leaving a cultural void that has led to a large number of farmer suicides in the global

South. People lose their sense of identity and their feeling of security in the world as their culture and practices are lost. This leads to a strong resentment toward transnational corporations.

This fight against transnational corporations is found at its height in the Ogoni region of southern Nigeria, where Shell Corporation is accused of exploiting the local indigenous peoples, destroying the natural environment, and causing environmental health problems that will endure for generations. A strong local social movement tried to fight back against the destruction of their local lands, but with very few people actually holding titles to their land, and with 80 percent of the Nigerian economy dependent upon petroleum production, the Ogoni people had little leverage to get international attention for their cause. Despite this, one of the movement leaders, Ken Saro-Wiwa, became a global figure in the environmental justice movement when he was jailed and eventually put to death by the Nigerian government for his part in the anti-Shell demonstrations. His execution speech is included among our selections and illustrates the often tragic outcomes that result when the values and traditions of local indigenous communities are discarded in exchange for corporate and elite profits. I quote his speech at length:

> My lord, we all stand before history. I am a man of peace, of ideas. Appalled by the denigrating poverty of my people who live on a richly endowed land, distressed by their political marginalization and economic strangulation, angered by the devastation of their land, their ultimate heritage, anxious to preserve their right to life and to a decent living, and determined to usher to this country as a whole a fair and just democratic system which protects everyone and every ethnic group and gives us all a valid claim to human civilization, I have devoted my intellectual and material resources, my very life, to a cause in which I have total belief and from which I cannot be blackmailed or intimidated...

> I and my colleagues are not the only ones on trial. Shell is here on trial ... The company has, indeed, ducked this particular trial, but its day will surely come and the lessons learned here may prove useful to it for there is not doubt in my mind that the ecological war that the Company has waged in the Delta will be called into question sooner than later and the crimes of that war be duly punished...

> On trial also is the Nigerian nation, its present rulers and those who assist them. Any nation which can do to the weak and disadvantaged what the Nigerian nation has done to the Ogoni, loses a claim to independence and to freedom from outside influence...

> We all stand on trial, my lord, for by our actions we have denigrated our Country and jeopardized the future of our children. As we subscribe to the sub-normal and accept double standards, as we lie and cheat openly, as we protect injustice and oppression, we empty our classrooms, denigrate our hospitals, fill our stomachs with hunger and elect to make ourselves slaves of those who ascribe to higher standards, pursue the truth, and honour justice, freedom and hard work.

> In my innocence of the false charges I face Here, in my utter conviction, I call upon the Ogoni people, the peoples of the Niger delta, and the oppressed ethnic minorities of Nigeria to stand up now and fight fearlessly and peacefully for their rights.

Kenule Beeson Saro-Wiwa was put to death, along with seven other Ogoni leaders, on November 11, 1995.

Natural Resource Rights

Several scholars have turned to the Cochabamba movement in Bolivia as an illustrative case of grassroots environmental movements in the global South (Olivera 2004). This movement of peasants, environmental groups, and local leaders fought against the privatization of water services in the Cochabamba region of Bolivia. Beginning as a grassroots, local movement, participants took their cause to international meetings like the World Social Forum, where they mobilized global environmental movement leaders like Maude Barlow to take up their cause. The central argument in this fight was that natural resources like water and air are common goods that belong to no one and everyone at the same time. By mobilizing international networks from the global democracy and international environmental movements, residents of Cochabamba maneuvered complex political institutions to become a central rallying point for indigenous, peasant, and grassroots environmental movements around the world. The movement became so central to the identity of Bolivia that Evo Morales, a leader of the Cochabamba movement, was elected as president of Bolivia in 2005. Morales's leadership has solidified the Cochabamba movement as a battle cry for indigenous farmers around the world who feel their access to natural resources are threatened by corporate interests.

Maude Barlow and her co-author, Tony Clarke, write in *Blue Gold* (2002):

> There was a time not so long ago when certain aspects of life and Nature were not considered commodities to be bought and sold in the marketplace. Some things were not for sale—things like natural resources (including air and water), genetic codes and seeds, health, education, culture, and heritage. These, and other essential elements of life and Nature, were part of a shared inheritance or rights that belonged to all people. In other words, they belonged to "the commons."

Creative policies have been proposed by some governments. South Africa's water law sets aside a basic allotment of water to each person as a human right and another allotment as a natural reserve for ecosystem services, and it allows the purchase of water above the basic level as a commodity. This kind of creative thinking may stop the elimination of local knowledge and management of natural resources and create partnership opportunities that respect local needs and traditions. As Barlow and Clarke encourage us to ask, genes, seeds, air, and water are up for sale to the highest bidder, but how did these common-pool resources become the property of those who are making the deals? Questions of governance and justice are at the center of such questions.

The "S" Word: Can Socialist-Democracy lead to Sustainable Development?

John Bellamy Foster has spent his career examining the relationship between environmental degradation, economics, and social justice—the three pillars of sustainable development. In a recent book, perhaps one of the crowning achievements of his career, he suggests that socialism as a governance system can serve as a model for the achievement of sustainable human development. How does this differ, you might ask, from sustainable development more generally? According to Foster, the only way development can be sustainable is to correct the current imbalances between environmental resource availability and broad-based human suffering. This can only be achieved by reorganizing our values around shared prosperity. It cannot be enough that many are benefitting from the overexploitation of nature; such an approach, according to Foster, will never be sustainable. Foster (2009) defines socialism as follows:

> Socialism has always been understood as a society aimed at reversing the relations of exploitation of capitalism and removing the manifold social evils to which these relations have given rise. This requires the abolition of private property in the means of production, a high degree of equality in all things, replacement of the blind forces of the market by planning by the associated producers in accordance with genuine social needs, and the elimination to whatever extent possible of invidious distinctions associated with the division of town and country, mental and manual labor, racial divisions, and gender divisions.

Foster argues that this is not enough, however: "The transition to socialism is possible only through a revolutionizing practice that *revolutionizes human beings themselves*" [emphasis in the original]. We must correct the extent to which we overexploit nature, and we must discontinue wherever possible our alienation from nature.

So, what does this mean in practice? The path isn't clear to most practitioners, but some common ground can be found in these readings and in the life stories of their authors. In the case of Wangari Maathai, Nobel Peace Prize recipient, we see a woman who watched the beautiful countryside of her youth disappear, and along with it, the livelihoods and traditions of her local community also disappeared. In the case of Ken Saro-Wiwa, Ogoni activist from Nigeria, the destruction of the delta made elites and Shell Corporation rich while leaving the Ogoni people struggling for their lives. In the case of the Indian farmers who have resorted to suicide in the face of corporate agriculture, local crops and farming traditions withered under the shadow of global export markets. In each of these cases, we find an imbalance between environmental extraction, local prosperity, and traditional practices. In most of these cases, the poor and ethnic minorities are the most common losers, while corporations and local elites prosper.

Bill McKibben writes: "The Left has embarked on a series of 'new democratic initiatives' that come as close as anything on the planet to actually incarnating 'sustainable development'" (Foster 2009). Perhaps Foster puts it best when he writes:

> ...there is little real prospect for the needed global ecological revolution, unless these attempts to revolutionize social relations in the struggle for a just and sustainable society, now emerging in the periphery, are somehow mirrored in movements for ecological and social revolution in the advanced capitalist world. It is only through fundamental change at the center of the system, from which the pressures on the planet principally emanate, that there is any genuine possibility of avoiding ultimate ecological destruction.

References

1. Barlow, Maude, and Tony Clarke. *Blue Gold: The Fight to Stop the Corporate Theft of the World's Water*. New York: The New Press, 2002.

2. Caniglia, Beth Schaefer. "Global Environmental Governance & Pathways to Environmental Justice." In *Environmental Injustice Beyond Borders: Local Perspectives on Global Inequalities*, edited by J Agyeman and J. Carmin. Cambridge, MA: MIT Press, 2010.

3. Catastrophe Map. http://catastrophemap.org/toxic-apocalypse-nigerian-oil-disaster.html.

4. Doyle, T., and S. MacGregor, eds. *Environmental Movements Around the World: Shades of Green in Politics and Culture.* Santa Barbara, CA: Praeger Press, 2013.

5. Foster, John Bellamy. *The Ecological Revolution.* New York: Monthly Review Press, 2009.

6. Gambrell, Jon. "Oil Thefts Threaten Nigeria's Economy, Environment." *The Associated Press.* http://news.yahoo.com/oil-thefts-threaten-nigerias-economy-environment-085738512.html.

7. Maathai, Wangari. 2004. As in selection.

8. Olivera, Oscar. *!Cochabamba!: Water War in Bolivia.* Cambridge, MA: South End Press, 2004.

9. Saro-Wiwa, Ken. 1995. As in selection.

10. Shiva, Vandana. *Stolen Harvest.* Cambridge, MA: South End Press, 2000.

11. Strong, Maurice. 1992 (from selections)

Opening Statement to the Rio Earth Summit

BY MAURICE STRONG

Mr. President, Secretary-General, Your Majesty, Your Excellency the President of Portugal, Your Excellencies the Prime Ministers of Norway and Tuvalu, Distinguished Leaders of Brazil present here, Distinguished Delegates, and the people we all serve.

First, may I extend my warm congratulations to you, Mr. President, on your election as President of this Conference. You have now become our President and I, and the members of our fine UNCED Secretariat team, look forward to serving under your leadership. I want also to express to you, to your Government and your people, our deep gratitude for the remarkable job you have done in preparing for this largest intergovernmental conference ever, and for the warmth and generosity with which you have welcomed us here. Our gratitude extends, too, to Governor Brizola and Mayor Alencar who have joined you so wholeheartedly in this.

Today, the capital of our planet moves to this beautiful city of Rio de Janeiro. There could be no better place to hold this historic Earth Summit. This great country of Brazil, which takes pride in being a part of the developing world, is a universe in itself, rich in the resources with which nature has endowed it and in the diversity, the vitality, the creativity and the charm of its people. It is, at the same time, one of the world's leading industrial countries and one of its most urbanized, while containing some of its greatest frontier areas. The EcoBrasil exhibition in Sao Paulo and EcoTech '92 here in Rio have demonstrated, too, the impressive quality and range of Brazil's scientific and technological capabilities. The economic, social and environmental challenges which Brazil is tackling with characteristic vigor and dynamism mirror the whole panoply of issues this Conference is addressing. And the initiatives Brazil has taken under your leadership, Mr. President, in dealing with some of your own critical environment and development problems have set an enlightened example to the international community. Today, all Brazilians can take special and well-deserved pride in their country and their President.

I commend you, Mr. President and Secretary-General Boutros-Ghali, whom I am so proud to serve, for your inspiring statements which have made clear the awesome nature of the challenges which confront this Conference. Indeed, it will define the state of political will to save our planet and to make it, in the words of the EarthPledge, a secure and hospitable home for present and future generations.

This is not a single issue Conference. Rather, it deals with the overall cause and effect system through which a broad range of human activities interact to shape our future.

Twenty years ago at Stockholm, representatives of 113 of the world's nations took the first steps on a new journey of hope for the future of our 'Only One Earth'. Today, in this beautiful city of Rio de Janeiro, you have come together, as representatives of more than 178 nations, in this unprecedented parliament of the planet, to take the decisions needed to rekindle that hope and give it new substance and impetus. For, despite significant progress made since 1972 in many areas, the hopes ignited at Stockholm remain largely unfulfilled.

As the World Commission on Environment and Development made clear and—I am so pleased that the distinguished Chairman of that Commission is here and will be addressing us this morning, Prime Minister Gro Harlem Brundtland—in its landmark report, 'Our Common Future', the environment, natural resources and life-support systems of our planet have continued to deteriorate, while global risks like those of climate change and ozone depletion have become more immediate and acute. Yet all the environmental deterioration and risks we have experienced to date have occurred at levels of population and human activity that are much less than they will be in the period ahead. And the underlying conditions that have produced this dilemma remain as dominant driving forces that are shaping our future and threatening our survival.

Undermining Earth's life-support system

Central to the issues we are going to have to deal with are: patterns of production and consumption in the industrial world that are undermining the Earth's life-support systems; the explosive increase in population, largely in the developing world, that is adding a quarter of a million people daily; deepening disparities between rich and poor that leave 75 per cent of humanity struggling to live; and an economic system that takes no account of ecological costs or damage —one which views unfettered growth as progress. We have been the most successful species ever; we are now a species out of control. Our very success is leading us to a dangerous future.

The concentration of population growth in developing countries and economic growth in the industrialized countries has deepened, creating imbalances which are unsustainable, either in environmental or economic terms. Since 1972 world population has grown by 1.7 billion people, equivalent to almost the entire population at the beginning of this century. 1.5 billion of these live in developing countries which are least able to support them. Each individual person is precious. We must honour, and the Earth must support, all its children. But, overall, this growth cannot continue. Population must be stabilized, and rapidly. If we do not do it, nature will, and much more brutally.

During the same 20 year period, world GDP increased by $20 trillion. Yet 15 per cent of the increase accrued to developing countries. Over 70 per cent went to the already rich countries, adding further to their disproportionate pressures on the environment, resources and life-support systems of our planet. This is the other part of the population problem: the fact that every child born in the developed world consumes 20 to 30 times the resources of the planet than a third world child.

The same processes of economic growth which have produced such unprecedented levels of wealth and power for the rich minority and hopes of a better life for everyone have also given rise to the risks and imbalances that now threaten the future of rich and poor alike. This growth model, and the patterns of production and consumption which have accompanied it, is not sustainable for the rich; nor can it be replicated by the poor. To continue along this pathway could lead to the end of our civilization.

Vicious circle of poverty

Yet the poor need economic and social development as the only means of relieving the vicious circle of poverty in which they are caught up. Their right to development cannot be denied; nor should it be impeded by conditions unilaterally imposed on the financial flows or trade of developing countries. The rich must take the lead in bringing their development under control, reducing substantially their impacts on the environment, leaving environmental 'space' for developing countries to grow. The wasteful and destructive lifestyles of the rich cannot be maintained at the cost of the lives and livelihoods of the poor, and of nature.

For the rich, the transition to sustainable development need not require regression to a difficult or primitive life. On the contrary, it can lead to a richer life of expanded opportunities for self-realization and fulfilment. More satisfying and secure because it is sustainable, and more sustainable because its opportunities and benefits are more universally shared.

Sustainable development—development that does not destroy or undermine the ecological, economic or social basis on which continued development depends—is the only viable pathway to a more secure and hopeful future for rich and poor alike.

Fortunately, that pathway is still an option, but that option is closing. This Conference must establish the foundations for effecting the transition to sustainable development. This can only be done through fundamental changes in our economic life and in international economic relations, particularly as between industrialized and developing countries. Environment must be integrated into every aspect of our economic policy and decision-making as well as the culture and value systems which motivate economic behaviour.

Some of the world's most precious resources and ecosystems are in acute danger—tropical forests, arctic tundra, coastal waters, rivers and other freshwater systems. They can only be protected and developed sustainably if they are valued fully and if the people who depend on them for their livelihoods have the incentives and the means to do so.

In our negotiations with each other, nature must have a place at the table, for nature will have the last word and our decisions must respect the boundary conditions it imposes on us as well as the rich array of resources and opportunities it makes available to us. As Sir Shridath Ramphal says in his book, *Our Country, The Planet*, commissioned for the Conference, 'In our drive for material betterment, we have become so indifferent to our roots in nature that we are in danger of tearing them out'. We have to face up to the dire implications of the warnings scientists are sounding. They point to the real prospect that this planet may soon become uninhabitable for people. If we respond only with rhetoric and gestures, this prospect could become a grim reality.

Preparations for the Conference have focused on the concrete actions required to effect the transition to sustainability. Pursuant to the mandate extended to it by the United Nations General Assembly in its Resolution 44/228 and under the masterful leadership of its Chairman, Ambassador Tommy Koh, the Preparatory Committee of this Conference, in more than two years of intensive preparations and negotiations, has fashioned the proposals that are now before you. In doing so, it has had the benefit of an extraordinary range of contributions, from the entire UN system, from preparatory conferences in every region, many sectoral conferences, national reports and the participation in various ways of an unprecedented number of institutions, experts and organizations, governmental and non-governmental. I join the Secretary-General in his tribute to all of those who have contributed to this process. I want especially to note that no international conference of governments has enjoyed a broader range of participation and greater contributions from non-governmental organizations than this one, and I salute them for this.

Critical issues

The results of this preparatory work are now before you. The majority of the proposals come with the recommendation, by consensus, of the Preparatory Committee. But some critically important issues remain for you to resolve here.

Let me mention some of the most important issues as I see them.

The 27 principles of the 'Rio Declaration', building on the Stockholm Declaration, clearly represent a major step forward in establishing the basic-principles that must govern the conduct of nations and peoples towards each other and the Earth to ensure a secure and sustainable future. I recommend that you approve them in their present form and that they serve as a basis for future negotiation of an 'Earth Charter', which could be approved on the occasion of the 50th anniversary of the United Nations.

Agenda 21 is the product of an extensive process of preparation at the professional level and negotiation at the political level. It establishes, for the first time, a framework for the systemic, co-operative action required to effect the transition to sustainable development. And its 115 pro-gramme areas define the concrete actions required to carry out this transition. In respect of the issues that are still unresolved, I would urge you to ensure that the agreements reached at this historic Summit move us beyond the positions agreed by Governments in previous fora.

The issue of new and additional financial resources to enable developing countries to imple-ment Agenda 21 is crucial and pervasive. This, more than any other issue, will clearly test the degree of political will and commitment of all countries to the fundamental purposes and goals of this Earth Summit. The Tokyo Declaration on Financing Global Environment and Development provides promising evidence that movement on this key issue is possible, despite the current dif-ficult economic climate.

The need to begin the process is so urgent, so compelling, that Governments, particularly those of the high-income countries, will have come, I trust, prepared to make the initial commitments that will be necessary to do this. It is clear that the North must begin to invest much more in progress for the developing world. Developing countries must leave here with confidence that they will have the support and incentives they need to commit themselves to the substantial reorienta-tions of policies and redeployment of their own resources called for by Agenda 21. For they are responsible for their own development and must provide most of the resources some 80 per cent -required to implement Agenda 21.

Additional funds

I hope, too, that you would agree that these new and additional funds may be channelled, at least initially, through a number of existing institutions and programmes, including an appropriately revised Global Environment Facility. This calls for a new sense of real partnership. Traditional notions of foreign aid and of the donor-recipient syndrome are no longer an appropriate basis for North-South relations. The world community must move towards a more objective and consistent system of effecting resource transfers similar to that used to redress imbalances and ensure equity within national societies. Financing the transition to sustainable development should not be seen merely in terms of extra costs, but rather as an indispensable investment in global environmental security.

Such investments also make good economic sense. It is no accident that those countries and corporations which use energy and materials most efficiently are also those which are most successful economically. The reverse is also true, for poor economic performance is almost invariably accompanied by poor environmental performance. The importance of eco-efficiency was the principal theme of the ground-breaking report 'Changing Course' prepared by the Business Council for Sustainable Development as its contribution to the Conference.

Nowhere is efficiency more important than in the use of energy. The transition to a more energy-efficient economy that weans us off our overdependence on fossil fuels is imperative to the achievement of sustainable developments. The removal of trade barriers and discriminatory subsidies would enable developing countries to earn several times more than the amounts they now receive by way of Official Development Assistance. Large-scale reduction of their current debt burdens could provide most of the new and additional resources they require to make the transition to sustainable development through implementation of Agenda 21.

We also need new ways of financing environment and development objectives. For example, emission permits that are tradable internationally offer a means of making the most cost-effective use of funds devoted to pollution control while at the same time providing a non-budgetary means of effecting resource transfers. Taxes on polluting products or activities, like the CO_2 taxes now being levied or proposed by a number of countries, could also be devoted to financing of international environment and development measures. While none of these promising measures may be ripe for definitive action at this Conference, I would urge the Conference to put them on the priority agenda for the early post-Rio period.

Poverty

The devastating drought in southern Africa and the continuing plight of the victims of conflict and poverty in so many African countries are a grim reminder of the need for the world community to give special priority to the needs of Africa and to the least-developed countries everywhere. The tragedy is that poverty and hunger persist in a world never better able to eliminate them. This is surely a denial of the moral and ethical basis of our civilization as well as a threat to its survival.

Agenda 21 measures for eradication of poverty and the economic enfranchisement of the poor provide the basis for a new world-wide war on poverty. Indeed, I urge you to adopt the eradication of poverty as a priority objective for the world community as we move into the 21st century.

Another important region which deserves special attention at this time is that comprised of the nations of the former Soviet Union and Eastern and Central Europe. These countries, which have suffered some of the most severe environmental devastation to be experienced anywhere, are now faced with the daunting task of revitalizing and rebuilding their economies. It is important to them, and to the entire world community, that they have the international support they will need to do this on an environmentally-sound and sustainable basis.

I want to pay tribute to those who have negotiated the Conventions on Climate Change and Biodiversity, which will be opened for your signature here. It has not been an easy process and some have important reservations about both instruments. They represent first steps in the processes of addressing two of the most serious threats to the habitability of our planet. Signing them will not, in itself, be sufficient Their real importance will depend on the extent to which they give rise to concrete actions and are followed quickly by protocols containing the special measures required to make them fully effective and the finances needed to implement them.

For both these issues deal with the future of life on Earth. Over the next 20 years, more than one quarter of the Earth's remaining species may become extinct And in the case of global warming, the Inter-governmental Panel on Climate Change has warned that if carbon dioxide emissions are not cut by 60 per cent immediately, the changes in the next 60 years may be so rapid that nature will be unable to adapt and man incapable of controlling them.

Convention

I also recommend that you mandate negotiation of a convention on desertification and deterioration of arid lands, which is threatening the lives and the livelihoods of so many people in the developing world, notably Africa. It is important, too, for this Conference, in negotiating the forestry principles placed before it by the Preparatory Committee, to provide for continuing progress towards an effective regime for conservation and sustainable development of the world's forests.

War and preparation for war are major sources of environmental damage which must be subjected to greater accountability and control. This should include much stronger legal instruments with clear provisions for enforcement which provide effective deterrence against future environmental aggressors.

The road to Rio has been enlightened and enlivened by a remarkable and diverse range of activities and dialogue - most have been highly supportive, some critical, some sceptical, but all testifying to the historic importance of this occasion and the hopes and expectations of people everywhere for what you will do here in the next two weeks. Many of the people and organizations participating in this global process will be with us here. Many more are gathering at the accompanying 'people's summit' at the Global Forum. I look forward to a positive and creative interaction between the Conference and these other people's fora.

Several other important events have occurred here just prior to the Conference. The World Conference of Indigenous Peoples met to share their experience and concerns. They are repositories of much of the traditional knowledge and wisdom from which modernization has separated most of us. They are custodians, too, of some of the world's most important and vulnerable ecosystems—tropical forests, deserts and arctic regions. We must hear and heed their voices, learn from their experience and respect their right to live in their own lands in accordance with their traditions, values and cultures.

Full and informed participation of people through democratic processes at every level, accompanied by openness and transparency, are essential to the achievement of the objectives of this Conference. Provision for such participation must be an essential feature of the response by Governments and institutions, national and international, to the results of the Conference.

Important constituencies

No constituencies are more important in all countries than women, youth and children. And the children who greeted us so beautifully at the door as we entered today—representatives of all the children whose world we are shaping here must surely be a particularly poignant reminder of the special responsibilities we carry towards them. To make their essential and distinctive contributions, the remaining barriers to the full and equal participation of women in all aspects of our economic, social and political life must be removed. Similarly, the views, concerns and the interests of our youth and children must be respected and they must be provided with expanding opportunities to participate in the decisions which will: shape the future which is so largely theirs.

By the early part of the 21st century, more than half the world's people will live in urban areas. Cities of the developing world are being overwhelmed by explosive growth at rates beyond anything ever experienced before. By the year 2025, the urban population of developing countries is expected to reach some 4 billion. In our host country, the proportion of people living in urban areas is already more than 70 per cent. The meetings of leading representatives of local governments, in which Mayor Alencar took such a leading role, which took place in Curitiba and Rio in the past week, have highlighted these issues and established the basis for the adoption of an Agenda 21 by many of the world's leading cities.

We are reminded by the Declaration of the Sacred Earth Gathering, which met here last weekend, that the changes in behaviour and direction called for here must be rooted in our deepest spiritual, moral and ethical values. We reinstate in our lives the ethic of love and respect for the Earth which traditional peoples have retained as central to their value systems. This must be accompanied by a revitalization of the values common to all of our principal religious and philosophical traditions. Caring, sharing, co-operation with and love of each other must no longer be seen as pious ideals, divorced from reality, but rather as the indispensable basis for the new realities on which our survival and well-being must be premised.

Science and technology have produced our knowledge-based civilization. Its misuse and unintended effects have given rise to the risks and imbalances which now threaten us. At the same time, it offers the insights we need to guide our decisions and the tools we need to take the actions that will shape our common future. The guidance which science provides will seldom be so precise as to remove all uncertainty. In matters affecting our survival, we cannot afford to wait for the certainty which only a post-mortem could provide. We must act on the precautionary principle guided by the best evidence available.

Full partners

To become full partners in the process of saving our planet, developing countries need first and foremost substantial new support for strengthening their own scientific, technological, professional, educational and related institutional capacities. This is one of the important and urgent features of Agenda 21. And I am delighted, Mr. President, that in your own opening remarks you invited the international community to follow up this Conference by establishing an appropriate and central part of that institutional network here in Rio. I commend it and I pledge you my support in achieving it.

Perhaps the most important common ground we must arrive at in Rio is the understanding that we are all in this together. No place on the planet can remain an island of affluence in a sea of misery. We're either going to save the whole world or no-one will be saved. We must from here on in all go down the same path. One country cannot stabilize its climate in isolation. No country can unilaterally preserve its biodiversity. One part of the world cannot live an orgy of unrestrained consumption while the rest destroys its environment just to survive. Neither is immune from the effects of the other.

There is an ominous tendency today to erect new iron curtains to insulate the more affluent and privileged from the poor, the underprivileged and the dispossessed. Iron curtains and closed national boundaries provide no solutions to the problems of an interdependent world community in which what happens in one part affects all.

Like it or not, from here on in, we're in this together: rich, poor, North, South, East and West. It is an exhilarating challenge to erase the barriers that have separated us in the past, to join in the global partnership that will enable us to survive in a more secure and hospitable world. The industrialized world cannot escape its primary responsibility to lead the way in establishing this partnership and making it work. Up to now, the damage inflicted on our planet has been done largely inadvertently. We now know what we are doing. We have lost our innocence. It would be more than irresponsible to continue down this path.

This Conference will, in the final analysis, only meet the needs for which it was called and the hopes and aspirations it has ignited throughout the world if the decisions taken here give rise to real and fundamental changes in the underlying conditions that have produced the civilizational crisis we now confront. If the agreements reached here do not serve the common interests of the entire human family, if they are devoid of the means and commitments required to implement them, if the world lapses back to 'business as usual', we will have missed a historic opportunity, one which may not recur in our times, if ever. We would thus bequeath to those who follow us a legacy of lost hopes and deepening despair. This we must not do.

The Earth Summit is not an end in itself, but a new beginning. The measures you agree on here will be but first steps on a new pathway to our common future. Thus, the results of this Conference will ultimately depend on the credibility and effectiveness of its follow-up. It is, therefore, of the highest importance that all Governments commit themselves to translate the decisions they take collectively here to national policies and practices required to give effect to them, particularly implementation of Agenda 21. The preparatory process has provided the basis for this and the momentum which has brought us to Rio must be maintained. And institutional changes, as the Secretary-General has said, to be made within the United Nations must provide an effective and credible basis for its continued leadership of this process.

Our essential unity as peoples of the Earth must transcend the differences and difficulties which still divide us. You are called upon to rise to your historic responsibility as custodians of the planet in taking the decisions here that will unite rich and poor, North, South, East and West, in a new global partnership to ensure our common future. The road beyond Rio will be a long and difficult one; but it will also be a journey of renewed hope, of excitement, challenge and opportunity, leading as we move into the 21st century to the dawning of a new world in which the hopes and aspirations of all the world's children for a more secure and hospitable future can be fulfilled. This unprecedented responsibility is in your hands.

Excerpt from *Blue Gold: The Fight to Stop the Corporate Theft of the World's Water*

BY MAUDE BARLOW AND TONY CLARKE

One of the prime driving forces behind transnational corporations and the expansion of the global economy has been the "growth imperative," and in recent years, people have begun to recognize that this principle is on a collision course with Nature itself. In their classic work *For the Common Good*, Herman E. Daly and John B. Cobb demonstrated that orthodox economics, based on the growth imperative, was rooted in a narrow definition of "capital" as human-made assets like goods and services, machines and buildings. Left out of the equation, said Daly and Cobb, was what they called "natural capital," the resources of the earth which make all economic activity possible. But the carrying capacity of the planet's ecosystem has its limits, especially given the rapid pace at which the natural world is being destroyed by industrial agriculture, deforestation, desertification, and urbanization. At this rate, Daly and Cobb warned, the collision could come within the next generation.

In India, feminist, physicist, and ecological activist Vandana Shiva takes the concept one step further by arguing that the growth imperative amounts to "a form of theft" from Nature and people. It is true, says Shiva, that cutting down natural forests and converting them into monocultures of pine for industrial raw materials generates revenues and growth. However, it also robs the forest of its diversity and its capacity to conserve soil and water. And by destroying the forest's diversity, communities of people who depend on the original forest for their sources of food, fodder, fuel, fiber, and medicine, as well as for protection from drought and famine, are also being robbed. Shiva goes on to show how the growth imperative, applied to industrial agriculture, also fails to provide more food, reduce hunger, or save natural resources. Industrial agriculture also operates as a form of theft from Nature and the poor. She would argue that the same can be said of the construction of huge, high-tech power dams and the diversion of river systems.

At the heart of this critique lie concerns about the increasing commodification of Nature and of life itself. There was a time riot so long ago when certain aspects of life and Nature were not considered commodities to be bought and sold in the marketplace. Some things were not for sale—things like natural resources (including air and water), genetic codes and seeds, health, education, culture, and heritage. These, and other essential elements of life and Nature, were part of a shared inheritance or rights that belonged to all people. In other words, they belonged to "the commons." In India, for example, space, air, energy, and water have traditionally been viewed as "incapable of being bound into property relations." They were not to be treated as private property but as "common resource property," and they were not to be subjected to market forces such as the laws of demand and supply. On the contrary, these dimensions of common life were deemed to be of universal importance, and in many respects, they were considered sacred. As such, they were to be protected and preserved by governments through the public sector or more directly by local communities themselves.

The commodification of water, in particular, is seen to be a direct assault on the commons. In a report by the Research Foundation for Science, Technology and Ecology (a New Delhi-based NGO directed by Dr. Vandana Shiva), water in India is understood to be "life itself, on which our land, our food, our livelihood, our tradition and our culture depends." j As "the lifeline of society," water is "a sacred common heritage ... to be worshiped, preserved and shared collectively, sustainably used and equitably distributed in our culture." In the traditional teachings of Islam, for example, the "Sharia," or "way," originally meant the "path to water," and the ultimate basis for the "rights of thirst," which apply to both people and Nature. Based on these traditional spiritual and cultural traditions, says the foundation, local communities in India have developed "creative mechanisms of water management and ownership through collective and consensual decision making processes" designed to ensure "sustainable resource use and equitable distribution."

But now, in this age of economic globalization, water is being commodified and commercialized in India, says the foundation, with alarming results. Under pressure from the IMF and the World Bank to secure revenues to pay down their debt load, the Government of India has been selling water rights to global water corporations, including Suez and Vivendi, and to major industries requiring heavy water use for their production operations. As a result, Indigenous local traditions of water management and harvesting are bypassed, giving way to increased "commercialization and over-exploitation of scarce water resources." What we are witnessing, reports the foundation, is "the enclosure of a hitherto 'common property resource' into private commodities." The impacts of this commodification of water amount to "irreversible losses to our environment and livelihoods of our people." What's more, these trends are being experienced not only in India but throughout most of the Third World

Indeed, the commodification, not only of water, but of other parts of Nature and of life itself, is a distinguishing feature of corporate-led globalization today. What was once understood to be "the commons" has become the last frontier in the expansion of global capitalism. As transnational corporations conquer markets around the world, new industries are emerging to commercialize the remaining elements of our common life A prominent example in recent years has been the biotechnology industry. Presenting themselves as "life science" industries, major biotech corporations like Monsanto and Novartis have been turning seeds and genes into commodities to be bought and sold as genetically engineered food and health products in global markets. Similarly, the global water giants have been busy transforming this life-giving resource into a commodity to be sold on a for-profit basis to those who have the ability to pay. In short everything is now for sale to the highest bidder, including seeds genes' and water. And the fundamental contradiction underlying the commodification of water was articulated by no less than the CEO of the global water giant Suez. "Water is an efficient product," said Gerard Mestrallet. "It is a product which normally would be free, and our fob is to sell it. But it is a product which is absolutely necessary for life."

Excerpt from *Stolen Harvest*

BY VANDANA SHIVA

I focus on India to tell the story of how corporate control of food and globalization of agriculture are robbing millions of their livelihoods and their right to food both because I am an Indian and because Indian agriculture is being especially targeted by global corporations. Since 75 percent of the Indian population derives its livelihood from agriculture, and every fourth farmer in the world is an Indian, the impact of globalization on Indian agriculture is of global significance.

However, this phenomenon of the stolen harvest is not unique to India. It is being experienced in every society as small farms and small farmers are pushed to extinction, as monocultures replace biodiverse crops, as farming is transformed from the production of nourishing and diverse foods into the creation of markets for genetically engineered seeds, herbicides, and pesticides. As farmers are transformed from producers into consumers of corporate-patented agricultural products, as markets are destroyed locally and nationally but expanded globally, the myth of "free trade" and the global economy becomes a means far the rich to rob the poor of their right to food and even their right to life. For the vast majority of the world's people—70 percent—earn their livelihoods by producing food. The majority of these farmers are women. In contrast, in the industrialized countries, only 2 percent of the population are fanners.

Food Security is in the Seed

For centuries Third World farmers have evolved crops and given us the diversity of plants that provide us nutrition. Indian farmers evolved 200,000 varieties of rice through their innovation and breeding. They bred rice varieties such as Basmati. They bred red rice and brown rice and black rice. They bred rice that grew 18 feet tall in the Gangetic floodwaters, and saline-resistant rice that could be grown in the coastal water. And this innovation by farmers has not stopped. Farmers involved in our movement, Navdanya, dedicated to conserving native seed diversity, are still breeding new varieties.

The seed, for the farmer, is not merely the source of future plants and food; it is the storage place of culture and history. Seed is the first link in die food chain. Seed is the ultimate symbol of food security.

Free exchange of seed among farmers has been the basis of maintaining biodiversity as well as food security. This exchange is based on cooperation and reciprocity, A farmer who wants to exchange seed generally gives an equal quantity of seed from his field in return for the seed he gets.

Free exchange among farmers goes beyond mere exchange of seeds; it involves exchanges of ideas and knowledge, of culture and heritage. It is an accumulation of tradition, of knowledge of how to work the seed. Farmers learn about the plants they want to grow in the future by watching them grow in other farmers' fields.

Paddy, or rice, has religious significance in most parts of the country and is an essential component of most religious festivals. The *Akti* festival in Chattisgarh, where a diversity of *indica* rices are grown, reinforces the many principles of biodiversity conservation. In Southern India, rice grain is considered auspicious, or *akshanta*. It is mixed with *kumkum* and turmeric and given as a blessing. The priest is given rice, often along with coconut, as an indication of religious regard. Other agricultural varieties whose seeds, leaves, or flowers form an essential component of religious ceremonies include coconut, betel, arecanut, wheat, finger and little millets, horsegram, blackgram, chickpea, pigeon pea, sesame, sugarcane, jackfruit seed, cardamom, ginger, bananas, and gooseberry.

New seeds are first worshipped, and only then are they planted. New crops are worshipped before being consumed. Festivals held before sowing seeds as well as harvest festivals, celebrated in the fields, symbolize people's intimacy with nature.[7] For the farmer, the field is the mother; worshipping the field is a sign of gratitude toward the earth, which, as mother, feeds the millions of life forms that are her children.

But new intellectual-property-rights regimes, which are being universalized through the Trade Related Intellectual Property Rights Agreement of the World Trade Organization (WTO), allow corporations to usurp the knowledge of the seed and monopolize it by claiming it as their private property. Over time, this results in corporate monopolies over the seed itself.

Corporations like RiceTec of the United States are claiming patents on Basmati rice. Soybean, which evolved in East Asia, has been patented by Calgene, which is now owned by Monsanto. Calgene also owns patents on mustard, a crop of Indian origin. Centuries of collective innovation by farmers and peasants are being hijacked as corporations claim intellectual-property rights on these and other seeds and plants.[8]

"Free Trade" or "Forced Trade"

Today, ten corporations control 32 percent of the commercial-seed market, valued at $23 billion, and 100 percent of the market for genetically engineered, or transgenic, seeds.[9] These corporations also control the global agrochemical and pesticide market. Just five corporations control the global trade in grain. In late 1998, Cargill, the largest of these five companies, bought Continental, the second largest, making it the single biggest factor in the grain trade. Monoliths such as Cargill and Monsanto were both actively involved in shaping international trade agreements in particular the Uruguay Round of the General Agreement on Trade and Tarriffs, which led to the establishment of the WTO,

This monopolistic control over agricultural production, along with structural adjustment policies that brutally favor exports, results in floods of exports of foods from the United States and Europe to the Third World. As a result of the North American Free Trade Agreement (NAFTA), the proportion of Mexico's food supply that is imported has increased from 20 percent in 1992 to 43 percent in 1996. After 18 months of NAFTA, 2.2. million Mexicans have lost their jobs, and 40 million have fallen into extreme poverty. One out of two peasants is not getting enough to eat.

As Victor Suares has stated, "Eating more cheaply on imports is not eating at all for the poor in Mexico."[10]

In the Philippines, sugar imports have destroyed the economy. In Kerala, India, the prosperous rubber plantations were rendered unviable due to rubber imports. The local $350 million rubber economy was wiped out, with a multiplier effect of $3.5 billion on the economy of Kerala. In Kenya, maize imports brought prices crashing for local farmers who could not even recover their costs of production.

Trade liberalization of agriculture was introduced in India in 1991 as part of a World Bank/ International Monetary Fund (IMF) structural adjustment package. While the hectares of land under cotton cultivation had been decreasing in the 1970s and 1980s, in the first six years of World Bank/IMF-mandated reforms, the land under cotton cultivation increased by 1.7 million hectares. Cotton started to displace food crops. Aggressive corporate advertising campaigns, including promotional films shown in villages on "video vans," were launched to sell new, hybrid seeds to fanners. Even gods, goddesses, and saints were not spared: in Punjab, Monsanto sells its products using the image of Guru Nanak, the founder of the Sikh religion. Corporate, hybrid seeds began to replace local farmers' varieties.

The new hybrid seeds, being vulnerable lo pests required more pesticides. Extremely poor farmers bought both seeds and chemicals on credit from the same company. When the crops failed due to heavy pest incidence or large-scale seed failure, many peasants committed suicide by consuming the same pesticides that had gotten them into debt in the first place. In the district of Warangal, nearly 400 cotton farmers committed suicide due to crop failure in 1997, and dozens more committed suicide in 1998.

Under this pressure to cultivate cash crops, many states in India have allowed private corporations to acquire hundreds of acres of land. The state of Maharashtra has exempted horticulture projects from its land-ceiling legislation. Madhya Pradesh is offering land to private industry on long-term leases, which, according to industry, should last for at least 40 years. In Andhra Pradesh and Tamil Nadu, private corporations are today allowed to acquire over 300 acres of land for raising shrimp for exports. A large percentage of agricultural production on these lands will go toward supplying the burgeoning food-processing industry, in which mainly transnational corporations are involved. Meanwhile, the United States has taken India to the WTO dispute panel to contest its restrictions on food imports.

In certain instances, markets are captured by other means. In August 1998, the mustard-oil supply in Delhi was mysteriously adulterated. The adulteration was restricted to Delhi but not to any specific brand, indicating that it was not the work of a particular trader or business house. More than 50 people died. The government banned all local processing of oil and announced free imports of soybean oil. Millions of people extracting oil on tiny, ecological, cold-press mills lost their livelihoods. Prices of indigenous oilseed collapsed to less than one-third their previous levels. In Sira, in the state of Karnataka, police officers shot farmers protesting the fall in prices of oilseeds.

Imported soybeans' takeover of the Indian market is a clear example of the imperialism on which globalization is built One crop exported from a single country by one or two corporations replaced hundreds of foods and food producers, destroying biological and cultural diversity, and economic and political democracy. Small mills are now unable to serve small farmers and poor consumers with low-cost, healthy, and culturally appropriate edible oils. Farmers are robbed of their freedom to choose what they grow, and consumers are being robbed of their freedom to choose what they eat.

Creating Hunger with Monocultures

Global chemical corporations, recently reshaped into "life sciences" corporations, declare that without them and their patented products the world cannot be fed.

As Monsanto advertised in its $1.6 million European advertising campaign:

> Worrying about starving future generations won't feed them. Food biotechnology will. The world's population is growing rapidly, adding the equivalent of a China to the globe every ten years. To feed these billion more mouths, we can try extending our farming land or squeezing greater harvests out of existing cultivation. With the planet set to double in numbers around 2030, this heavy dependency on land can only become heavier. Soil erosion and mineral depletion will exhaust the ground. Lands such as rainforests will be forced into cultivation. Fertilizer, insecticide, and herbicide use will increase globally. At Monsanto, we now believe food biotechnology is a better way forward.[11]

But food is necessary for all living species. That is why the *Taittreya Upanishad* calls on humans to feed all beings in their zone of influence.

Industrial agriculture has not produced more food. It has destroyed diverse sources of food, and it has stolen food from other species to bring larger quantities of specific commodities to the market, using huge quantities of fossil fuels and water and toxic chemicals in the process.

It is often said that the so-called miracle varieties of the Green Revolution in modern industrial agriculture prevented famine because they had higher yields. However, these higher yields disappear in the context of total yields of crops on farms. Green Revolution varieties produced more grain by diverting production away from straw. This "partitioning" was achieved through dwarfing the plants, which also enabled them to withstand high doses of chemical fertilizer.

However, less straw means less fodder for cattle and less organic matter for the soil to feed the millions of soil organisms that make and rejuvenate soil. The higher yields of wheat or maize were thus achieved by stealing food from farm animals and soil organisms. Since cattle and earthworms are our partners in food production, stealing food from them makes it impossible to maintain food production over time, and means that the partial yield increases were not sustainable.

The increase in yields of wheat and maize under industrial agriculture were also achieved at the cost of yields of other foods a small farm provides. Beans, legumes, fruits, and vegetables all disappeared both from farms and from the calculus of yields. More grain from two or three commodities arrived on national and international markets, but less food was eaten by farm families in the Third World.

The gain in "yields" of industrially produced crops is thus based on a theft of food from other species and the rural poor in the Third World. That is why, as more grain is produced and traded globally, more people go hungry in the Third World. Global markets have more commodities for trading because food has been robbed from nature and the poor.

Productivity in traditional farming practices has always been high if it is remembered that very few external inputs are required. While the Green Revolution has been promoted as having increased productivity in the absolute sense, when resource use is taken into account, it has been found to be counterproductive and inefficient.

Perhaps one of the most fallacious myths propagated by Green Revolution advocates is the assertion that high-yielding varieties have reduced the acreage under cultivation, therefore preserving millions of hectares of biodiversity. But in India, instead of more land being released for conservation, industrial breeding actually increases pressure on the land, since each acre of a monoculture provides a single output, and the displaced outputs have to be grown on additional acres, or "shadow" acres.[12]

A study comparing traditional polycultures with industrial monocultures shows that a polyculture system can produce 100 units of food from 5 units of inputs, whereas an industrial system requires 300 units of input to produce the same 100 units. The 295 units of wasted inputs could have provided 5,900 units of additional food. Thus the industrial system leads to a decline of 5,900 units of food. This is a recipe for starving people, not for feeding them.[13]

Wasting resources creates hunger. By wasting resources through one-dimensional monocultures maintained with intensive external inputs, the new biotechnologies create food insecurity and starvation.

Stealing Nature's Harvest

Global corporations are not just stealing the harvest of farmers. They are stealing nature's harvest through genetic engineering and patents on life forms.

Genetically engineered crops manufactured by corporations pose serious ecological risks. Crops such as Monsanto's Roundup Ready soybeans, designed to be resistant to herbicides, lead to the destruction of biodiversity and increased use of agrochemicals. They can also create highly invasive "superweeds" by transferring die genes for herbicide resistance to weeds. Crops designed to be pesticide factories, genetically engineered to produce toxins and venom with genes from bacteria, scorpions, snakes, and wasps, can threaten non-pest species and can contribute to the emergence of resistance in pests and hence the creation of "superpests." In every application of genetic engineering, food is being stolen from other species for the maximization of corporate profits.

To secure patents on life forms and living resources, corporations must claim seeds and plants to be their "inventions" and hence their property. Thus corporations like Cargill and Monsanto see nature's web of life and cycles of renewal as "theft" of their property. During the debate about the entry of Cargill into India in 1992, the Cargill chief executive stated, "We bring Indian farmers smart technologies, which prevent bees from usurping the pollen."[16] During the United Nations Biosafety Negotiations, Monsanto circulated literature that claimed , that "weeds steal the sunshine."[17] A worldview that defines pollination as "theft by bees" and claims that diverse plants "steal" sunshine is one aimed at stealing nature's harvest, by replacing open, pollinated varieties with hybrids and sterile seeds, and destroying biodiverse flora with herbicides such as Monsanto's Roundup.

This is a worldview based on scarcity. A worldview of abundance is the worldview of women in India who leave food for ants on their doorstep, even as they create the most beautiful art in *kolams, mandates,* and *rangoli* with rice flour. Abundance is the worldview of peasant women who weave beautiful designs of paddy to hang up for birds when the birds do not find grain in the fields. This view of abundance recognizes that, in giving food to other beings and species, we maintain conditions for our own food security. It is the recognition in the *Isho Upanishad* that the universe is the creation of the Supreme Power meant for the benefits of (all) creation. Each individual life form must learn to enjoy its benefits by farming a part of the system in close relation with other species. Let not any one species encroach upon others' rights.[18] The *Isho Upanishad* also says,

> a selfish man over-utilizing the resources of nature to satisfy his own ever-increasing needs is nothing but a thief, because using resources beyond one's needs would result in the utilization of resources over which others have a right.[19]

In the ecological worldview, when we consume more than we need or exploit nature on principles of greed, we are engaging in theft. In the anti-life view of agribusiness corporations, nature renewing and maintaining herself is a thief. Such a worldview replaces abundance with scarcity, fertility with sterility. It makes theft from nature a market imperative, and hides it in the calculus of efficiency and productivity.

Food Democracy

What we are seeing is the emergence of food totalitarianism, in which a handful of corporations control the entire food chain and destroy alternatives so that people do not have access to diverse, safe foods produced ecologically. Local markets are being deliberately destroyed to establish monopolies over seed and food systems. The destruction of the edible-oil market in India and the many ways through which farmers are prevented from having their own seed supply are small instances of an overall trend in which trade rules, property rights, and new technologies are used to destroy people-friendly and environment-friendly alternatives and to impose anti-people, anti-nature food systems globally.

The notion of rights has been turned on its head under globalization and free trade. The right to produce for oneself or consume according to cultural priorities and safety concerns has been rendered illegal according to the new trade rules. The right of corporations to force-feed citizens of the world with culturally inappropriate and hazardous foods has been made absolute. The right to food, the right to safety, the right to culture are all being treated as bade barriers that need to be dismantled.

This food totalitarianism can only be stopped through major citizen mobilization for democratization of the food system. This mobilization is starting to gain momentum in Europe, Japan, India, Brazil, and other parts of the world.

We have to reclaim our right to save seed and to biodiversity. We have to reclaim our right to nutrition and food safety. We have to reclaim our right to protect the earth and her diverse species. We have to stop this corporate theft from the poor and from nature. Food democracy is the new agenda for democracy and human rights. It is the new agenda for ecological sustainability and social justice.

Trial Speech

BY KEN SARO-WIWA

My lord,

We all stand before history. I am a man of peace, of ideas. Appalled by the denigrating poverty of my people who live on a richly endowed land, distressed by their political marginalization and economic strangulation, angered by the devastation of their land, their ultimate heritage, anxious to preserve their right to life and to a decent living, and determined to usher to this country as a whole a fair and just democratic system which protects everyone and every ethnic group and gives us all a valid claim to human civilization, I have devoted my intellectual and material resources, my very life, to a cause in which I have total belief and from which I cannot be blackmailed or intimidated. I have no doubt at all about the ultimate success of my cause, no matter the trials and tribulations which I and those who believe with me may encounter on our journey. Neither imprisonment nor death can stop our ultimate victory.

I repeat that we all stand before history. I and my colleagues are not the only ones on trial. Shell is here on trial and it is as well that it is represented by counsel said to be holding a watching brief. The Company has, indeed, ducked this particular trial, but its day will surely come and the lessons learnt here may prove useful to it for there is no doubt in my mind that the ecological war that the Company has waged in the Delta will be called to question sooner than later and the crimes of that war be duly punished. The crime of the Company's dirty wars against the Ogoni people will also be punished.

On trial also is the Nigerian nation, its present rulers and those who assist them. Any nation which can do to the weak and disadvantaged what the Nigerian nation has done to the Ogoni, loses a claim to independence and to freedom from outside influence. I am not one of those who shy away from protesting injustice and oppression, arguing that they are expected in a military regime. The military do not act alone. They are supported by a gaggle of politicians, lawyers, judges, academics and businessmen, all of them hiding under the claim that they are only doing their duty, men and women too afraid to wash their pants of urine.

We all stand on trial, my lord, for by our actions we have denigrated our Country and jeopardized the future of our children. As we subscribe to the sub-normal and accept double standards, as we lie and cheat openly, as we protect injustice and oppression, we empty our classrooms, denigrate our hospitals, fill our stomachs with hunger and elect to make ourselves the slaves of those who ascribe to higher standards, pursue the truth, and honour justice, freedom, and hard work. I predict that the scene here will be played and replayed by generations yet unborn. Some have already cast themselves in the role of villains, some are tragic victims, some still have a chance to redeem themselves. The choice is for each individual.

I predict that the denoument of the riddle of the Niger delta will soon come. The agenda is being set at this trial. Whether the peaceful ways I have favoured will prevail depends on what the oppressor decides, what signals it sends out to the waiting public.

In my innocence of the false charges I face Here, in my utter conviction, I call upon the Ogoni people, the peoples of the Niger delta, and the oppressed ethnic minorities of Nigeria to stand up now and fight fearlessly and peacefully for their rights. History is on their side. God is on their side. For the Holy Quran says in Sura 42, verse 41: "All those that fight when oppressed incur no guilt, but Allah shall punish the oppressor." Come the day.

Nobel Laureate Acceptance Speech

BY WANGARI MAATHAI

Your Majesties
Your Royal Highnesses
Honourable Members of the Norwegian Nobel Committee
Excellencies
Ladies and Gentlemen

I stand before you and the world humbled by this recognition and uplifted by the honour of being the 2004 Nobel Peace Laureate.

As the first African woman to receive this prize, I accept it on behalf of the people of Kenya and Africa, and indeed the world. I am especially mindful of women and the girl child. I hope it will encourage them to raise their voices and take more space for leadership. I know the honour also gives a deep sense of pride to our men, both old and young. As a mother, I appreciate the inspiration this brings to the youth and urge them to use it to pursue their dreams.

Although this prize comes to me, it acknowledges the work of countless individuals and groups across the globe. They work quietly and often without recognition to protect the environment, promote democracy, defend human rights and ensure equality between women and men. By so doing, they plant seeds of peace. I know they, too, are proud today. To all who feel represented by this prize I say use it to advance your mission and meet the high expectations the world will place on us.

This honour is also for my family, friends, partners and supporters throughout the world. All of them helped shape the vision and sustain our work, which was often accomplished under hostile conditions. I am also grateful to the people of Kenya - who remained stubbornly hopeful that democracy could be realized and their environment managed sustainably. Because of this support, I am here today to accept this great honour.

I am immensely privileged to join my fellow African Peace laureates, Presidents Nelson Mandela and F.W. de Klerk, Archbishop Desmond Tutu, the late Chief Albert Luthuli, the late Anwar el-Sadat and the UN Secretary General, Kofi Annan.

I know that African people everywhere are encouraged by this news. My fellow Africans, as we embrace this recognition, let us use it to intensify our commitment to our people, to reduce conflicts and poverty and thereby improve their quality of life. Let us embrace democratic governance, protect human rights and protect our environment. I am confident that we shall rise to the occasion. I have always believed that solutions to most of our problems must come from us.

In this year's prize, the Norwegian Nobel Committee has placed the critical issue of environment and its linkage to democracy and peace before the world. For their visionary action, I am profoundly grateful. Recognizing that sustainable development, democracy and peace are indivisible is an idea whose time has come. Our work over the past 30 years has always appreciated and engaged these linkages.

My inspiration partly comes from my childhood experiences and observations of Nature in rural Kenya. It has been influenced and nurtured by the formal education I was privileged to receive in Kenya, the United States and Germany. As I was growing up, I witnessed forests being cleared and replaced by commercial plantations, which destroyed local biodiversity and the capacity of the forests to conserve water.

Excellencies, ladies and gentlemen,

In 1977, when we started the Green Belt Movement, I was partly responding to needs identified by rural women, namely lack of firewood, clean drinking water, balanced diets, shelter and income.

Throughout Africa, women are the primary caretakers, holding significant responsibility for tilling the land and feeding their families. As a result, they are often the first to become aware of environmental damage as resources become scarce and incapable of sustaining their families.

The women we worked with recounted that unlike in the past, they were unable to meet their basic needs. This was due to the degradation of their immediate environment as well as the introduction of commercial farming, which replaced the growing of household food crops. But international trade controlled the price of the exports from these small-scale farmers and a reasonable and just income could not be guaranteed. I came to understand that when the environment is destroyed, plundered or mismanaged, we undermine our quality of life and that of future generations.

Tree planting became a natural choice to address some of the initial basic needs identified by women. Also, tree planting is simple, attainable and guarantees quick, successful results within a reasonable amount time. This sustains interest and commitment.

So, together, we have planted over 30 million trees that provide fuel, food, shelter, and income to support their children's education and household needs. The activity also creates employment and improves soils and watersheds. Through their involvement, women gain some degree of power over their lives, especially their social and economic position and relevance in the family. This work continues.

Initially, the work was difficult because historically our people have been persuaded to believe that because they are poor, they lack not only capital, but also knowledge and skills to address their challenges. Instead they are conditioned to believe that solutions to their problems must come from 'outside'. Further, women did not realize that meeting their needs depended on their environment being healthy and well managed. They were also unaware that a degraded environment leads to a scramble for scarce resources and may culminate in poverty and even conflict. They were also unaware of the injustices of international economic arrangements.

In order to assist communities to understand these linkages, we developed a citizen education program, during which people identify their problems, the causes and possible solutions. They then make connections between their own personal actions and the problems they witness in the environment and in society. They learn that our world is confronted with a litany of woes: corruption, violence against women and children, disruption and breakdown of families, and disintegration of cultures and communities. They also identify the abuse of drugs and chemical substances, especially among young people. There are also devastating diseases that are defying cures or occurring in epidemic proportions. Of particular concern are HIV/AIDS, malaria and diseases associated with malnutrition.

On the environment front, they are exposed to many human activities that are devastating to the environment and societies. These include widespread destruction of ecosystems, especially through deforestation, climatic instability, and contamination in the soils and waters that all contribute to excruciating poverty.

In the process, the participants discover that they must be part of the solutions. They realize their hidden potential and are empowered to overcome inertia and take action. They come to recognize that they are the primary custodians and beneficiaries of the environment that sustains them.

Entire communities also come to understand that while it is necessary to hold their governments accountable, it is equally important that in their own relationships with each other, they exemplify the leadership values they wish to see in their own leaders, namely justice, integrity and trust.

Although initially the Green Belt Movement's tree planting activities did not address issues of democracy and peace, it soon became clear that responsible governance of the environment was impossible without democratic space. Therefore, the tree became a symbol for the democratic struggle in Kenya. Citizens were mobilised to challenge widespread abuses of power, corruption and environmental mismanagement. In Nairobi's Uhuru Park, at Freedom Corner, and in many parts of the country, trees of peace were planted to demand the release of prisoners of conscience and a peaceful transition to democracy.

Through the Green Belt Movement, thousands of ordinary citizens were mobilized and empowered to take action and effect change. They learned to overcome fear and a sense of helplessness and moved to defend democratic rights.

In time, the tree also became a symbol for peace and conflict resolution, especially during ethnic conflicts in Kenya when the Green Belt Movement used peace trees to reconcile disputing communities. During the ongoing re-writing of the Kenyan constitution, similar trees of peace were planted in many parts of the country to promote a culture of peace. Using trees as a symbol of peace is in keeping with a widespread African tradition. For example, the elders of the Kikuyu carried a staff from the *thigi* tree that, when placed between two disputing sides, caused them to stop fighting and seek reconciliation. Many communities in Africa have these traditions.

Such practises are part of an extensive cultural heritage, which contributes both to the conservation of habitats and to cultures of peace. With the destruction of these cultures and the introduction of new values, local biodiversity is no longer valued or protected and as a result, it is quickly degraded and disappears. For this reason, The Green Belt Movement explores the concept of cultural biodiversity, especially with respect to indigenous seeds and medicinal plants.

As we progressively understood the causes of environmental degradation, we saw the need for good governance. Indeed, the state of any county's environment is a reflection of the kind of governance in place, and without good governance there can be no peace. Many countries, which have poor governance systems, are also likely to have conflicts and poor laws protecting the environment.

In 2002, the courage, resilience, patience and commitment of members of the Green Belt Movement, other civil society organizations, and the Kenyan public culminated in the peaceful transition to a democratic government and laid the foundation for a more stable society.

Excellencies, friends, ladies and gentlemen,

It is 30 years since we started this work. Activities that devastate the environment and societies continue unabated. Today we are faced with a challenge that calls for a shift in our thinking, so that humanity stops threatening its life-support system. We are called to assist the Earth to heal her wounds and in the process heal our own—indeed, to embrace the whole creation in all its diversity, beauty and wonder. This will happen if we see the need to revive our sense of belonging to a larger family of life, with which we have shared our evolutionary process.

In the course of history, there comes a time when humanity is called to shift to a new level of consciousness, to reach a higher moral ground. A time when we have to shed our fear and give hope to each other.

That time is now.

The Norwegian Nobel Committee has challenged the world to broaden the understanding of peace: there can be no peace without equitable development; and there can be no development without sustainable management of the environment in a democratic and peaceful space. This shift is an idea whose time has come.

I call on leaders, especially from Africa, to expand democratic space and build fair and just societies that allow the creativity and energy of their citizens to flourish.

Those of us who have been privileged to receive education, skills, and experiences and even power must be role models for the next generation of leadership. In this regard, I would also like to appeal for the freedom of my fellow laureate Aung San Suu Kyi so that she can continue her work for peace and democracy for the people of Burma and the world at large.

Culture plays a central role in the political, economic and social life of communities. Indeed, culture may be the missing link in the development of Africa. Culture is dynamic and evolves over time, consciously discarding retrogressive traditions, like female genital mutilation (FGM), and embracing aspects that are good and useful.

Africans, especially, should re-discover positive aspects of their culture. In accepting them, they would give themselves a sense of belonging, identity and self-confidence.

Ladies and Gentlemen,

There is also need to galvanize civil society and grassroots movements to catalyse change. I call upon governments to recognize the role of these social movements in building a critical mass of responsible citizens, who help maintain checks and balances in society. On their part, civil society should embrace not only their rights but also their responsibilities.

Further, industry and global institutions must appreciate that ensuring economic justice, equity and ecological integrity are of greater value than profits at any cost.

The extreme global inequities and prevailing consumption patterns continue at the expense of the environment and peaceful co-existence. The choice is ours.

I would like to call on young people to commit themselves to activities that contribute toward achieving their long-term dreams. They have the energy and creativity to shape a sustainable future. To the young people I say, you are a gift to your communities and indeed the world. You are our hope and our future.

The holistic approach to development, as exemplified by the Green Belt Movement, could be embraced and replicated in more parts of Africa and beyond. It is for this reason that I have established the Wangari Maathai Foundation to ensure the continuation and expansion of these activities. Although a lot has been achieved, much remains to be done.

Excellencies, ladies and gentlemen,

As I conclude I reflect on my childhood experience when I would visit a stream next to our home to fetch water for my mother. I would drink water straight from the stream. Playing among the arrowroot leaves I tried in vain to pick up the strands of frogs' eggs, believing they were beads. But every time I put my little fingers under them they would break. Later, I saw thousands of tadpoles: black, energetic and wriggling through the clear water against the background of the brown earth. This is the world I inherited from my parents.

Today, over 50 years later, the stream has dried up, women walk long distances for water, which is not always clean, and children will never know what they have lost. The challenge is to restore the home of the tadpoles and give back to our children a world of beauty and wonder.

Thank you very much.

Excerpt from *The Ecological Revolution*

BY JOHN BELLAMY FOSTER

How are we to meet this challenge, arguably the greatest that human civilization has ever faced? A genuine answer to the ecological question, transcending Arendt's tragic understanding of world alienation, requires a revolutionary conception of sustainable human development—one that addresses both human self-estrangement (the alienation of labor) and world alienation (the alienation of nature). It was Ernesto "Che" Guevara who most famously argued, in his "Man and Socialism in Cuba," that the crucial issue in the building of socialism was not economic development but human development. This needs to be extended by recognizing, in line with Marx, that the real question is one of sustainable human development, explicitly addressing the human metabolism with nature through human labor.[12]

Too often, the transition to socialism has been approached mechanistically as the mere expansion of the means of production, rather than in terms of the development of human social relations and needs. In the system that emerged in the Soviet Union, the indispensable tool of planning was misdirected to production for production's sake, losing sight of genuine human needs, and eventually gave rise to a new class structure. The detailed division of labor, introduced by capitalism, was retained under this system and extended in the interest of higher productivity. In this type of society, as Che critically observed, "the period of the building of socialism ... is characterized by the extinction of the individual for the "sake of the state."13

The revolutionary character of Latin American socialism, today, derives its strength from an acute recognition of the negative (as well as some positive) lessons of the Soviet experience, partly through an understanding of the problem raised by Che: the need to develop socialist humanity. Further, the Bolivarian vision proclaimed by Chávez has its own deep roots of inspiration, drawing on an older pre-Marxian socialism. Thus, it was Simón Bolívar's teacher Simón Rodríguez who wrote in 1847: "The division of labour in the production of goods only serves to brutalize the workforce. If to produce cheap and excellent nail scissors, we have to reduce the workers to machines, we would do better to cut our finger nails with our teeth." Indeed, what we most admire today with regard to Bolívar's own principles is his uncompromising insistence that equality is "the law of laws."[14]

The same commitment to the egalitarian, universal development of humanity was fundamental to Marx. The evolution of the society of associated producers was to be synonymous with the positive transcendence of human alienation. The goal was a many-sided human development. Just as "all history is nothing but a continuous transformation of human nature," so "the *cultivation* of the five senses is the work of all previous history." Socialism, thus, appears as the "complete emancipation of the senses," of human sensuous capacities, and their wide-ranging development. "Communism, as fully developed naturalism," Marx wrote, "*equals* humanism, and as fully developed humanism equals naturalism."[15]

The contrast between this revolutionary, humanistic-naturalistic vision and today's dominant mechanical-exploitative reality could not be starker.

We find ourselves in a period of imperialist development that is potentially the most dangerous in all of history.[16] There are two ways in which life on the planet as we know it can be destroyed—either instantaneously through global nuclear holocaust, or in a matter of a few generations by climate change and other manifestations of environmental destruction. Nuclear weapons continue to proliferate in an atmosphere of global insecurity promoted by the world's greatest power. War is currently being waged in the Middle East over geopolitical control of the world's oil, while carbon emissions from fossil fuels and other forms of industrial production are generating global warming. Biofuels offered up today as a major alternative to pending world oil shortages are destined only to enlarge world hunger.[17] Water resources are being monopolized by global corporations. Human needs are everywhere being denied: either in the form of extreme deprivation for a majority of the population of the world, or, in the richer countries, in the form of the most intensive self-estrangement conceivable, extending beyond production to a managed consumption, enforcing lifelong dependence on alienating wage labor. More and more, life is debased in a welter of artificial wants dissociated from genuine needs.

All of this is altering the ways in which we think about the transition from capitalism to socialism. Socialism has always been understood as a society aimed at reversing the relations of exploitation of capitalism and removing the manifold social evils to which these relations have given rise. This requires the abolition of private property in the means of production, a high degree of equality in all things, replacement of the blind forces of the market by planning by the associated producers in accordance with genuine social needs, and the elimination to whatever extent possible of invidious distinctions associated with the division of town and country, mental and manual labor, racial divisions, and gender divisions. Yet the root problem of socialism goes much deeper. The transition to socialism is possible only through a revolutionizing practice that *revolutionizes human beings themselves*.[18] The only way to accomplish this is by altering our human metabolism with nature, along with our human-social relations, transcending both the alienation of nature and of humanity. Marx, like Hegel, was fond of quoting Terence's famous statement: "Nothing human is alien to me." Now it is clear that we must deepen and extend this to: *Nothing of this earth is alien to me*.[19]

Mainstream environmentalists seek to solve ecological problems almost exclusively through three mechanical strategies: (1) technological bullets; (2) extending the market to all aspects of nature; and (3) creating what are intended as mere islands of preservation in a world of almost universal exploitation and destruction of natural habitats. In contrast, a minority of critical human ecologists have come to understand the need to change our fundamental social relations. Some of the best, most concerned ecologists, searching for concrete models of change have therefore come to focus on those states (or regions) that are both ecological and socialistic (in the sense of relying to a considerable extent on social planning rather than market forces) in orientation. Thus, Cuba, Curitiba and Porto Alegre in Brazil, and Kerala in India are singled out as the leading lights of ecological transformation by some of the most committed environmentalists, such as Bill McKibben, beat known as the author of *The End of Nature*.[20] More recently, Venezuela has been using its surplus from oil to transform its society in the direction of sustainable human development, thereby laying the foundation for a greening of its production. Although there are contradictions to what has been called Venezuelan "petro-socialism," the fact that an oil-generated surplus is being dedicated to genuine social transformation rather than feeding into the proverbial "curse of oil" makes Venezuela unique.[21]

Of course, there are powerful environmental movements within the center of the system as well to which we might look for hope. But severed from strong socialist movements and a revolutionary situation, they have been constrained much more by a perceived need to adapt to the dominant accumulation system, thereby drastically undermining the ecological struggle. Hence, revolutionary strategies and movements with regard to ecology and society are world-historical forces at present largely in the periphery, in the weak links and breakaways from the capitalist system.

I can only point to a few essential aspects of this radical process of ecological change as manifested in areas of the global South. In Cuba, the goal of human development that Che advanced is taking on a new form through what is widely regarded as "the greening of Cuba." This is evident in the emergence of the most revolutionary experiment in agroecology on earth, and the related changes in health, science, and education. As McKibben states, "Cubans have created what may be the world's largest working model of a semisustainable agriculture, one that relies far less than the rest of the world does on oil, on chemicals, on shipping vast quantities of food back and forth. . .. Cuba has thousands of *organopónicos*—urban gardens—more than two hundred in the Havana area alone." Indeed, according to the World Wildlife Fund's *Living Planet Report*, "Cuba alone" in the entire world has achieved a high level of human development, with a human development index greater than 0.8, while also having a per capita ecological footprint below the world's average.[22]

This ecological transformation is deeply rooted in the Cuban revolution rather than, as frequently said, simply a forced response in the Special Period following the fall of the Soviet Union. Already in the 1970s, Carlos Rafael Rodriguez, one of the founders of Cuban ecology, had introduced arguments for "integral development, laying the groundwork"—as ecologist Richard Levins points out—for "harmonious development of the economy and social relations with nature." This was followed by the gradual flowering of ecological thought in Cuba in the 1980s. The Special Period, Levins explains, simply allowed the "ecologists by conviction," who had emerged through the internal development of Cuban science and society, to recruit the "ecologists by necessity," turning many of them, too, into ecologists by conviction.[23]

Venezuela, under Chavez, has not only advanced revolutionary new social relations with the growth of Bolivarian circles, community councils, and increased worker control of factories, but has introduced some crucial initiatives with regard to what István Mészáros has called a new "socialist time accountancy" in the production and exchange of goods. In the new Bolivarian Alternative for the Americas (ALBA), the emphasis is on *communal exchange*, the exchange of activities rather than exchange-values.[24] Instead of allowing the market to establish the priorities of the entire economy, planning is being introduced to redistribute resources and capacities to those most in need and to the majority of the populace. The goal here is to address the most pressing individual and collective requirements of the society, related in the first place to physiological needs, and hence raising directly the question of the human relation to nature. This is the absolute precondition of the creation of a sustainable society. In the countryside, preliminary attempts have also been made to green Venezuelan agriculture.[25]

In Bolivia, the rise of a socialist current (though embattled at present), embedded in the needs of indigenous peoples and struggling for control of basic resources such as water and hydrocarbons, offers hope of another kind of development. Evo Morales, the socialist president of Bolivia, has emerged as one of the world's most eloquent defenders of the global environment and indigenous rights. The cities of Curitiba and Porto Alegre in Brazil point to the possibility of more radical forms of management of urban space and transportation. Curitiba, in McKibben's words, "is as much an example for the sprawling, decaying cities of the Erst world as for the crowded, booming cities of the Third World." Kerala, in India, has taught us that a poor state or region, if animated by genuine socialist planning, can go a long way toward unleashing human potentials in education, health care, and basic environmental conditions. In Kerala, McKibben observes, "the Left has embarked on a series of 'new democratic initiatives' that come as close as anything on the planet to actually incarnating 'sustainable development.' "[26]

To be sure, these are mainly islands of hope at present. They constitute fragile new experiments in social relations and in the human metabolism with .nature. They are still subject to the class and imperial war imposed from above by the larger system. The planet as a whole remains firmly in the grip of capital and its world alienation. Everywhere we see manifestations of a metabolic rift, now extended to the biospheric level.

It follows that there is little real prospect for the needed global ecological revolution, unless these attempts to revolutionize social relations in the struggle for a just and sustainable society, now emerging in the periphery, are somehow mirrored in movements for ecological and social revolution in the advanced capitalist world. It is only through fundamental change at the center of the system, from which the pressures on the planet principally emanate, that there is any genuine possibility of avoiding ultimate ecological destruction.

Calls for a Green New Deal to be carried out by the Obama administration reflect, if nothing else, a growing constituency for major ecological change. This, however, will only be substantively realized to the extent that there is a major revolt from below in support of social and ecological transformation, pointing beyond the existing system.

For some, this vision of far-reaching ecological transformation may seem to be an impossible goal. Nevertheless, it is important to recognize that there is now an *ecology* as well as a political economy of revolutionary change. The emergence in our time of sustainable human development, in various revolutionary interstices within the global periphery, could mark the beginning of a universal revolt against both world alienation and human self-estrangement. Such a revolt, if consistent, could have only one objective: the creation of a society of associated producers rationally regulating their metabolic relation to nature, and doing so not only in accordance with their own needs but also those of future generations and life as a whole. Today, the transition to socialism and the transition to an ecological society are one.

CPSIA information can be obtained
at www.ICGtesting.com
Printed in the USA
LVOW04s1334130118
562735LV00005B/12/P